ADVANCE PRAISE FOR PERSIST

"The butch/femme dynamic is desire and trust; it's a dance of ... Butches and femmes share a sens ...ued family, and kinship—no matter what our genders might be. There is no doubt in my mind that this book will soon be recognised as a major contribution to the shelves of our queer literature. And it's totally gonna be a must-have bedside reader for many. This is a smart, loving book by some terrific writers. They all know what it means to live and love as butch/femme beyond the stereotypes, and they've made their diesel femme Auntie Kate very proud of them. Kiss, kiss."
—Kate Bornstein, author of *Gender Outlaw*

"The death of butch-femme has been greatly exaggerated. This beautiful collection captures the intensity of gender variant communities now while continuing to make important links to pioneers from the past. Here we meet femme sharks and cowboys, faggy butches, studs and futches. This book is like a pocketknife: it is useful, sharp and in the right hands it can do anything."
—Jack Halberstam, author of *Female Masculinity* and *In a Queer Time and Place: Transgender Bodies, Subcultural Lives*

ARSENAL PULP PRESS | VANCOUVER

Persistence

All Ways Butch and Femme

edited by IVAN E. COYOTE
& ZENA SHARMAN

PERSISTENCE
Copyright © 2011 by the contributors

ARSENAL PULP PRESS
#101–211 East Georgia St
Vancouver, BC
V6A 1Z6
arsenalpulp.com

The publisher gratefully acknowledges the support of the Canada Council for the Arts and the British Columbia Arts Council for its publishing program, and the Government of Canada (through the Book Publishing Industry Development Program) and the Government of British Columbia (through the Book Publishing Tax Credit Program) for its publishing activities.

"A Butch Roadmap" and "Hats Off" were previously published in *Missed Her,* by Ivan E. Coyote.

Cover illustration by Elisha Lim
Book design by Shyla Seller

Printed and bound in Canada on recycled paper

Library and Archives Canada Cataloguing in Publication:

  Persistence : all ways butch and femme / [edited by] Ivan E. Coyote and Zena Sharman.

Issued also in electronic format.
ISBN 978-1-55152-397-2

  1. Lesbians--Identity. 2. Gender identity. 3. Lesbians--Biography. I. Coyote, Ivan E. (Ivan Elizabeth), 1969-
II. Sharman, Zena, 1979-

HQ75.5.P47 2011   306.76'63   C2011-901943-4

We would like to dedicate this book to all the femmes and butches who came before us. We want to thank you for your strength and your spirit, for your red fingernails and your fishnet stockings and your neckties and white button-down shirts. We want to thank you for your bravery and your broken hearts and busted-up knees and bad backs. We want to thank you for keeping on, for rising above, for remembering, and for what you left behind. We want to thank you for making us possible. We want to thank you for being, for believing, and for persisting.

Contents

Forward!

Foreword by Joan Nestle

> *Dedicated to the contributors to* The Persistent Desire: A
> Femme-Butch Reader *who have died since the book was
> published in 1992: Mabel Hampton, 1902–89; Marge
> McDonald, 1931–86; Audre Lorde, 1934–92; Deanna
> Alida, d. 1991; Jeanie Meuer, d. 1991; Blue Lunden,
> 1936–99; Ira Jeffries, d. 2010. My buddies, my mentors,
> my critics, my erotic comrades. So many years of courage
> and creations, touch and yearning and defiance and love,
> of complex histories of culture, gender, and desire. Your
> buddy misses you.*

When Ivan and Zena told me of their soon-to-be-published collection, which you now hold in your hands, I did not react well.
Their title was too close to that of my own work, *The Persistent
Desire: A Femme-Butch Reader*, published by Alyson Books, and
I wanted them to choose a title that reflected their own historical
positioning. For the many years since the publication of *Persistent Desire*, I had refused to do a sequel, as I believed that it was
a book born out of its own time's struggles over erotic territories
and gender certainties. Now, after having read this manuscript,
I believe I made the right decision to contribute this foreword.
The voices of another generation, of other cultural positions,
new possibilities of gender discourse, and erotic adventuring are

presented here, and these extend in complex ways the passionate and embattled conversation of the now out-of-print *Persistent Desire*. I asked the two editors if I could write a foreword that would give the reasons and some of the processes behind my work. While I was the editor and a contributor, *Persistent Desire* was the creation of all its writers—all sixty-seven of them who generously and excellently transformed the public face of gender and erotic conversation in the lesbian community from the 1990s on. I met two of those original contributors once again in these new pages—Jewelle Gomez and Jeanne Córdova. Their words remind me of their original gift of comradeship, so freely given in harder times (the 1970s and 1980s)—harder, I mean, in the ability to have full and open discussions of gender and sexual differences within our own communities. I am afraid, given the present political climate in North America, that we are in for a new definition of hard times.

It's worth mentioning that I am now seventy and just this year had my third bout of a major cancer. I sometimes ask laughingly—how many cancers can a girl have? I am afraid I will find out, and so I look upon this foreword as a way to look backward, to fix in a more permanent (though life just laughs at such endeavours) form, the journey behind that pink-and-grey book cover showing a fem's[1] large thigh sheathed in seamed stockings pushing its way between the legs of her butch lover; my black slip riding high and Deb's urban boots holding their own, both of us cradled in rich New Hampshire meadow grass, and all captured in the lens of Morgan Gwenwald, that fine photographer of all things lesbian. My fem body, scarred in ways I had not imagined then, looks upon its younger self with gratitude for the kindness

---

1 In my own writing, I prefer using "fem," the word as I imagined it when I first entered this community in the late 1950s. I had no knowledge that it was based on a French word, and "femme" still feels like an affectation to me, but I have often lost this battle for experiential and class purity to my editors.

of that 1992 gay publisher who did not flinch at such an image. Even one's thighs are historical documents. Time has shifted not just the contours of my body but the streets I walk, the skies I see. Eleven years ago, under the threat of aggressive breast cancer, I left New York's upper west-side streets and moved to Melbourne, Australia, to be with my woman poppa, Dianne Otto. I am writing this in a room far away from the Greenwich Village streets where it all began, at least in a public way, back in 1958 when I walked into my first lesbian bar on 8th Street.

In her essay "Never Be Hungry Again," Leah Lakshmi Piepzna-Samarasinha tells us, "Sometimes I feel like I've been writing the same story since I started writing." How fitting, I thought. Ever since my work "Marcia's Room" was first published in 1980, I have been trying to translate the language of desire of one time to another, trying to hold the forces of erasure and judgment at bay long enough to make known the wonders of the butches and fems I met in the working-class bars of the 1950s—both to honour how they held this woman's body in often work-worn hands and raised her hips to such deeply sought caresses, to such deeply sought penetrations—but even more, to honour and make into history women's communities of gender difference and hard-won autonomies of survival and pleasure. Out of my history—as a bar fem, as a gay liberationist, as a member of the first lesbian feminist groups in New York City—as a political dissenter from the deadly McCarthy era of the 1950s to the anti-war movements and the civil rights marches of the 1960s; out of my teaching in the revolutionary educational program called SEEK (Search for Elevation, Education, and Knowledge); out of my relationship with Mabel Hampton, the first lesbian I had ever known, who took me into her past with her wife Lillian Foster, back into the 1920s lesbian communities of Harlem and the Bronx; out of the life of Regina Nestle, my sometimes sex-worker and most-of-the-time bookkeeping mother, came the will to keep the ledger books open for what was acceptable lesbian, women's, gay, social-justice history.

Perhaps you have heard of the Sex Wars, perhaps you think it is all an overstatement now that we live in a time of endless war, but I can tell you that at times it felt as if we were fighting for our lives, for the lives of our imaginations, for the right to think and talk about sexual difference and play of power out loud, for the right to question gender essentialisms, for the right to simply say *our desires are more complex*, and somehow, as Carole Vance[2] so brilliantly put it, to walk the streets between pleasure and danger. I am talking of the 1982 Barnard Conference on Sexuality when a huge act of censorship went unchallenged—except by those hurt by the erasure of their work—because the group Women Against Pornography considered the artwork and some of the speakers unacceptable and told the college authorities that sex perverts were taking over the conference, and the university believed them. (The original censored program is held in the Lesbian Herstory Archives in Brooklyn, NY, along with images from the lesser-known sex-radical speak-out we held as soon as the conference ended, in which one of the readers was a young woman named Judith Butler.)[3] A picket line of women wearing Women Against Pornography black T-shirts greeted us on that first sunny morning of the conference. They were giving out leaflets about the unacceptable speakers at the conference: Dorothy Allison, Pat Califia, Gayle Rubin, Amber Hollibaugh, and me. Our crime was that we spoke of butch-fem, we spoke

---

2   Carol Vance, anthropologist and epidemiologist, is co-director of the Institute for the Study of Sex in Society and History in New York; she is also the editor of *Pleasure and Danger: Exploring Female Sexuality* (1984), the papers of the Scholar and Feminist IX Conference, *Toward a Politics of Sexuality*, of which I am speaking. She is a leading thinker in the intersections between human rights and sexuality.

3   Judith Butler, author of *Gender Trouble: Feminism and the Subversion of Identity* (1990), and many other ground-breaking works, has become one of the world's most exciting thinkers on issues of gender, performative language, and post-modern feminism.

of S/M, we were an affront to the new order. This was the only picket line I ever crossed.

At the opening session, two things happened that influenced my decision to do *Persistent Desire*. I found myself standing behind the women who had worked so hard on the images and text for the program as the Barnard College president explained that the program had been pulled from every packet because it was too controversial, too explicit. Tears ran down the faces of those women as they suffered their public shaming. Disgusted, I walked toward the exit only to be stopped by one of the leaders of Women Against Pornography who told me in words I'll never forget: "If you write about butch-fem in the past, we will let you do it; but if you write about it today, you are on the enemy list." Oh, girl, what a mistake you made! All I can say is that none of us were unscathed by the public attacks and that some of the finest thinkers on gender and queer erotics in our communities were deeply wounded in these conflicts. I wanted to do an international, vast exploration of butch-fem lives to open up the conversation, let other voices from other histories as well as from the present day tell their stories, let their faces and bodies be seen, let new readers judge for themselves what was important about this way of desiring, being, playing, resisting, and cherishing—about its past and ongoing engagement with feminisms.

After the late 1970s, I developed a project that would eventually lead to some of the most moving and provoking moments of *Persistent Desire*. I decided to put together a slide show, the old-fashioned kind with a Kodak projector, slide trays, and a roll-up screen. This was the grassroots technology that I used to speak to gay and lesbian communities wherever they would have me and to bring them images and voices from lesbian history before 1969, with an emphasis on working-class butch-fem lives. With my shoe box-shaped cassette tape recorder, I sat at the working table of the Archives (also my dinner table) and listened to hundreds of hours of old-time butches (and fewer hours of old-time fems) telling their stories from the 1940s and '50s. I listened to women like Sandy Kern, who hugged her first girlfriend during a blackout in 1945 on a Brooklyn stoop; to Jules Bruno, telling tales of her run-ins, as a young butch, with the police and of the first time she used a dildo—still one of my favourite narratives in all of lesbian history for its poetry, humour, bravado, and its portrait of an older fem woman clear about what she wanted, and all told within the bar-culture realities of the early 1960s. I was compiling what James Baldwin called, in his book *Notes of a Native Son*, a "geography of the Old Country." He was speaking of the Jim Crow era American south in the early and middle twentieth century, while ours was the old country of vice-squad raids, police round-ups in lesbian and gay bars, physical assaults on dark streets, and all the paraphernalia of a time when homophobia was the law of the land. But that law did not stop Marge McDonald, another of the voices in *Persistent Desire*, from driving all over the night streets of Columbus, Ohio, in 1955 trying to find the one women's bar "where I could finally meet one of my own kind." This was the tension I wanted to recreate—of oppression and persistence. I still wonder why I've spent so much of my life seeking out these stories and telling my own. I believe it's because I found profound moments of the human heart in them, because the women sitting before me often had so little of what my society considered wealth or safety, and amidst laughter, poses, flirtations, and devastating pain, they told me of the worlds of touch and community they had managed to create—the new homes, both of gender and of neighbourhood, they had created, breaking countless caste systems along the way, and the rages and ecstasies that threatened them every day. This was human stuff, important enough for the whole world to know about.

I started the slide show with images from the 1941 US government-sponsored medical study, *Sex Variants*, compiled by George W. Henry, MD, with its eighty case studies of people described as gender variants—women, men, and intersexed. In

the back of the book were the line drawings done by the contributing doctors, who measured the nipples and labia, the rectums
and penises of the people interviewed to show their biological
abnormalities. Replete with the racism of its times, the book
grew out of the government's amazement at their "discovery" of
so many "sexual deviants" during the two World Wars. When
the measured body parts of our elders appeared on the screen, I
talked about other lineages of biological determinism: the colo-
nial masters' measuring of the skull sizes of African-Americans
to prove their inferiority and allowable candidacy for slavery;
the weighing of the brains of women at the turn of the nine-
teenth century to prove their lack of intelligence and, therefore,
their need for masculine custodial care; the Nazis' careful mea-
surements of the width of Jewish nostrils to establish their difference from the norm and suitability for extermination. I wanted
this history of how our bodies were treated by the State and by
science to be part of lesbian, queer history. I asked my audiences
to be careful of arguments based on biological destiny. I still
do. (Never will I fight for gay rights on the basis of the argument that *I was born this way*.) Henry's book, with its clinical
language, also gave me clues to the butch-fem history I was looking for. With a different reading, these records of "pathology"
hinted at lives of resistance, passion, and accomplishment.

Marian J:
Marian is a large, middle-aged mulatto woman of me-
dium height. Her well developed breasts and hips suggest
the gentle mammy but her square shoulders, erect posture, decisive gait and fearless attitude give the impression of being distinctly masculine attributes ... For forty
years Marian has been a professional entertainer and for
twenty years she was a favorite in European society ...

Two hours later, the audience had seen images from McCarthy-era, government-led purges of sex-deviants and from the *Well of Loneliness* censorship trial of the 1920s, during which Lady Troubridge (Una Vincenzo) urged Radclyffe Hall (her partner and the book's author) on to full disclosure with the words, "I am sick to death of ambiguities." They had seen images from *The Captive*, one of the first plays with a lesbian theme, which was presented on Broadway in 1928 and closed by the vice squad, and had heard of how butch-fem women protected each other during bar raids. My audiences listened to the voices of Audre Lorde, Sandy Kern, Jules Bruno, and Mabel Hampton while viewing photos of these women from the 1950s. I showed them images of Doris (Blue) Lunden as a baby butch in New Orleans in the 1950s, as a pregnant butch, as a feminist butch peace activist, and as a grandmother. While listening to a tape of '50s bar music, the audiences watched as 100 images of butch and fem women from the early and mid-twentieth century were projected onto the screen. In small towns, in university towns, in gay and women's centres, in living rooms and church halls, in the back rooms of bars, and at the Berkshire Conferences on the History of Women—wherever I was invited, I took this multimedia presentation of my version of lesbian history. At every showing, women would come up and tell me of their past experiences, of how they used to "pass" and not talk about their butch or fem selves, about how they had destroyed the old lesbian paperbacks because they were so terrified of being that ugly thing created by both the State and by those who should have known better. They brought photographs and asked me to put them into the slide show.

I had set out to conquer my own and others' shame, and I did my work, my greatly loved work, with my best feminist self, with appreciation for the complexities of each queer person's life. *The Persistent Desire* could only have been conceived after I had been a lesbian feminist for some years. Thus, through writing letters to old friends, making announcements in community publications, gathering responses to the slide show, working with the Lesbian Herstory Archives (which now holds all the materials I've collected and created), I amassed a huge manuscript, because I was convinced of the importance of each voice. Only the patient editing wisdom of Lynne Yamaguchi Fletcher at Alyson Books allowed me to pare down the manuscript to slightly over 500 pages.

We needed this vast archive, I believed, because one of the goals of *Persistent Desire* was to reconstitute lives fragmented by the small-minded, by those trapped by gender or class conventions, by those so taken with prevailing ideologies of liberation that they repeated new mantras of dismissal. In 1979, at the first ever National Women's Studies Association Conference held on the grounds of the University of Kansas, with its endless fields open to endless skies, women were giddy with the community-building of lesbian-feminism. We were there to do a presentation about the Archives, but during the afternoon before our talk, I attended a slide show created to combat homophobia. All was going well, as we took pleasure in the cleverness of the images— we were so sunny with self-possession—until a slide with the words, "Old-fashioned stereotypes of lesbians," came out of the darkness—and then, "Butch-fem is no longer a reality of lesbian lives; it was born out of a desperate time." These words were accompanied by caricatures of women representing such desperation. The laughter stopped in my throat; perhaps I was the only '50s bar lesbian there, perhaps others were passing, but all of a sudden the wonder of the camaraderie of shared, new world-visions turned to dust. I let my anger be known at this ahistorical and self-betraying public relations device, the same anger I felt when a leading, glamorous American lesbian writer of the 1980s said, "We're not all truck drivers, you know." Again, I saw the urge to achieve conventional respectability falsifying and denying a past; I saw the looming dangers of over-simplifications and further betrayals of communities that had made our present possible, but even more, I saw a dead-end way of looking at marginalized sexually different communities of gender, both those of the past and of the 1990s present. I didn't think feminism demanded this of us. Just the opposite.

Persistent Desire was almost all I wanted it to be: a historical collection spanning fem-butch utterances from 1893 to the 1990s; an international anthology containing contributions from Mexico, the Philippines, Australia, England, Canada, Cuba, and Chile; and full of fem-butch display and gender provocation, with twenty-six pages of grainy black-and-white photographs. I have it in my hands now, and I can barely put it down. Many of the writers, narrators, and poets in the book were an important part of my mid- and late-twentieth century life; they were friends and colleagues in the deepest sense of the words: Liz (Elizabeth) Kennedy and Madeline Davis, who contributed one of their early chapters from *Boots of Leather, Slippers of Gold*; Cheryl Clarke, whose poem "Of Althea and Flaxie" said all I was trying to do with the collection; Amber Hollibaugh and Cherríe Moraga, whose essay, "What We're Rollin' Around in Bed with: Sexual Silences in Feminism," became a classic moment of honest talk about sexuality and feminism; Jewelle Gomez, who wrote a wonderful poem about same-gendered difference, "Flamingos and Bears: A Parable"; the pioneering grass-roots lesbian scholar Judith Schwarz, who wrote about the butches she had known in 1963 working night-shift, cutting negatives in the labs of Technicolor, Inc., in San Francisco; Dorothy Allison; Kitty Tsui; Pam Parker; Chea Villanueva—I touch you all still. As if the subject itself was transitioning out of my hands into new times, Pat Califia's poetry speaks of "Gender Fucks," and Gayle Rubin, in her measured brilliance, looks to the future in "Of Catamites and Kings: Reflections on Butch, Gender, and Boundaries." All of us had stood our ground, watching each other's backs when the attacks came, believing in the necessity of the work we were doing. The ground was shifting, however; new histories were emerging.

NEW FEM TERRITORIES

The year is 2009, the occasion is the Melbourne launch of the book *Femmes of Power: Exploding Queer Femininities* by Del LaGrace Volcano and Ulrika Dahl, the place is a queer bar with a small stage and red overhead lighting, much like the bars I went to in the '50s (except without the police surveillance), with many people of many genders. I was invited to the stage by Ulrika, a high fem who held the room in her most capable hands.

"Thank you, Ulrika. My words tonight, my expression of fem power, grows out of the courage of the young fem-butch trans people, lesbian-feminist people, peace and gender activists both Palestinian and Israeli, with whom I spoke in Haifa, Tel Aviv, and Jerusalem two years ago. It is inspired by the courage of Raouda Marcos, the founder of ASWAT, the organization of Palestinian gay women, who fights for the lives of all her people on so many fronts. In 2008, I found the poetry of Mahmoud Darwish, the Palestinian poet who died at age sixty-seven on August 9, 2008 in exile and who lived his life labelled as a 'present-absent alien' by the Israeli government. I will carry his words on this fem body for the rest of my life. Dear Poet, how did I find you, through the dusty roads of unknown histories, you whose words live on so many tongues? I was so ignorant of the love you poured into your differently metered lines, of your swirling solid notes of exile, of the white mare that runs down into the valleys no longer safe, that drinks from your fathers' wells, now empty of their sense of self. I came as a stranger, a Jewish fem stranger, into your cadences of loss and exultation, into your Andalusian sunsets and endless stony roads that lead to children carrying fathers on their backs, to endless journeys past familiar olive trees but with no rest allowed, no fruit given.

"I stood in front of the grey looming wall that divided life from life, that marked the loss of history for one people and the loss of a soul for another. That impenetrable wall, with its razor wire far above us, froze my fem queer body. And that is why I am here tonight. For many years, I have written, mapped, tracked the power of my fem desire, the strength of my thighs to grip the wanted body and shake it loose of its hard places, to offer my fullness of desire and flesh as a way through, as a break in the wall, as a yearning that refuses solid borders and policed boundaries. I have revelled in the thrust of penetration, the opening in the wall. In other writings, I have charted how desire for a certain kind of touch can push a woman off the map. And on that deserted sandy road in East Jerusalem facing the wall's solid brutality, I had an inkling of a new fem politic, something beyond my earlier years of celebration of the fem-butch courage that had walked the hate-filled streets of Joseph McCarthy's America. How does a fem face history; how does my body, which always speaks of my desires, confront the atrophy of national compassion that so marks our world? A port of entry, a simple thing, a taking in, an opening in the wall. Over ruins so huge they threaten to blot out all hope, your words find me. I have tasted your heat, seen the olive trees in exile, decorative in the gardens of the usurpers. What a strange two the world would think us, a 1950s Jewish fem from the Bronx and the dying Palestinian poet who lives in every Arabic mouth—but the only way I can live in a world where such a wall exists is to take your words into my mouth. A port of entry, a simple thing, a taking in, an opening in the wall."

The poet, Mahmoud Darwish, speaks: "This is my language, collars of stars around the necks of lovers, my steps are of wind and sand/my world in my body and what my hands possess/I am the traveler and the path."

Remember when I said that *Persistent Desire* was almost all I wanted it to be? I had wanted more fem voices and I still do, and after reading *Persistence: All Ways Butch and Femme*, I see that others were better suited to the new century. Since my book's publication, readers have come up to me and asked if I knew that some of the butch writers in it were "transitioning." The lesbian world of genders was changing all around me: in language and style, in biology as destiny being recreated or refused, in new kinds of masculinities, new kinds of erotic partnerships that delight in shifting bodies, new expressions of fem power, of snapping jaws, new combinations of identities alongside disavowals of all fixed gender selves, through fems and butches speaking for themselves, uncoupled, and differently gendered people weaving their complex selves through ancestral homes. At seventy, I have looked into the future, I have heard the new-old cries of don't box us in, don't be sure of how all this is going to turn out, we will forge new liberations in a time of endless war, we will work toward social justice in this world, carrying these complex bodies of desire with us, as much acts of the imagination as flesh and bone. We have cast off the anchors.

I wish you well on your journeys, so important for all of us. Thank you, Ivan and Zena, for giving me this vista.

Note: Copies of the 1992 edition of *The Persistent Desire* can still be found in used book stores, and it has been included in an EBSCO scanned collection for libraries. I must add that the Lesbian Herstory Archives, which I co-founded in 1974, made my work possible in all ways.

ACKNOWLEDGMENTS

First of all, we would like to thank the dedicated and hardworking folks at Arsenal Pulp Press for believing in this book and helping us take it out of our hopes and into our hands. Arsenal's ongoing commitment to publishing queer voices continues to inspire. We also would like to thank Joan Nestle, not only for the heart-bending foreword that she wrote for this book, but also for being such a brave and eloquent mentor and role model for both of us, then, now, and always. Every movement needs its leaders, and we are truly blessed to have her as one of ours: as a writer, as an activist, a theorist, and a femme. Joan, we thank you. This book exists partly as a gift to you for everything you have given us.

We would like to thank Elisha Lim for the beautiful original piece of art that graces the front cover of this book. We would also like to acknowledge the commitment and hard work of each and every writer contained in these pages. Speaking honestly and with an open heart about issues as close to the bone as one's own identity is never an easy thing, and we sincerely thank you all for taking that risk with your stories.

We would like to extend our thanks as well to the independent bookstores that will stock this book, and their staff. You help complete the equation: putting the right books into the right hands and onto shelves in cities and towns where, even today, books from the margins would otherwise go unfound. We would especially like to thank Little Sister's bookstore and Janine Fuller for their tireless work against censorship of queer books at our borders, and in our country. Our heartfelt appreciation must also be extended to the many radical librarians out there, who will see to it that books like this find their way into the hands of those who need them the most.

Lastly, we would like to thank the butch and femme communities on this continent and around the world. This book is by us, for us, and for those who will come after. You are our family.

Introduction

Ivan E. Coyote and Zena Sharman

STUMBLING ONTO BUTCH

I remember the day I first saw the word "butch" in print. How it stuck out of the sentence I found it in, like a purple-black thumbnail, like a blood smear on a hammer head. I was twenty-three years old, standing in the cramped and steamy space between shelves at the old Little Sister's bookstore in Vancouver, holding a freshly inked copy of *The Persistent Desire: A Femme-Butch Reader*. Butch. The word seemed somehow simultaneously archaic and revolutionary. Lost as I was at the time in an androgynous sea of second-wave lesbian feminists, the word butch seemed so … dangerous, so not what my lover and her Women's Studies separatist friends would approve of, so … male-identified.

I had learned a lot since leaving my small-town northern working-class roots and moving to the big city five years earlier. I had come out of the closet everybody but me had always known I was in, and found community in Vancouver's activist scene. I had learned *Robert's Rules of Order*, non-violent peaceful resistance, and ways to smash the patriarchy. I learned that men were the enemy, and that being male-identified was counter-revolutionary at best—and at times, tantamount to treason. I had also learned to remain silent about what I fantasized while fucking my lovers, silent about what I really felt when I stepped into a strap-on harness, silent about why I avoided mirrors when naked. We were going to change the world. I was a good queer. A good feminist. How could I be butch? How could this word feel so good when I lifted it onto my shoulders? What would Andrea Dworkin think? Still, I bought *The Persistent Desire* and secreted it home, stashed it right between my 1992 edition of *Practical Problems in Mathematics for Electricians* and *The Complete Guide to Repairing and Maintaining Your Ford Engine*.

Twenty years later, "butch" fits like my favourite boots, like my oldest belt. Other words have been thrown about, and some even stuck for a while, but butch persists. It is the only thing I have always been. I have been out for twenty-four years and a butch for forty-one.

READING MY WAY INTO FEMME

As a kid, I used to carry my library books home in a little red wagon. This was partly a product of my bookish nature and partly because my single mother didn't own a car, and we lived in a small northern town with a lousy transit system. Thirty-odd years later, my reading habits haven't changed much. I'm still a bookworm. In fact, I've read my way into everything that's ever mattered to me—feminism, social justice, queerness, femme.

I don't remember the first time I read the word femme, but it was probably in some dusty corner of the university library— the HQ section, to be exact, which is where you can find all of the books the librarians classify under the broad category called "Family, Marriage, Women, and Sexuality." It's a veritable treasure-trove of writing about queers and perverts and gender warriors and freaks (and, to my great delight, is likely where this anthology will be found).

I was a twenty-something grad student doing a sort of independent study called "Am I queer or just a bi-curious co-ed?" Until then, I'd always written off my girl crushes as some sort of romantic quirk, a never-acted-upon marker of just how progressive a feminist I really was. It turns out I was a big old homo, but it took me a while to figure that out. After all, I'd never seen a lesbian who looked like me. The only dykes I'd ever met were middle-aged, sensibly dressed professors in comfortable shoes. I liked and admired them, but they didn't look like my future.

That all changed when grad school brought me to the big city, where I got to know beautiful tattooed femmes and lithe sissy boys with drag-queen alter egos, and I met handsome butches who set my heart aflutter. Suddenly I could see myself in "queer." I started going to the gay bar, took up go-go dancing for a queer punk band, and read everything I could get my hands on. It was in books like *The Persistent Desire* and *Brazen Femme: Queering Femininity* that I found words for who I was, and through these a lineage, a community, my heroes. Nearly ten years later, femme is more than just a word on a page. It's who I am.

BROADENING THE JOINING

When we first sat down to write the introduction for this book, we did what both of us have traditionally done when setting out to say something that matters to us: we started with the dictionary. Since we were looking for the most contemporary, hip, and down-with-the-people definitions of the words femme and butch, we passed over the *Oxford English Dictionary* in favour of the Internet. But even the interwebs couldn't get it quite right. The word "stereotype" was bandied about a lot. Butch was used as a synonym for dominant, and most definitions of femme had a lot more to say about outfits and accessories than identity and politics. This would never do. Our experience of these words and the people who use them was so much bigger than that.

The stories in these pages resist simple definitions. The people in these stories defy reductive stereotypes and inflexible categories. The pages in this book describe the lives of an incredible diversity of people whose hearts also pounded for some reason the first time they read or heard the word butch or femme.

This book is a testament to the many beautiful ways butch and femme can be lived and embodied. It is our homage to the bodies that lived it before us, and it is our gift to those just discovering themselves.

Audre Lorde said: "When we define ourselves, when I define myself, the place in which I am like you and the place in which

I am not like you, I'm not excluding you from the joining—I'm broadening the joining."[1]

We hope this book will broaden the joining. We hope it will stretch and break and reform those tired and tiring definitions into the words and worlds we see around us. We hope this book will be opened in big-city bookstores by small-town butches and dragged home in wagons by bookworms blossoming into femmes. We hope that you find parts of yourself in these pages and a sense of history and community and belonging between its covers. And we hope you persist.

---

1   Audre Lorde, *Sister Outsider: Essays and Speeches* (Berkeley, CA: The Crossing Press, 1984), 10.

Ride

Anna Camilleri

I've heard it said that injury is far worse if a body knows it's
about to be hurt, and instinctively braces itself taut and tight like
a stretched elastic band. It's an autonomic response—like blood
flow or arousal—it's not a thinking thing, it just happens. That
day, the safe distance between trivia about the endlessly fascinating human body and the mortality of my own was erased.

Half of Vaughan Avenue was torn up. Orange pylons and
signs designated two narrow lanes and a reduced speed of thirty
kilometres an hour. There wasn't enough room to share the lane
with a vehicle, so I slipped my bike into the centre, pedalled fast
through a cloud of dust: lips pressed shut, eyes drawn shut to
narrow slits.

The only thing that had been fluttering through my mind was
how much I dislike the smell of tar. I wondered about the lungs
of workers who mix and lay it, day in, day out. I could see up
ahead to where the pylons ended.

I heard the car behind me, felt the heat of it. It was close, too
close. Ass in the air, I pedalled harder.

Then I had a mouthful of gravel and knuckles that looked
like they had been dragged across a cheese grater. I tried to pick
myself up, but my body folded underneath me like a marionette
that had been cut loose from its tethers. Blood pooled under
my tongue. The taste of iron blended with the odour of freshly
pressed tar smelled strangely like fire. There was blood on the
road, burning in my body, but I couldn't isolate the source. Cars
drove past.

I spotted my bicycle twenty feet away from where I lay, its
metal frame bent in half at the crossbar. It dawned on me that I
had been hit by a driver who had not stopped. Right before I lost
consciousness, lying belly down on the spine of the road, unable

to move, I remember thinking, *This isn't a good place to hang out. You need to move.*

It was the rasp of her voice that drew me back, and her hands at my temples, sweeping hair away from my face.

"Anna?"

"Hi ... What are you doing here?"

A smile came through in the creases of her eyes. "Just happened to be in the area—looks like you need a hand."

I hadn't seen her in six years, but asked after her periodically. She had become a tool-and-die maker in prosthetics manufacturing, was shacked up with a sweet young thing out in suburban Toronto, and in her second year of sobriety. Despite the mess I was in, I remembered the heat between us, felt it as though no time had passed: autonomic response—it's not a thinking thing, it just happens.

Those long nights when we didn't sleep until after the sun came up. Living on strong coffee and forevers. After some choice words about not putting up with any more shit, I left her standing there on the fire-escape one day, dragging hard on a cigarette, looking like James Dean in *Rebel Without a Cause*, only more brooding.

I willed myself not to turn back; I didn't. Told myself that I'd forget her; I didn't.

I was nineteen when we met, the city kid, all grown up at an early age, full of vitriol and righteousness and, underneath all of that, a soft underbelly with romantic dreams and convictions where everything was life or death and there was no such thing as relative value—everything was important, dire, immediate. She had ten or so years on me—but who was counting?—and had high-tailed it out of northern Manitoba when she was a teenager, farm-handed her way across the country until she landed in Toronto. Said it was the ugliest place she ever loved.

She had a low-riding boat of a car, a '67 Cutlass Supreme that she fussed over as though she had carried it herself for three trimesters, with gleaming wheel hubs and a mint-condition interior that she conditioned with Armor All every weekend. The sum total of her bathroom products included a bar of soap that doubled as shampoo, a toothbrush, toothpaste, and a deodorant stick. Two whole Rubbermaid containers contained nothing but car-care products.

On the days I arrived home before her, I could hear her coming up the hill in her Cutlass, even with the din of traffic from St. Clair Avenue and transport trucks rumbling north and south on Dufferin Street (which was more pothole than street).

She'd drop her tool belt, wrap her arms around me and say, "Did the day treat you right, babe?"

"Right enough," I'd say. "Did you give 'em hell today?"

"Sure did, darlin', sure did. Plenty for the both of us."

She rode side-saddle next to me in the ambulance, and when we arrived in admissions, she answered the intake worker's question about the nature of our relationship with the word "family."

We left the hospital six hours later with a prescription for antibiotics, a long list of soft-tissue injuries that would heal, and strict orders that I not be allowed to sleep for more than three hours at a stretch for the next twenty-four hours (to make sure I didn't have a concussion).

In my apartment, she ran a bath, undressed me, and helped me into it. Her gaze didn't wander from my eyes. "I'm right on the other side of the door. Holler if you need me, darlin', I mean Anna."

She arranged for friends to care for me over the next couple of days, and just before she left said, "I'm not glad you were hit, but I'm glad I was there." She planted a kiss on my forehead and turned to leave, but stopped short of the door. "I ask after you too. You know that, right?"

This time, it was my turn to watch her walk away.

ANNA CAMILLERI has been hailed as a "storytelling siren" (Pride Toronto); "tough, visceral and funny" (*Atlanta Journal Constitution*) and a "cultural agitator " (*Now Magazine*). She has performed across Canada and the US in theatres, festivals, and universities over the past fifteen years, and she is a founding member of SweLL, a collaborative performance project with Ivan E. Coyote and Lyndell Montgomery. Camilleri is writer/performer of the one-woman shows *Still Breathing Fire* and *Sounds Siren Red*, author of *I Am a Red Dress*, editor of *Red Light: Superheroes, Saints, and Sluts,* co-editor of *Brazen Femme: Queering Femininity*, co-author of *Boys Like Her: Transfictions*, and writer/director of two nationally broadcast CBC radio works. Her books are included in the University of Toronto's Fisher Rare Books Library Queer Canadian Literature collection, and she is artistic director of Red Dress Productions, a company that creates and disseminates original interdisciplinary performance and works with/in communities on large-scale, community-engaged public artworks. As lead visual artist, she recently completed *Flux*, a 27 x 5 foot (8.2 x 1.5 m) mosaic, working with members of the 519 Church Street Community Centre, and is currently engaged in a creative writing residency with students at the Triangle Program, Canada's only alternative high school for LGBTQ youth. Anna can be found online at *annacamilleri.com* and *reddressproductions.blogspot.com.*

My First Lover Was Not a Lesbian

Kimberly Dark

My first lover was not a lesbian. One night after we made love, she stared at the ceiling, pondering.

"At least I'm not a lesbian," she said.

I raised myself to one elbow on the bed. My skin was still sticking to her skin, the sheet tangled between us. I stared for a moment, incredulous. "Is that so?" I finally managed.

She nodded, shrugged.

"You ever been in love with a man?" I asked her.

"No."

"With a woman?"

"Sure."

"Have you ever felt really attracted to men?"

"No." She was getting annoyed.

"Are you attracted to women?"

She glared at me.

"Take me, for example." I offered, coquettishly. "I am a woman, you know." I pressed myself against her and kissed her earlobe. She growled a bit, finished with my foolishness. She rolled on top of me and kissed me hard, long.

"Yes, I had noticed that," she confirmed in a softened tone, once the kiss was finished. Her body on my body, moist thighs pressing against mine, hands holding my wrists, where she pinned me for this kiss of retribution, she conceded, "Okay, so maybe I'm bisexual."

I guffawed, but then she silenced me again, in the best way she knew how. I can't say I minded the disagreement—or the resolution. But being as I am, I didn't let it go.

The next day, I tried to explain to her how her distance from other women appeared. Surely, I thought, I could make her see the way she signalled her queerness to others, despite her closeted ways.

"Women look at each other. We stand close to each other," I explained.

"Not straight women," she replied.

"Especially straight women," I insisted.

"Yeah, well, not women like me," she said firmly.

"I think that was the point, darling," I rolled my eyes.

The truth is, her public distance from me made me tense. It made her tense. She tried to pass as a straight woman, and because this was stressful, she just looked like an awkward dyke trying not to gawk at some woman she found attractive. If she had allowed me to show my affection, at least she wouldn't have looked pitiful.

It was ridiculous that she thought she could pass for straight. She was tall and athletic, with a muscular female swagger, no makeup, short hair, and sensible shoes. She had a tendency to say "Um-mmm" when a pretty woman walked by. This last part seemed involuntary, or she'd have corrected it, I'm sure. So, instead of acting like a couple deserving of one another's affection, we acted like we were having an illicit affair. We glanced at each other playfully from across the room. We played footsies under the dinner table and flirted at a distance, electricity between us. I was young, and being queer still seemed potentially dangerous to me too, though less so than it did for her. Something was different in our experiences, and I was slowly putting it together. As a girly-girl, my queerness could be cute. Hers could be threatening. She knew it without knowing what she knew. And, of course, our flirtations were all the more obvious because of the tension. Inexperience made me insensitive to her troubles, but I was learning quickly. See, I can pass for straight. But she only pretends she can. She pretends that no one looks at her and thinks "dyke." She envied my femme invisibility and was angered when I refused to use it.

A person could hear this story and sympathize with my closeted darling. It's possible that the travails of the time prompted my lover's inability to claim her butchness, to claim her queerness. It wasn't as easy to live openly in 1983 as it is now. We lived in Southern California, but she had grown up in suburban Virginia—that matters too. People weren't as evolved then in their queer consciousness. Today, we can all be held to a higher standard.

And yet, gay culture and living were already established in the 1980s—gay America was post-criminalization, post-institutionalization, post-Stonewall. But what does it matter if something exists, if you've never seen it? Gay America was an unknown destination on my map, and on hers. I was new, and while my lover could've found gay culture in 1983, she'd never looked. Why would she? She was not a lesbian, even though she slept with women and expressed her female gender femininity-free. She knew what she was just as surely as she knew what I was when she saw me, but she never called herself lesbian, gay, queer, or any other such thing.

Location and queer visibility can influence a person. While she was sixteen years my senior, she had known fewer openly gay people in Virginia than I had, living in Southern California. But then, all the gay people I knew were men: hairdressers, interior designers, and models. (Oh yes, just as you imagine, the gays were everywhere. And they were beautifully dressed—and tanned.) Gay men were fashionable, but all I ever heard about lesbians was that they were ugly, unfortunate women. They had no sense of style. Lesbians were worse than invisible in my youth; they were maligned. It's not only important that one sees queers, but that one hears positive messages about diversity.

So ironically, my butch lover was not a lesbian, but I was pretty sure I was. I was different in so many ways. She was my first lover, and I stood in the bathroom the morning after we first made love saying the word "lesbian" over and over to the mirror just to feel it, to see if it would stick. I didn't know where I would possibly find others like her—women to whom I could be *that* attracted. It took a few years to find the next one, probably because I never gave up femininity in order to be visible as queer. (My next butch lover was also in Southern California, and she had a long lesbian-feminist history attached to her identity. What an education—but that's another story.)

Is it any wonder that we know what we know when we know it? History is not linear; our collective understanding of social phenomena lurches forward and falls back again, always intersecting variously with the individual paths we tread, the ways we understand ourselves, where we grow up, and how we're taught to feel about being "other." Nowadays, queer identities have become more mainstream, so that even a person in a rural or fundamentalist Christian community might've seen "the gays" on TV or the Internet. Of course, the persistent array is not all positive; it's still easy to find people disrespecting each other and calling it normal.

The ready information about alternate identities multiplies, but at the same time, representations of queerness homogenize. We become sitcom characters and news-show sound bites. Femmes are the hot object-of-the-masculine-gaze lesbians, the female lesbians, and now we bear the burden of those identities rather than the burden of full invisibility. I definitely feel less invisible as a dyke in my queer community than I did twenty years ago, but no better understood by hetero culture. Butches and femmes are still the only two pop-media flavours of female queer. And butches are, well, like men. At least, that's what most straight folks seem to think. We've all been simplified for public consumption. That's the error I stand most vibrantly against: I am gorgeously complex—we all are.

Respect for complexity is still what's wanted, and it's what I work for. Part of the privilege of femme-invisibility is that I can choose when I become complex—I have slightly more control over how others perceive me. My first lover was well aware of this, and she still prefers to cultivate her own invisibility as a queer person. She and her current femme partner live in South Carolina, and they joke about how their families think it's "real nice" that they can live together like that, two gals without husbands. It's real nice that the one can coach the other on proper femininity, being that she's always had a little trouble with it, and all. No one focuses too closely on her lack of progress with feminine ways. And that's how they find peace together. I'm all for peace. In my case, I find it in queer community, by being of service when I can, and by celebrating complexity. I've certainly moved beyond saying the word "lesbian" to myself in the mirror. I tell stories on stage. When my son was about nine years old, someone asked him what I do for a living and, after a thoughtful pause, he replied, "She talks to people. She's kind of a professional lesbian."

We know what we know when we want to know it—and when it's available to know. Language, explanations, and appearances undulate and shimmer like water. The way we understand things changes. I claim the word "queer" exactly because it's complicated. My current lover, however, doesn't embrace the word queer. She's butch. She's lesbian. She says "queer" is for younger people or for academic types. Why would I argue that point? I may be a professional lesbian, but I certainly don't have all the answers. I just do what I can. I'm the non-threatening-looking queer, the gender-normative hottie who's aging into the gender-normative nurturing mother-type. I can be queer in a way that won't make you wince. I get it. Some femme dykes are upset by their invisibility as queers, but I accept it. I try to use it for the greater good, and I look for humour and grace in those moments when the more butch and androgynous among us make fun of my femininity. Finding respect for femininity is a whole 'nother issue; they don't know who they're dealing with—yet. I just go right on talking to people and complicating myself right in front of them. I'm happy to be part of the queer culture that's now available in the media and on the Internet, a culture that was accessible only through books and individual encounters, twenty years ago.

It may be easier to be "gay," but it's still pretty rough to be different. Butch-femme couples like my first lover and her current partner can still cultivate a relative invisibility. It's easy because they don't use any fancy language that would make straight people uncomfortable; folks have been doing it like that silently for generations. They're good neighbours; whatever it is they're doing, they don't do it in the streets and scare the horses. And, at the same time, because of all the boldness that came before me, it's easier for women like me to be more visibly queer. My first lover is not a lesbian, but I am—contrary to what people might guess before they get to know us.

KIMBERLY DARK is a writer, mother, performer, and professor. She is the author of five award-winning solo performance scripts, and her poetry and prose appear in a number of publications. For more than ten years, Kimberly has inspired audiences in fancy theatres, esteemed universities, and fabulous festivals. She's been exploring butch and femme roles and attractions on stage across North America and Europe since her first theatre show—*The Butch/Femme Chronicles: Discussions With Women Who Are Not Like Me (and Some Who Are)*—was released in 1998. Her 2009 release, *Dykeotomy*, returned to butch-femme sex and dating in an era of multiplied gender. *The Salt Lake Tribune* says: "Dark doesn't shy away from provocative, incendiary statements, but don't expect a rant. Her shows, leavened with humour, are more likely to explore how small everyday moments can inform the arc of our lives." The *High Plains Reader* in Fargo, ND, says: "Dark's skill as a storyteller gets to your heart by exposing hers." Find her at *kimberlydark.com*.

Coming Back Around to Butch

Miriam Zoila Pérez

My first real girl-crush was a butch. Well, she didn't call herself that (and maybe never has), and she was in the closet (just like I was), but it was something about her short hair, expertly chosen jeans and T-shirts, boyish lines, and masculine sensibilities that drew me to her. When D and I met, I still believed there was an imaginary line down the middle of the clothing store that meant only the right side was for me. She was the fashion role model I'd never had and even took me to buy my first baseball cap.

I'd ignored minor crushes like these for years: my thirteen-year-old mind wandering to thoughts of kissing my drama teacher and seventeen-year-old me secretly wanting to kiss my math tutor. But this one I couldn't ignore, even though it was more than two years of friendship before my feelings for her finally forced me to come out.

The line between wanting to date her and wanting to look like her felt tenuous, and looking back, I'm pretty sure any attempts at being sexual would have failed miserably. But my complicated feelings for D taught me this crucial lesson: I needed to figure out who I wanted to be before I could figure out who I wanted to be with.

I was barely a dyke then, let alone butch, but it was the lure of female masculinity that drew me out and into the queer world.

When I was coming out, butch was no longer new. There was both popular knowledge and an underground cultural understanding of what it meant to be butch—and there were books written from both perspectives. I may not have known it intimately, as a late-blooming queer who grew up in an extremely straight southern-US town, but I knew enough to feel self-conscious about claiming butchness.

You see, I was never a tomboy. There, I said it. I was never a goddamn tomboy; I never resisted the dresses my mom wanted me to wear, never hid in my dad's closet trying on his clothes. I did gender conformity without any real fight, and when I came out to my mom, she used it against me—"But you were always so feminine!"

Maybe I didn't have the fight in me, maybe I wanted to fit in more than I wanted to know myself, but until I was well past twenty, I wore my hair long, with earrings dangling, and makeup on my face. I wore spaghetti-strap tank tops and flowing skirts. I flaunted my cleavage.

The butch narrative I had absorbed, the one I began to furtively read about as I came out, wasn't mine. I wasn't a rough-and-tumble butch kid, all scabby knees and hardness, fighting against mom over Sunday dresses. I wasn't good at sports, didn't have trouble being friends with girls, didn't feel more "boy" than "girl." So when I slowly started easing toward the masculine side of the spectrum, I was self-conscious as hell. I felt like an impostor. I felt like a phony. I had similar feelings when I came out as lesbian, but my fantasies about women quickly assuaged my fears of being a queer fraud.

With my gender presentation, I couldn't get over the feeling that I was trying too hard. Even as I slowly shed the layers of femininity in my presentation, the self-consciousness still affected what labels I used. I knew what butch was, and I still felt it couldn't be me. I had dated men. I wore a pink dress to prom. I was short and chubby and more giggly than tough.

It was a fierce femme who bossy-bottomed me into the role of butch top. It was easy to be the butch to C's femme, and she delighted in my enjoyment of her high heels, pretty dresses, and makeup. In those moments, when my insecurity was stronger than my sense of self, the contrast between my budding masculinity and her strong, well-articulated femininity were just what I needed to feel whole, strong, even butch. C didn't change me, exactly, but our gender-play heavy sex gave me room to figure out what my gender could look like in those private spaces we shared.

There are people who believe you can't be butch without a femme, that you need the two ends of the spectrum all the time to be in balance. For me, that was only half-true. I did need the strength of my lover's femininity to bring me into my own identity. I did need the contrast with her to let me see myself. But now that I'm there, I haven't forgotten the tomboys I had crushes on in the early days. I still fantasize about fucking them—but now, not exactly as a girl. I needed my own sense of gender first so that I could come back to them.

We were at T's mom's apartment in Los Angeles the first time I painted her nails. I took the cheap, runny fire-engine red polish out of the bathroom cabinet and into the bedroom, kneeling on the scratchy carpet at the foot of the bed. T sat at the edge of the mattress, and I took each of her fingers into my hand, carefully removing the old chipped pearl-coloured polish she had messily applied herself. The acetone stung my nostrils, and I inhaled the scents of sleepovers and beauty parlours as I covered each nail with the bright red polish. You wouldn't know it by looking at us, but I, with my short hair, white undershirt, and men's jeans, was the expert manicurist in the room. T, with her chin-length curly hair, eye shadow, and purple low-cut blouse was the newbie to all things girly.

I'd had years of practice painting nails—my own and others— I had countless manicures and pedicures under my belt, courtesy of my mom, a once-a-week regular at the nail salon. After years of keeping my nails painted and long (between compulsive bouts of nail biting), I was happy to save my skills for a girlfriend-pampering session. T was impressed by my skillful use of the nail polish applicator, and I had a good excuse to worship her feet.

T and I both play with gender, and sometimes our orbits seem to be on opposite sides of the universe. But butch-femme doesn't really suit us, even though gender play propels our relationship.

The first time sex between T and I was ever really good—you know, the room-spinning, grin-plastering, sweaty kind—I gave our gender play credit.

It was Halloween, a holiday second only to Pride for its ability to release us queers from convention and let the real divas or dappers out for a night on the town. I had been using Halloween as an excuse to do just that for the last few years and each time, my drag became more convincing and less of a costume. T also used it as an excuse to dress in full rockabilly femme gear: black dress with deep cleavage, high heels, and red lipstick—the works. We were glued together that night, making out on the dance floor of the crowded bar, my tube-sock-enhanced package against her bare thigh. Later, when we finally undressed in the privacy of my room, the awkwardness fell away, propelled by the intensity of the night out as our better selves. We might not be a conventional butch-femme couple, but I'll be damned if our gender play isn't hot as hell.

It was almost a year before I talked to anyone other than my first girlfriend about gender. We'd actually just broken up when I met S—who I affectionately referred to as my gender friend—at a conference in Massachusetts. S and I were walking through the lobby after a few beers at the hotel bar when the conversation turned to shopping. We bonded over the difficulty of finding clothing to fit our frames—short and on the chubby side—when we wanted to wear mostly men's clothes.

That conference was an exhilarating weekend of bits and pieces of gender conversation, something I was starved for after hesitantly coming out as genderqueer to my girlfriend only a year before. When the weekend was over, S gave me a business card with her contact info and a note scribbled on the back: *Don't forget to share outfits through the mail. I need more faggy butches in my life.*

Faggy butch was good. It accurately described my pink button-down shirts, my giggles, the fact that I talk with my hands. I once saw a tape of myself in which I made a gesture that looked more like it belonged in *A Chorus Line* than in the middle of an interview. Faggy butch was like genderqueer—not quite this or that, a little of both, maybe. A friend once said to me, "I access my femininity through my masculinity."

I feel lucky to have grown up in a world with butch pioneers, and I feel lucky that I had an idea about what being butch might have meant. But instead of making me feel part of the community, these constructions of what butch was—stereotypes, really—pushed me away from the word and the identity. Instead, I chose a newer term, genderqueer, which had yet to be defined; it was in flux, it was a new frontier. I may not have been butch "enough," but genderqueer was all mine to rewrite and redefine.

I still like the word "genderqueer," still claim it and own it and love the way it makes room for me, in all my complexities. But I'm coming back around to butch. Maybe it's because the years of pink prom dresses are further and further behind me, maybe it's because I'm learning from butch elders who talk in terms that make room for me, giggles and all. Maybe it's also because the people I know have no idea (unless I tell them) that I was never a tomboy. They only know me—my short hair, tightly bound chest, and button-down shirts.

I think every new generation feels the need to reject their elders, reject what came before them, and feel that they are the new gender rebels. We invent terms, we create new spaces, and sometimes, we come back to where our big brothers started—home.

MIRIAM ZOILA PÉREZ is a twenty-six-year-old Cuban-American writer, blogger, and reproductive justice activist. After growing up in North Carolina and leaving as soon as she was old enough, Pérez has lived in various East Coast cities for the last eight years. She is a trained doula and the founder of *RadicalDoula.com*, a blog where she writes about the intersections between birth activism and social justice. Pérez is also an editor at *Feministing.com*, a leading feminist blog and online community. Her writing has appeared in numerous online and print publications, including *Bitch*, *The Nation*, *The American Prospect*, and *ColorLines*. Her essays have been included in the anthologies *Yes Means Yes: Visions of Female Sexual Power and a World without Rape* and *Click: When We Knew We Were Feminists*. Pérez is a member of the Board of Directors of the Astraea Lesbian Foundation for Justice.

A Dad Called Mum

Anne Fleming

A long time ago, I was going to make a butch video. I was going to have a shot of just the ankles and feet of a row of dykes and ask the audience to identify the butch feet, the butch ankles. I was going to show a row of knees. A row of butts. I was going to show butch women's mothers talking about what they thought of how their daughters dressed. I was going to do a matching game: which mother belongs to which daughter? I was going to do quick cuts of butches identifying themselves: "Well, I would say I'm sort of, you know, a faggy butch?" "Butch." "I feel sorta guy-like, like I'm not a guy, but I'm not *not* a guy. Maybe that makes me trans, I don't know." "Gay butch." "Flipped butch." "Butch-a-licious!" "Fuckin' bull dyke." "Boi."

I was going to show kid pictures of now grown-up butches. I was going to show butches singing. I was going to show butches not being able to open jars and passing them to their femme partners.

I think it's safe to say now I'll never make that video.[1] But it sure would be fun.

What I wanted to show, I guess, is that butch is a self-definition. That it's not about the body but the spirit, or not about the body but the way that body moves. (Imagine it: the row of ankles, the femmes' toenails.) Because lot of times you'll look at photos and go, "Her? She's not that butch."

Because sometimes it's a competition.

When I was a kid, I used to wear my dad's ascots when nobody was home.

---

1   But someone else has! See "Butch Tits," by Jen Crothers (*http://jencrothers.com/films/butch-tits/*.)

Isn't there something campy about the word "butch"? Isn't there something inherently mocking in it? Isn't the word "butch" basically un-butch? That is to say, if you are butch, you are not really masculine, you are only pretending masculinity? (Aha. But pretend masculinity is the best kind.)

There was a butch-femme couple at the church where my mom was the adult education coordinator. They made her sad. They were aping heterosexual sex roles.

One time when I was eight, I was allowed to wear pants to the soirée of a conference my dad was attending in Banff. The pants were allowed because, with them, I would be wearing a shirt with puffed sleeves. Happily, my shoulders made the shirt look piratical rather than femmy, and a girl about my age thought I was a boy and asked me to dance. What was I going to do? I danced.

Five years later, at a dance at music camp, when the DJ called a snowball, another girl who thought I was a boy asked me to dance. When I held back she took it for the boy equivalent of coyness and pulled harder. "Come on. Dance." But there were kids who knew me in the crowd. Kids who would say something, kids who would out me as a girl, and I worried about how she'd feel then. I didn't dance.

At the same camp, there was a girl in my cabin with auburn hair and a dry sense of humour who, unasked, and somewhat mystifyingly, cleaned my trunk for me. (Trunk. You know. That thing with a lid you pack off to summer camp.) Messiness was a kind of butch incompetence she could help out with. If she found the cut-offs with the blood stains in the crotch, she never said. Looking back on it, I recognize her as a femme.

There was a butch woman who lived at the Y in Kitchener in the 1980s. She was in her late sixties, probably, when I was in my twenties. She was really handsome. Grey hair. Plaid shirt. Jeans. What a dull description that is. But I can't tell you how much that meant to me, seeing her outside the Y, smoking.

For my twelfth birthday, my friends took me to a Blue Jays game, and then we stayed overnight at Anne Bunting's house. Somebody asked whose body type would we most like to have? I assumed everyone would say what I would say: Anne Bunting's. The most boyish. The narrowest hips. But they all said Katie Wilkins. Hourglass. They wanted hips, all my tomboy friends.

When I was seven, I had red jeans and a matching jean jacket. I should add that these were my only jeans. My mother did not believe in jeans for girls. I loved those jeans—loved the jacket, too, but not with the jeans. Too femmy. I had already heard, I don't know how many times, kids asking me, "Are you a boy or a girl?" Up till then, I'd always answered, "girl." I had a vague sense that it was a trick question. If I said "boy," they'd say, "Bullshit, why are you trying to trick me?" One day, while wearing my red jeans and hanging out in the ravine across from the Dog Ladies' house (yup, you guessed it, the Dog Ladies were the neighbourhood "spinsters"), I said, "boy." And the kid who'd asked, a boy, asked, "Oh, yeah? How come you got no dick?" pointing at the flatness in my crotch.

We weren't supposed to go to the ravine by ourselves, but it was our main activity. We lit fires under the Mount Pleasant bridge. We built jumps for our bikes. We climbed high in the willows and dropped twigs on passers-below. One day, when we were in grade five, we were under the bridge, and some grade seven kids came along. They'd been drinking. One of them put me in a headlock while another lit matches and threw them at my head. They talked about me in the third person: he, him. They thought I was our group's ringleader. Katie Wilkins got her grade-eight brother to come to our rescue, and the grade seven kids took off.

At twenty-one, I worked at a winter outdoor-education centre in central Ontario. We had school groups up for two or three days at a time. One evening, I was sitting by the fire, reading or knitting—everyone knit there, the men and the women—and a group of twelve-year-old girls came in from their cabin to go to the washroom. They saw me there and walked over to chat. "We thought you were a guy when we came in last night," one of them said.

"And we thought you were cute!" They cracked themselves up.

"Were you a tomboy when you were our age?" the most tomboyish of them asked.

Yes, I told them. I was.

"Don't most people grow out of it?" she said.

Well ... no.

The last five years or so, I've been doing a lot of reading to research my next novel, and I've found loads of fantastic stuff, including a pamphlet from 1620 called *Hic Mulier; Or, The Man-Woman*[2] and tales like this one from *The Tradition of Female Transvestism in Early Modern Europe*, dated 1694: "Two maid-servants of a Delft regent amused themselves ... One of them donned the clothing of her master, his trousers, his stockings and his shoes, finishing her costume by placing his fur hat on her head. The other dressed in her mistress's clothes, pretending to be 'his' wife. Elegantly attired in this way, they went to a nearby village where they visited friends, then to a waffle stall, and finally to an inn, where they hired a violinist to play for them, dancing until late into the night."[3]

---

2   The pamphlet's flavour is summed up on its title page: *Being a Medicine to Cure the Coltish Disease of the Staggers in the Masculine-Feminines of Our Times, Expressed in a Brief Declamation.*

3   From Rudolf M. Dekker and Lotte C. Van de Pol, *The Tradition of Female Transvestism in Early Modern Europe* (New York: St. Martin's

The summer I was seventeen, I said to my friend Val, with whom I spent almost all my time, that I didn't know what love felt like. "What does it feel like?" I asked rhetorically. "What does it feel like to say, 'I love you'"?

So I said it. "I love you." It didn't feel like anything.

"Me?" said Val.

"No, no. I was just trying out the phrase." It was true. But was I in love with Val? It never occurred to me that I could be.

At university, the winter I was eighteen, you could almost always get into the bar without being ID'd if you showed a second-year student card. One night I borrowed a friend's card as usual, but the guy at the door thought I looked young and asked for other ID. *Fuck*, I thought. *What am I going to do?* I couldn't show my own ID; it had a different name. I didn't have Jane's ID with me, didn't think of that. Flustered, I gave him my own ID. He looked at it. He looked at me. His face got a look I know, the oh-my-god-I-got-this-person's-gender-wrong look. He let me in.

I find myself telling these anecdotes—and there are more of them—over and over, as a way of asserting something: The time I got called "sir" when I was wearing a skirt; the two bank tellers, one in the small farming community of Woodstock, Ontario, the other at a big-city dyke-central intersection, who said to me, "Anne. That's a funny name for a boy."

What am I trying to assert?

That there's something about me that is read as masculine—a gait, a manner, a mien—even when I am not trying, even when there are contrary indicators like long hair, skirts, or earrings. That this "read" matches my own sense of self. Until I was in my mid-thirties, my mother and I had this recurring argument: "Why are you trying to look like a boy?" she would ask. "I'm

Press, 1989).

not," I would say. "I am trying to look like myself." That there are girls and women who get this—who love this—whose eyes sparkle at this, and who know, long before I do, just what it's about.

That I have what feels like a natural, in-born masculinity that even my mother's long, relentless siege could not vanquish or disguise. That I like and honour this masculinity. That it exists universally in women throughout time and space.

Whatever feelings I may have had about being masculine—that I was an ugly girl but would make a good-looking boy, for instance—they were all instantly resolved when I finally, in bed with my best friend, figured out I was a dyke. Suddenly, my life made sense. Suddenly, I wasn't an ugly straight girl, I was a handsome baby dyke. I already loved my own masculinity. Now I could own it. Now I was part of a community, too, and part of a tradition. In 1983, masculinity in lesbians was the norm, even de rigueur (much to the chagrin of femmes who had to butch up to be recognized and authenticated, including the woman dating my male upstairs neighbour, whose hair, my roommate and I noted, was getting dykier and dykier, the woman who called me at the Leaping Lesbian radio show I hosted with a request to play: "Do I Move You?", the woman who asserted her right to re-femme in the 1990s, the same woman I've adored for twenty-one years).

But it's not the same for everyone.

I had a friend from summer camp who, when in high school, would answer the phone in a deep voice, and then, when she heard it was me, let her voice come out the way it "naturally" did. She'd moved from her mom's to her dad's house, and I figured from this voice thing that she had to answer the phone as Dennis, not Denise. But I didn't ask, and she didn't say. Years later, we both came out, and I heard the story of how she'd lived as Dennis during high school, how she'd told people she was the handyman at our girls' camp, and how her girlfriend's father had got her charged with fraud for using a male alias.

Years later again, I wrote a play based on my imagining of all this. I sent it to Dennis. I had written the play as a dialogue between the character and the court-ordered counsellor and Dennis brought up a line of the counsellor's: "Have you ever considered a sex change?" There was a pause on the phone. S/he was about to say something big, something important. And then there was a knock at my door—my parents, arriving from Toronto. I had to go. I never did hear what s/he had to say. Always regretted it.

Years after that, my first book came out, and Dennis came to the Toronto launch. He'd thought about that sex change and he'd had it. He'd transitioned. His voice was deep. He had facial hair. His pecs and shoulders were bigger. He finally felt like he could be himself. Was himself. What had happened for me upon coming out had happened for him upon transitioning.

I confess I didn't totally get it. We understand the world by extension of ourselves. It's hard to get why people feel differently. It's hard to believe they even do.

I interviewed a guy who was coming to Vancouver to do a one-man show called *FTM*. He'd been a dyke for a long time, but he'd had this profound and longstanding feeling that his body wasn't right. He had dreams he was shaving. In his dreams, his body was male. In his psyche, he was male. Interviewing him was the first time I got how that was a difference between us. I've thought a lot since about how, if my body conformed less well to my ability to appear butch to my satisfaction—if I had bigger hips or gi-normous boobs or a girlier face—I might have felt the same as him. I might have felt that my body and soul did not match up. And I am finding that age is feminizing me. I weigh more, for one thing, and the chub on my face femmes me up in a way I don't much like. I have to take birth control pills so I don't bleed all the time. Sometimes I wonder if I couldn't just take testosterone instead.

Three years ago, I wrote this:

"Kate, your dad's here," one of the kids calls out at my daughter's preschool.

"No," says one of the teachers. "That's Kate's mum."

Sometimes it will be Kate herself who says, "I don't have a dad. That's my mum."

But I always feel stuck. The kid's not wrong. She's made an accurate assessment: masculine-identified parent. But Kate's not wrong, either. I'm a lesbian dad. And I'm trapped by nomenclature.

What should we call ourselves? My partner, Cindy, wanted a parental name for herself—"Mom" or "Mommy." Because my family of origin was already saying I wouldn't be a parent when our child was born but rather a "nursemaid," calling ourselves Mommy and Anne wasn't going to work.

Mom and Dad? Dad I liked, but *Mom and Dad* is just a little too ... Mom and Dad, you know? A little too mainstream America. On the other hand, it's pretty subversive because we're not Mom and Dad from mainstream America. Ultimately, it seemed as though it would require too much public explanation: "Hi. I'm not actually male, but my daughter calls me Dad because that's the parental identity I relate to the most." Maybe it's just because I'm chicken that I didn't go for "Dad." I couldn't imagine going to visit the relatives and having to explain gender identity. I didn't want to face the scorn and derision, fury, and outrage I would endure from my father and brothers in particular, the embarrassment my sister and nephews might feel—the scorn, derision, fury, outrage, and embarrassment that our child might endure at my being called Dad all turned me against it. And now that Kate is four, there are lots of times I'm happy we didn't opt for that. Like when we're on our way into the women's washroom, where I'm already suspect, but where I feel most comfortable peeing and taking my daughter to pee, or when I'm in the women's change room at the pool, I'm kind of glad she's not calling me Dad.

We looked at names from other languages. My cousin's

partner is Appa to her children—Korean for Dad—but that didn't feel right to me, either. Cindy thought that she wouldn't be able to say my idea for a hybrid name—Mumpa—without laughing. Mop? Also too comical. Wasn't that what the Rubble's kangaroo used to say on *The Flintstones*? Mop-mop? I kind of liked Pomo, but decided it was too clever. It's not fair to set up a two year-old (or even a seven-year-old) to call you something that they won't "get" until they're twenty, something that is an inside joke to adults. Pa-Ma sounds like you're saying "Palmer" with an English accent. Moppa is one friend's version of a hybrid that we heard about too late. I was already, reluctantly, Mum.

What I have found interesting about this whole thing is that it's made me realize how the word "Mom" has a specific, limited denotation, which is about …

I never finished the sentence. That's where I stopped. *The word "Mom" for me has a specific, limited denotation, which is about …*

Femininity is the short answer, but not adequate, which is why I gave up on the essay rather than find the right word.

"Why can't you just do with 'Mom' what you do with 'woman'?" Cindy asks me. That is, why can't you ask the world to expand its definition of Mom to include someone who is not feminine? I don't have an answer. "I just can't," is the answer. And yet, it is what I have done. I'm a dad called "Mum."

Which turns some heads. When people see us, they see masculine-presenting adult, feminine-presenting adult, and kid. They assume straightness—and then Kate calls me Mum. One clerk in a convenience store was so shocked he couldn't stop laughing the whole time we paid for our milk. He was nice; it wasn't mean laughter, he was just so freakin' surprised.

When she doesn't call me Mum, we pass. Like last week, a taxi driver in Paris tells us we should really go to gay Pride, the kids love it. He shrugs: *Go figure, but hey, what the kids love, that's what you do.*

We're always wondering, when do we say something? When do we come out? When do we let it go? People think Kate is a boy too. There's an example being set here. We want to say, "These divisions between boy and girl, man and woman—they're artificial and inadequate and they lead to injustice." We don't want to always think of the world in gendered terms. And yet, to be butch and femme is to be gendered, which seems important to shake up once in a while, regularly. Frankly, I get a little lost in thinking about it.

Funny thing is I now have a kid who is gender non-conforming. So I get to be completely not my mom and say, "What do you want to wear?" "Hair cut? Sure. Let's go."

One of the things we struggle with is trying to stop coding things as boy things or girl things. Loving spaceships is not a boy thing or a girl thing. Neither is loving Lego, or sparkly toenail polish, or pink, or bikes with flower decals. Or bikes with flame decals. Being butch doesn't mean I can't knit. And being femme doesn't mean Cindy can't be the jar-opener in the family.

When I was twenty-four, I read *The Persistent Desire*. In its pages, I found a kind of home. I found ways of articulating what I already knew: that the butch-femme couple at my mom's church wasn't aping anything—they were taking something, transforming it, and making something new that was their own. That butch is not a faked or pretended masculinity but a distinct masculinity, with its own fluidity and give, depending on who's inhabiting it.

ANNE FLEMING is the author of *Anomaly*, a novel, and *Pool-Hopping and Other Stories*. She divides her time between Vancouver and Kelowna, where she teaches creative writing at the University of British Columbia's Okanagan Campus.

A Beautiful Creature

Karleen Pendleton Jiménez

"It's the most feminine thing you could do," she blurts out at the bar.

I cringe. It's her explanation of why butches don't get pregnant, present company excepted. The butch takes a swig of beer and watches for the impact of her words. I hate this part of being butch. On any given night, I am thrown into the mix of butch-on-butch competition and insecurity, when all I want to do is dance. We know each other's vulnerabilities. She knows which issues draw my defensiveness. Throwing the word "feminine" in my direction has the desired effect.

It didn't feel very feminine. I can't say that I know what feminine feels like, but that wouldn't be what I imagine. A femme might or might not choose pregnancy as an example of her own femininity.

In the first few months, there was a complete overhaul of my body. My system was designing the little factory that would build my baby. My blood volume increased. My heart pounded, leaving me breathless after I climbed up just one flight of stairs. I could barely consume a slice of toast without the sickness filling my stomach.

In the middle months, I was reborn. I could eat everything. I would run an errand only to find myself in a bakery scarfing down some buttery pastry. My body felt warm and powerful. I glowed. My reflection in the mirror was vibrant. I hadn't looked that good since I was twenty-two—or maybe I had never looked that good. People smiled at me on the street. Men blushed and turned away.

In the last few months, my stomach stretched to the limit and the weight made my feet throb. My bones loosened and became sore. I couldn't bend over to tie my shoelaces. I'd close my eyes and see myself as a twelve-year-old again, following my brothers around. I could hear them instructing me, warning me, "Suck it up. Don't be a baby."

The due date came and went, but the baby didn't want to emerge. The midwives told me to walk as far as I could, to ease her out. I walked half the city in the summer rain, my belly hanging over my drenched jeans, to no avail.

And the birth? The induction. I remember carnage. There are photos full of blood. I remember the doctor sewing me back up for what seemed like an hour, as I held my new baby proudly on my chest. I remember that she apologized a few times for the damage to my body. Forceps. Unavoidable. Sorry.

My definition of butch involves chivalry. I want to be courageous, gallant, to show the highest respect for a woman. I think of an idealized knighthood, where such characteristics are valued and groomed. I would protect my lover from an enemy, risk physical harm.

I was nine years old the first time I held another girl. It was nighttime around the campfire, and the counsellors were telling gruesome stories to freak out the kids. The girl beside me—with hazel eyes and long braided hair—asked if I would hold her because she was scared. I had never imagined such a request. My instinct kicked in immediately. I wrapped my arms around her. I ceased being frightened myself because I could only think about how proud I felt to protect her. It didn't matter if I was cold, or if the rock that I was sitting on was hard and uncomfortable. Everything, for an instant and for the first time in my life, felt right. I was a little knight beside the campfire.

I have to admit that there is actually little, in my twenty-first-century North American life, that calls for mortal risk. The scary stories, after all, weren't real. My every-day gallantry probably has more to do with enduring minor physical discomfort for the benefit of the person beside me, especially a femme (but only if she wants it). Offering a chair, offering to do an errand or a chore, offering to share my food. Little tokens. That's all. Gifts that make me feel strong, generous, and loving.

If anything, pregnancy was my most courageous act. I endured the burden of growing a whole life underneath my skin. I risked my life to make another. It's the only time I've ever been admitted to a hospital. I listened to my baby's heartbeat rise and then slow, dangerously slow. I panicked. I looked up at the doctor and agreed to have my body cut open for the baby. Without question. I've never been so brave. I've never fulfilled my ideal role of butch with such certainty.

"Were you embarrassed?" one of my buddies asked after the fact, wondering why I kept fairly quiet about the pregnancy. No. I was nervous. I was uncomfortable. I averted my eyes when I saw another butch I knew at the fertility clinic. "Please don't tell anyone that you saw me here," I pleaded.

I had a plan when I started high school. I was going to wear girls' clothes. I was going to a new school in a different city, and I thought it was my chance to look normal. I would have no history. They wouldn't know that all I wore in junior high were jeans, jerseys, and soccer shorts. It never occurred to me to do otherwise until the day a boy in my science class told me that people thought I was weird for wearing guys' clothes. I wasn't following the rules. I didn't really know they existed. But I could fix that, and no one would have to know.

I had faith in pink sweaters to hide my masculine strut across the playground. I was just as oblivious to the stares of my classmates as I had been in my basketball sweats. The other students made bets about what gender I was. The ambiguity was hilarious to them. It wasn't about winning the bet; the entertainment value was derived from debating the issue, making a case based on observable evidence.

I was their joke. Having a butch in class was funny on its own, but a butch trying desperately to look like a girl was hysterical. It was all the more humiliating that I was wearing bright-coloured blouses with ruffled collars in an attempt to appease them. I couldn't protect myself in those clothes. When I came out a few years later, I got rid of feminine attire for good. I finally got to enjoy being attractive as a masculine woman, having women want me for precisely the same queerness that had previously been used against me.

"You're going to have to wear a dress now," my friend laughs, "a big, long matronly dress." The first time I heard this, I chuckled along with the friend or acquaintance who had thought of the image. But then it kept happening. After work, on the phone, at a party, one woman after another kept coming up to me and sharing her vision: Since I was pregnant, I would have to wear a dress. They were only partly kidding, as I had seriously transgressed my role as a butch by getting pregnant, and now it was time for me to pay my dues. For months, they kept urging me to oblige them, "Come on, just once."

I was nervous about the transformation of my butch body into something lush and womanly when I got pregnant, but it hadn't crossed my mind that it would entail wearing a dress. The comments were meant in fun—they weren't pressuring me as a woman to conform to social expectations; I was more like a man in drag on a wild night. Even though I understood their relatively harmless intentions, I could not shake the high school kid in me who had tried so hard to be okay.

Maybe I was embarrassed to be pregnant. I didn't want to look like a butch who was trying to be a girl again, didn't want to be in the in-between place where I didn't know how to defend myself, where I felt part monster, part joke.

A pregnant woman's body is hardly the model of conventional femininity. Bigger breasts aside, there is the massive hard ball of a stomach, more like my dad's beer belly than a soft, rounded lady's tummy. It's true that some people find it attractive, but at least as many, if not more, are turned off by it. If the shape is not particularly feminine, if the work of pregnancy is often sweaty and sore and gruelling, then what is it exactly that makes it, in that butch's opinion (and she's not alone), the ultimate in femininity?

I think it's because pregnancy is the physical manifestation of having been fucked. And specifically, fucked by a man. I think people reduce femininity to the one simple act. By the same token, the ultimate in masculinity is to be the one who does the fucking. Such conflation renders my butch pregnancy invisible, as it simultaneously devalues every femme in the world who does not have a baby. Their rich, complicated femininity is considered inferior to the more significant act of giving birth. This version of femininity is violent, tearing away at the legitimacy of our lives.

If femininity is taboo for butches, being fucked is even worse. As far as I can tell, a lot of us are, in fact, getting fucked by our girlfriends, but very few of us are willing to admit this openly. We barely confess to having needs of our own, or to crying, or to owning a piece of women's clothing. This information can only be shared in whispers between friends after a couple of beers. There is no place for my pregnant body in this context. Walking down the street with my massive belly, I became the emblem of a fucked butch. The images of the famous pregnant man all over the magazines didn't allow me to feel any less offensive or afraid.

But as I agonized over who I had become, men and women of all ages and ethnicities would smile at me on the street. They offered little gestures of their good wishes for me. I was pregnant and had finally joined the heterosexual club. Being butch could be overlooked because of the miracle of the baby. These were the people who had only ever noticed me as a queer or not noticed me at all. Meanwhile, friends and acquaintances expressed their surprise over my pregnancy—often joyous surprise, loving and supportive surprise, but surprise nonetheless—prompting my girlfriend and I to wonder about the state of butches as fully functional creatures of the earth. Are we not supposed to procreate? Are we somehow neutered by our gender expression? Are we eunuchs?

I understand that many butches have had to fight against traditional female roles. They have had to defend both their masculinity and sexuality against the family, friends, and community members who urged them to marry and have children like proper women. Sometimes our very survival lies in our ability to embrace our butch identity and reject social norms. I hope that as we struggle to make space for alternative lives, we don't inadvertently give up the possibility of giving birth.

As a Chicana, I wasn't going to buy in to this fate. I cut my teeth at Berkeley in the early 1990s, where Chicana feminism informed courses, politics, relationships, and house parties. There were plenty of butches in the community, butches who read Audre Lorde and Gloria Anzaldúa. We modelled our identities on woman-of-colour feminism. We were masculine, but still tied to a woman-centred politics. We read feminist manifestos, even if we struggled with bodies that were not altogether female.

We shared a family-centred politics as well; if you are Chicana, you care about family. That's how we have survived for so long against institutional racism. We depend on the support of our families when everyone else fails us. Even if this closeness wasn't always apparent in our actual families, the research said it was so. Our queer group on campus was called La Familia, and we made a pact to not give up on our families, even if it took them a while to learn how to accept us. I was a student of Cherrié Moraga's when she had her baby and wrote a memoir about it. Being a Chicana butch meant that I was a woman and that I could, and perhaps should, make family, an alternative vision of family, but family nonetheless.

My vision of family begins with my mother. As my mother's daughter, there was no question about whether or not I would have a baby. I was in love with my mother, a big, round woman with dark brown eyes and hair. She knew everything. She was so smart that people from all over the community would call her to ask for advice. While she talked on the phone for hours lying on her bed, I would cuddle up beside her. I pushed my head into her armpit and rested my hand on her stomach.

In my earliest memories, I would follow her around shopping or on errands, clutching the seam of her pants. That was my spot, behind my mama's leg, where I could peek out at new people. She taught me how to read when I was three and at ten told me I could get a PhD if I wanted to. She loved good humour, and my brothers and I would sit in the car on long drives and tell ridiculous stories to hear her laughter. She loved each of us, even though we three were entirely different from one another: one Democrat, one Republican, one Libertarian. She was shy in public and would tell me how much she admired my confidence and easiness with conversation.

We fought, too big screaming matches especially when I was a teenager. She would be yelling and crying in her light blue nightgown, crossing the living room toward me with her pain. She could be a crazy woman. I remember once thinking that I would tell her I was going to move out, but the sound got stuck in my throat. I couldn't move away from her. The intensity of our relationship made me feel connected, cared for, alive. In my mother's arms, I was not a tomboy, a queer, or a butch. I was just a kid hungry for her attention, for her approval, and for her love.

When she died a dozen years ago, it became even more important for me to have a baby. Losing my mother has been the biggest tragedy of my life. If I could no longer have a mother, then I needed to become one.

But first, I had to get through a pregnancy.

A butch pregnancy.

I have never felt so detached, so removed from the planet. Added to my state of gender nervousness was the physical obstacle growing inside. My massive stomach held me at a distance from everyone else.

At seven months pregnant, I board the subway to get home. It's crowded on a Friday evening, and I am thankful for the young Latino teenager who gives up his seat for me. I silently note that there must be a mother responsible for his good manners.

I look across the aisle at a South Asian man ready for a night on the town. I can smell his sharp, spiced cologne mixed with pheromones on high alert. His hair is gelled up stiff. He is wearing a gold linked chain around his neck, a cream silk shirt, black pants, and pointy Italian shoes. I breathe him in and sigh. He is ready to impress a woman on a date and, hopefully, will make love to her later that night. I smile. I like the smell of his daring. It makes me nostalgic for my body without a heavy baby inside, my body that is fit and ready to romance a girl. I miss my clothes, my dress shirts and slacks that now won't fit around my breasts or belly. I can barely get up to waddle out the door at my stop, and manage this only with the nagging feeling that my bladder wants to expel its tiny amount of pee.

I am eight months pregnant. It's a summer night and I've curled my girlfriend's fingers around my own and led her to our bedroom. I have become an expert at making love to my girlfriend. A dozen years of perfecting the dance. I know exactly when to bite her skin, when to caress her, when to pound her, and when to hold her. I know how to move inside, and I know how to rub and pull and make her body rise.

It's hard to find a position to reach her. Should I sit cross-legged or on my knees or lie on my side? What angle affords me the longest timeframe before my legs or arms get cramped and I lose steam? I twist into a spot and push all the blankets off the bed. I get to work. I feel my confidence return; I feel a little butch again. Even if I barely sense the warmth of my own body, I can take good care of my femme, and I am proud of that. But my fingers begin to go numb.

It's been happening for the last couple of months. I lose feeling in my right hand. The nerve is squeezed somewhere in my arm, and the midwife and Google tell me it's a common side-effect of pregnancy. Damn it. I depend on the delicate precision of my fingers. I hunger to touch and feel my girl. Damn. I don't stop moving my fingers. I can tell by the rhythm of my lover's breathing that they continue to do the job. I close my eyes and concentrate. I depend on the focus of my brain, even as my fingers lose all feeling.

Is a butch still a butch without her clothes, her body, her libido, her physical strength? Who was I in those moments? I felt far away from other butches and far away from myself. I felt calm, too. The pregnancy, despite its limitations, was peaceful. The hormones had kicked in. The urgency left my bones. I could feel the bliss of the new life in my body as my mind drifted into daydreams of the birth. I inhabited a spacey land, where I didn't care about anything except the movement of the baby inside. But as much as I enjoyed the tranquility, I might have panicked if I thought it would go on forever. For my entire life, my knowledge of the world has been grounded in a sense of myself as a butch. When I couldn't see myself any more, I became a body without any meaning attached to it. I felt vague, adrift.

Hilary takes portraits of me. She puts on a sun dress, lifts her heavy black Nikon, and stretches her arms. When she photographs you, she leads your body from one position to the next as she snaps the shots.

"Sit on the chair. Now stand, straddle it," she directs. "Lift your head, turn, now look away, and turn back once more. Good."

She searches a body, a face, the eyes for something she understands about its history, vulnerability, desire. You could stand right next to her and take a photo of the same person, but you wouldn't be able to capture the intimacy of her images.

On the day before my due date, I gather all the butch garments that will still cover my body—a tie, leather suspenders, XXL T-shirts, stretchy blue jeans, an exercise bra—and head outside.

It is a cool summer day, cloudy, the sunlight is diffused evenly across our backyard patio. Perfect photo weather, according to Hilary. It's a last chance to catch the picture of my pregnant body.

I slip in and out of clothing quickly, avoiding the curiosity of the neighbours in the apartment building beside us. They are busy with their barbecue; the smells of charcoal and burgers float over us.

Hilary guides me methodically through the shots. I look past the reflection on the lens, into the tiny hole of the aperture, and wait for the instant when the shutter snaps open and shut. I can see Hilary there, following the lines of my body. I sit up. I raise my chin. I smile. I look at her shamelessly with lust. I reach behind my head and lie down. I curl up into a ball. I give her my fiercest face. I frown. I plead. I worry. I daydream.

I find myself on my girlfriend's contact sheets. I find myself through her eyes: a femme's vision of a butch. In some shots, I don't look pregnant at all. I still look like the young boyish dyke she picked up a dozen years ago. In others, my belly is bigger than a basketball. My proportions are alarming. My skin looks soft. My face is tired but relaxed. My gaze is vulnerable. My dark eyes are wide open, inviting her to capture me, but carefully—please be careful. I don't look like other pregnant women. I look like an entirely different creature. A queer creature. A beautiful creature.

KARLEEN PENDLETON JIMÉNEZ is a writer, professor, mother, Chicana, butch, and dyke. A California kid who was swept away years ago by a Canadian femme, she makes her home in Toronto. If you're interested in reading more or viewing her children's film *Tomboy*, visit her website: *people.trentu.ca/kpendletonjimenez/index.html*.

Never Be Hungry Again

Leah Lakshmi Piepzna-Samarasinha

I know what femme is, and it's about honour.

Femmes are my oxygen. My water. I have fallen for queer masculinity that still gets it up for femmes since I was sixteen, but you, you are my daily love letter. You are my Trader Joe's dried chili mango, $1.99 in my purse, every day. Something sweet and fiery and full of flavour; I can reach for it, and it will feed me, sustain me, keep me going. Every day, gorgeous, perfect, needed. I reach for you. Femmes are my wealth. If I shine, it's because of you.

When I met you, I fell in love with you utterly. Never wanted to fuck you, not once (didn't let myself), but I fell in fierce, femme, best-friend-forever love with you. Dizzy. Delish. Tasty. Luscious. All the words that are satisfying in your mouth.

I friend-dated you. Prepped my outfits careful because I knew you would notice every little thing about them, love them best. Got myself ready like I got myself ready for dates with lovers, ready to be on and perfect and attentive. The first time we hung out, your teal suede pointy flats matched my teal knotted peep-toe slight heels, and it felt like a sign. We lay giggling in your Craigslist four-poster iron bed heaped with pillows and scarves from the homelands. Took two hours to get our outfits together, three to put on five layers of eyeshadow, were five hours late to pick up the shark we were trying to bust out of her horrible relationship, who was pissed, tapping her foot waiting on the corner. Made it to the gay Arab club on Market and 6th, and dirty danced together like it wasn't a thing.

You disappeared, and I found you chain-smoking outside, flirting with that Tunisian butch union organizer. One of us got finger fucked through the crotch hole in her fishnets in the corner. But the best part of the night was the silent smooth ride home in your black Honda Accord that had nothing wrong with it. Together, dizzy and happy from the night out, safe and alive. Whichever one of us was less drunk would get us home over the bridge safe. I got it down, memorized how to drive home next to every one else drunk-driving home to Oakland. The quiet— us next to each other after a night of being drunk wild girls with some kind of uncertain wind between our thighs—it's all I needed. That was what I loved about us: that we were drunk and insane and loving, screaming, laughing, half-naked brown girls. It's just like Lisa Jones said. Give me an army, a gang of girls. A million sistas ain't enough.

My pack, my prayer, my everyday, my everyday till it blows up and out. Sometimes I feel like I've been writing the same story since I started writing, about love that stays and love that blows up no matter how careful you tend it.

When I left ten-percent South Asian Toronto for an East Bay so magical for queer people of colour but so utterly lacking in South Asians, you became my desi community. My weird, queer, slutty, abuse-surviving desi community. From the north and south tips of the subcontinent, the two most bombed and fucked-up South Asian countries that Indians don't even care about or really consider desi. We ended up in North Oakland. Cupping weirdo colleges, writing dates, terrible day jobs, tequila doesn't make you hungover, weed and cable on the couch, zine writing, your tears, my shoulder, my tears, your shoulder. We were famous for going to gay yoga where we were the only two South Asians, and I would moan louder than anyone in the room when I was releasing my tension, and you would laugh at me, and then we would go to the desi halal cheeseburger-and-wings joint where we would have bacon-optional bacon-avocado cheeseburgers with fries. We zipped up our hoodies over our slutty outfits and tattoos before we went to the Palestinian all-night liquor store so somehow we could still be good brown girls even when we were buying Zima at one a.m.

When I got dumped on tour via text message, you took two of the shots the bar owner gave us, made me throw them back, then screamed at me, "Scream it out!" I screamed. "*HE SAID HE WAS GOING TO COOK ME SOUP!*" When I was so broke that summer, living off of a six-week ill-paid art ed contract and reading tarot cards in my living room, I would ask you for twenty bucks, or ten, whatever, it's okay if you don't want to, just a little, so I could put a gallon of gas in my car. You gave me forty dollars, looked me in the eyes, and said, "I never want you to be hungry."

When you left me for good, I mourned for you worse than I had for lost lovers. I would hold it together all day through my stupid work day and commute, and then, when I got off BART and made it past the lights in the station, I would start crying and wouldn't be able to stop. Wracking. Grabbing my belly sobs. I would pull the car into my favourite spot right in front of my house on 40th, and I would cry those can't-stop tears because I would remember the crazy way you would flip a U-ey and back into the spot in front of my door in the craziest Oakland-driving move ever, glint in your eye. So I wouldn't have to walk around the corner past the drunk guys at the bus stop in my mini-skirt, so you could make sure I got home safe.

I mourned for you worse than lovers. Because femmes are each other's wealth. Riches. Gold and fake gems that glint purple, amber. Food in the pantry. Massage on tired brown limbs. The effortless bliss of each other. My rock, my oxygen, my dearest and most passionate love.

You left, and I am hungry. And I will feed myself and feed others and be fed. But part of the hunger's consummation is this. Because femme is about honour. And I honour this love.

LEAH LAKSHMI PIEPZNA-SAMARASINHA is a queer disabled Sri Lankan writer, teacher, and cultural worker. The author of *Consensual Genocide* and co-editor of *The Revolution Starts at Home: Confronting Intimate Violence in Activist Communities*, her work has appeared in the anthologies *Yes Means Yes, Visible: A Femmethology, Homelands, Colonize This, We*

Don't Need Another Wave, Bitchfest, Without a Net, Dangerous Families, Brazen Femme, Femme, and *A Girl's Guide to Taking Over The World.* Her second book of poetry, *Love Cake,* and first memoir, *Dirty River,* are forthcoming. She co-founded Mangos With Chili, a national queer and trans people-of-colour performance organization, is a lead artist with Sins Invalid, and teaches with June Jordan's Poetry for the People. In 2010, she was named one of the Feminist Press's "40 Feminists Under 40 Who Are Shaping the Future" and nominated for a Pushcart Prize. She comes from a long line of border jumpers, scholarship winners, middle-class Sri Lankan feminists, working-class Ukrainian-Irish ladies with hard hands and three jobs, radical teachers, queers, crips, hustlers, storytellers, and survivors.

Femme Butch Feminist

Jewelle Gomez

> *In 1943 Althea was a welder/very dark/very butch/and*
> *very proud/loved to cook, sew, and drive a car/and did not*
> *care who knew she kept company with a woman ...*
> —*Cheryl Clarke, from "Of Althea and Flaxie"*

Everything I know I learned from poets. Before black lesbian, feminist activist Cheryl Clarke first published her poem "Of Althea and Flaxie" in 1982, the voice of women like this classic femme-butch couple was rarely heard outside the smoky bars of coloured neighbourhoods or in the finished basements of "single" women. The poem became part of a three-woman performance piece that was produced in New York and California through the mid-1980s, making Althea and Flaxie iconic lesbian muses. Women used the poem as a reference point for seduction and named their cats after them. It is a ballad that never failed to evoke smiles of joy and pride, as well as tears when, in the final stanza, Flaxie lays her proud butch to rest without the lace Althea's family demanded.

What is the message? In addition to its skillful dramatic poetics, Clarke's piece serves as a powerful personal framework for thinking about butch and femme identities and how they have been constructed, deconstructed, and reconstructed over the centuries. It is also a good entry point for thinking about how any of us perceives ourselves when we look in a mirror. One way I begin what is surely a much larger exploration than can be accomplished in one essay is to explore the immediate elements presented by Clarke's lyrical opening lines and discuss what these elements continue to tell women (whether we identify as butch, femme, or neither) almost thirty years after we first thrilled to hear them.

Clarke says so much in those opening lines, it is as if the world of butch-femme identity is encoded for posterity, waiting for us to crack the book open. Most directly and surprisingly we're told that Althea is a butch—in itself a bold proclamation, given the political period in which it was published and Clarke's reputation as a feminist. Then she makes it clear that "butch" is not a one-dimensional suit Althea puts on to be like a man. Althea also "loved to cook, sew, and drive a car."

We are also told she is proud. She's dark-skinned, not the traditional heroic description in most literatures, and not often depicted as deserving to be proud. She's a welder—a working-class figure—another aspect of US culture that is often overlooked or devalued. Clarke does the same with the character Flaxie, who "loved to shoot, fish, [and] play poker." The final result is a ballad celebrating complex, admirable, and attractive characters that—in just a few lines—puts the lie to things I had been taught (explicitly and implicitly) about feminists, lesbians, butches, and femmes.

This declaration of Althea's value is gold, and because there has been more attention given to femmes lately (including a biennial conference), I'll focus more on Althea's significance, though both characters represent the same method of dismantling lesbophobia. We still need to be reminded to treasure Althea decades later because the media and most parental and authority figures continue to propagate the stereotypes that make queers hate ourselves and each other, even when we can't recognize that's what we're doing. The dominant culture's distaste for us feeds our own anxiety and makes many marginalized people experience the need to demonstrate our "sameness" by trying to blend in—as happened in the Civil Rights and the Women's Liberation Movements.

To see this at work today, we need only look at the representations of women of colour, lesbians, and, especially, butch women. There are few representations and certainly not much variety among them. I don't need to name names, but even print and broadcast material created by women about women and lesbians manages to make sure that no one has to be afraid of the dark(ness) or of a real butch or a fat femme. The urge to homogeneity is a deadening disease; even queers catch it.

But how did we get here? When I first met Joan Nestle, who lived around the corner from me in New York City in the 1980s, she used to do her public readings wearing a black slip. She talked about her mother's and her own sexuality, revealing the shame of her past and her hope for our future. But who could hear what she said? She was a not-skinny, adult woman in a black slip, and it felt like she was talking directly to each woman in the room. We had never heard these words before.

So I read her work about being Jewish and working-class, about sexual desire and about femme and butch identities. A world of expression opened up to me that explained most of what I knew to be true; our identities are complex, and my attractions generally followed a specific direction: tailored women who did not wear lipstick. But Joan said out loud that we should be able to choose our healthy desires without shame.

For centuries, girls have been relentlessly and brutally channelled into the servitude of vanity (does anyone think those beauty pageants for five-year-old girls isn't obscene brainwashing?) in order to maintain a focus on: 1) embracing the market; 2) pleasing men; and 3) stopping us from changing the world. If some nations in the East historically or currently contained their women in burkas or bound feet, the West made manacles out of lipstick, pantyhose, mini-skirts, and magazine covers. A natural backlash against those advertising-agency constrictions sent many lesbian feminists running for the plaid shirts, coveralls, and Birkenstock sandals that everyone loves to make fun of today. What this disdain tells me, however, is just how powerful a uniform can be, as well as how scared people are when women refuse to look (and act) like Barbie dolls.

The evolution of feminist thought finally circled us back to the idea of informed choice, which Joan Nestle was proposing. Now women get to decide what we want to look like and insist that our looks are not the sum-total of the package. For femmes, that evolving feminist thought reacquainted us with something we kind of knew already: men and women might mistake us for "just girls" when they see our makeup and fashions, but we were/are actually guerrilla warriors, fighting undercover in the war to save women from the continuing campaign to make us irrelevant fluff.

But enough about me. For a butch, the experience is almost the polar opposite. Where femmes seem to be incognito in a hetero-sexual world, butches are a lightning rod. I can walk down the street with as many femmes as I can find and rarely a single bigot notices. But put me on the arm of an identifiable (i.e., not soft or ambiguous) butch and we're immediately targets. "Femme with butch" is a potent combination that makes the fearful and in-secure take notice. Just as potent is a butch woman alone; her presence speaks before she even opens her mouth to say: "I don't follow your 'women rules,'" and "My life is my own." That's an immediately dangerous space to occupy.

In retrospect, it's not surprising that second-wave feminists thought that butch and femme identities were retro imitations of heterosexual behaviour. We were not born into a feminist world with roadmaps and political advisors; we were all learning how to be feminists in the twentieth century as we were doing it! One thing we have learned now in the twenty-first century is that changing the world doesn't happen overnight; it requires a life of commit-ment and examination and recommitment. Today, young queers who whine about all the bad things feminists did (as if we were a monolithic voting bloc) mostly don't know what they're talking about and use their lack of knowledge as an excuse not to have a seriously considered political perspective. Actually, they wouldn't be talking at all if those "bad" feminists had not been there before them (sometimes making mistakes) to open things up.

But I'm not bitter. Earlier feminist activists rarely experienced the full range of class and ethnic expression that supported femme and butch identities, so how to frame our discussions of them was almost impossible before Nestle published her work. (Gender identity wasn't even part of the general lexicon until the '90s.) The earliest explicit literary butch for me was Stephen from the Radclyffe Hall novel *The Well of Loneliness* (1928), and she was not often looked upon as a role model. Stephen has "the curious suggestion of strength in her movements, the long line of her limbs—she was tall for her age—and the pose of her head on her over-broad shoulders." So identifiable was her butchness, the book was banned in the United States when it was published. Stephen came from the top of the upper crust; however, the author's depiction of her as full of self-loathing (Hall's deliberate attempt to elicit sympathy from the larger world) was too destructive not to be rejected by second wave feminists. But Stephen became a hero to girls like me in the 1960s, who were trying to figure out our feelings. And she certainly did wear a suit well. Stephen not withstanding, butch-femme identities were perceived as "lower class," even when that wasn't said out loud, which made them easier to target and reject for feminists finding their way.

Nestle carefully crafted a reinterpretation of femme and butch identities that made it possible for lesbians to look at ourselves in the mirror again (or in the shine of our boots). Once free to imagine ourselves as more than simply a reflection of an oppressive het culture, the binary of heterosexuality was forever transformed. When Nestle broke that silence, the idea of butch and femme was no longer excised from our political vocabulary. Nestle's writing put the pride back into the lip gloss and sharp creases.

What do we see when we look at ourselves? That all depends on how one defines identity. If identity is a box meant to contain all that you are, then any identity (Irish, secretary, mother,

Christian) is anxiety-provoking at best and soul-killing at worst. That box can lead to one of two paths: on one path, you totally embrace and enshrine the identity—a position that often leads to absolutisms (i.e., girls do this, but they don't do that; Christianity only means this sex position).

Conversely, insistence on a box can lead to a total rejection of received identities, which is often the case with contemporary women and men living on the fruits of feminism, who understandably chafe at the idea of containment. With that rejection, however, we often get a personal life devoid of context or history; that, in turn, erodes any political power-base that could demolish existing oppressive cultural behaviours or institutions. (Whew! That's exhausting even to say!) For example, in the "no-identity-reject-the-box-at-all-costs" world, sexism or child abuse become "incidents" that affect individuals, rather than a series of choices by a dominant culture that injures a class of people such as women or children. The assumption is that each individual has the opportunity to overcome such incidents on her/his own. Imagine what human rights advances would *not* have been made during the Civil Rights Movement if too many African-Americans had decided that ethnicity is a purely intellectual/political construct, and there's really no such thing as being black in America. (This interesting discussion takes place in the halls of academe today, but rarely on the street corners where the unemployed congregate.)

What would it be like if each transgendered person felt, "I've chosen this personal path, and it's my work alone to keep people from discriminating against me," rather than identifying with a whole class of transgendered people and doing the work as a group to challenge discrimination? Dynamic political activism (i.e., feminism) to improve the condition of women (and ultimately all people) can't yet regain a foothold in the twenty-first century without women and men willing to acknowledge and open the identity "box."

If, however, identity is seen as a door, not a box, then you've got a very different and an extraordinary adventure. Like Althea, we are all quite complex, and the butch identity opens, like a door, onto so many additional aspects of her. A butch, just like a femme, is able to be soft and hard at the same time. Remember that in the 1940s, a woman driving a car was still not the norm, so just depicting a butch who can "cook, sew, and drive a car" was creating a very expansive identity. It tells us many things about who a butch woman might be—not the least of which is that she can be both angry and amused when straight women challenge her in a public bathroom. She can feel embarrassed and, at the same time, empowered as she recognizes a teachable moment.

The femme Flaxie is also not a simplistic interpretation of any woman—she loves to play poker, not bridge; again a signal of atypical complexity for a woman of the time. Clarke deliberately signals the depth of these women's identities, easily making a not-so-easy point: each door in identity opens onto another part of ourselves. When I look at myself, I see, in no particular order: femme, lesbian of colour (Ioway, Wampanoag, Cape Verdean), writer, raised poor, raised female, now middle-class, child-free, feminist, former Bostonian, current Californian, left-handed, plus-size, older ... and the list of my identities can go on. One identity does not negate the other, something we often forget. Each of the identities and its history helps shape who I am; my being an ex-Catholic is as valuable to consider as is my being a person of colour.

Our acknowledgment and exploration of those identities, and the past that comes with them, are what makes us whole. What makes Althea and Flaxie such powerful figures in a poem (merely forty-eight lines long) is the author's insistence that they be full characters, not one-dimensional stereotypes. We need to demand the same for ourselves as we embrace our own identities. What makes the poem and its ideas important is that the relentless, insidious, and poisonous demand that women stay in somewhat singular boxes is always out there, tugging at us. It is in the fairytales read to us at bedtime, in advertisements, the movies, and TV shows. It is in our parents' voices, the novels that win international prizes, the plays on Broadway. The poison is there in how kids get assigned tasks at home, and it's still there in who gets hired to do what job in the university or on the construction site. The number of women welders is, I dare say, not that much higher today than it was in Althea's lifetime; in fact, it may be lower—at least we were needed in the factories during World War II. When we dismiss the poison of discrimination in our waters we die from it; or worse we adapt and don't know when we've become toxic ourselves.

We may escape cultural moulds when we're adolescent girls and our parents think being a tomboy is cute. We might reject the cultural call when we're finally out on our own at college or hanging with our BFFs at the piercing parlour. But the siren song (that mythological female creatures use to lure men to their deaths) is always there, and the volume gets turned way up when we look for meaningful work or have kids or want our parents to take us seriously or we get closer to middle age.

What about sex? The fear of sex, or erotophobia as Amber Hollibaugh named it, is a basic underpinning of culture of the United States (founded by Puritans, lest we forget). That fear manifests itself in many perverse ways in heterosexuals, not the least of which includes, for example, embarrassment at seeing scantily clad gay men on a Pride float or a completely irrational hatred of LGBTQ people being allowed to marry. If queer people got married, they'd go on a honeymoon, right? And we all know what happens on a honeymoon!

One of the significant things that femme-butch couples do is remind everyone that lesbians are having sex. Women aren't really supposed to enjoy sex anyway, according to some religious clergy of all denominations and right-wing conservatives who think sex is just for procreation, etc., and we certainly aren't supposed to enjoy it with each other. When you see a femme and butch dancing, you know there's sex involved. That yin-yang attraction says everything before we even French kiss at the last note of the song. The energy is unmistakable and irresistible. How our desire is constructed—physically, emotionally, psychologically—is something for those PhD heads lounging around Gender (formerly Women's) Studies Departments to explore. But you cannot mistake the pull you feel when you meet your other; that combination of qualities that always gets under your skin is often more easily seen when identified as butch or femme. The butch-femme dyad makes sexual desire much more obvious and therefore dangerous for women who, as a class, are already identified as sexual prey in our culture.

My attraction to butches is less about how they appropriate so-called masculine trappings and more about the interaction between the masculine (or yang) with the feminine (or yin). The transgression is inherent in the combination of elements and fans the flames of desire. Until we have better language to talk about "masculine" and "feminine," our conversations about identities will be fraught with misunderstanding and frustration and keep us from adequately exploring the differences in desire and gender. In the 1970s, the feminist movement first made us aware that our language was inadequate to change the world. The transgender movement has re-highlighted these limitations of language and opened up a great place for re-examining of how we need to avoid the male-female polarities in our actions, in our thinking, and in our linguistics. But that's another essay.

And what about breasts? The idea of Althea in her welder's mask is appealing to me because she is a woman in a non-traditional position; she's a welder. That Althea is very butch and loves to sew is sexy as hell to me! When my spouse, Diane, dresses up in her favourite vest and bolo tie, I love the slight bulge of her breasts beneath the fabric. Some butches are not enamoured of their breasts; they don't fit a self-image that may be based on a number of factors, including historic and idealized images, or binding may feel sexy to them or exemplify what they will endure to be butch. My interest in Diane is in her womanliness *and* her butchness, the place where it all comes together and signifies her past and her present, and her crossing of cultural boundaries.

Maybe because I grew up in a lower working-class, coloured community, where butches and femmes were an ordinary expression of sexual identity, I was confused by the controversy when I later encountered it in the women's community. Every lesbian of colour I knew recognized Audre Lorde's crisp butches and fluttery femmes in her book *Zami: A New Spelling of My Name*. Cheryl Clarke's Althea and Flaxie spoke out for those of us who recognized our desire and the choice to embrace our complexity. They are the power couple who aren't afraid to be women of a different stripe. They don't see identity as a singular thing—girls one way and boys another. They mix up what it means to be women in ways that create dramatic tension and intrigue us.

Do we still need them? Early explorations of butch and femme by feminist writers and activists such as Cheryl Clarke and Joan Nestle, as well as Amber Hollibaugh, Elizabeth Kennedy, Madeleine Davis, Lillian Faderman, and Ann Bannon, laid the groundwork for our insistence that lesbians are not a singular, monolithic idea to be shaped simply by the dominant culture's fears and fantasies about women. As I celebrate my sixty-second year, and butches are reclaiming their identities out loud, I look back at the writings that shaped my liberation and worry that those building blocks will be forgotten or that the continued political ramifications of women's identities and clothing will be overlooked. Before we were born, Althea and Flaxie laid the groundwork for the fullest expression of ourselves.

Femme and butch manifestations are often more muted in the

upper classes as well as among younger and middle-class lesbians, but the impulse to those identities is often there. And even those not identifying as either butch or femme benefit from the space made in our culture by those identities. The working-class and ethnic roots of the femme-butch couple create a more immediately gratifying experience; it is a stylish, vibrant image that reflects the flamboyance of survival, the heat of lesbian erotic desire, and our loud demand for respect.

Can we still hear them? I believe in the evolution of style, expression, and politics. Continuing to listen for the echoes of earlier voices and celebrating the paths we've already walked is not simply a trip down memory lane; it is vital to strengthening who we will become. Other than the iconic couple Phyllis Lyon and Del Martin, I had no elders to look to for ideas or imagery. Who knew that ordinary lesbians could live to be eighty and revel in their flagrant, transgressive pasts? Althea and Flaxie are fictional ordinary lesbians who represent who we might grow up to be, how we can hold onto all of the things that make us who we are, and they make it clear how we've changed the world since 1943. This knowledge enables me to continue believing that social change is still possible and that I'm a part of it. Thirty years after reading "Of Althea and Flaxie," I'm relieved to see the persistence of our lesbian desire is still out and proud.

SOURCES

Clarke, Carol. *The Days of Good Looks: Prose and Poetry 1980 to 2005*. New York: Carroll & Graf, 2006.

Hall, Radclyffe (Radclyffe-Hall, Marguerite). *The Well of Loneliness*. New York: Anchor Books, 1990.

Hollibaugh, Amber. *My Dangerous Desires: A Queer Girl Dreaming Her Way Home*. Durham, NC: Duke University Press, 2000.

Lorde, Audre. *Zami: A New Spelling of My Name*. Trumansburg, NY: The Crossing Press, 1982.

Nestle, Joan. *A Restricted Country*. San Francisco: Cleis Press, 2003.

JEWELLE GOMEZ is the author of seven books, including the double Lambda Literary Award-winning lesbian novel, *The Gilda Stories* (whose vampire grows up to be a soft butch). Her forthcoming novel is entitled *Televised*. Follow her on Facebook, Twitter (@VampyreVamp), and at *jewellegomez.com*.

Home/Sickness: Self Diagnosis

romham padraig gallacher

i want to spend less time ruminating on this subject and more time simply being, so i'd like to get this off my chest. Despite this beard, lower voice, fur, scars, or anything else about this particular butch[1], i didn't give up on butch or on any part of my community when i started injecting testosterone. i didn't give up on butch during any of my sometimes malaise-soaked, sometimes more politically nuanced self-and-community-imposed absences from butch spaces. i didn't give up on butch when i had a breast reduction, or when forced by family history to get a hysterectomy. You can certainly invite me in or kick me out, but butch isn't an identity for me requiring some kind of social approval or massage; it's something i've loved, cuddled, struggled with, and known, always. Butch for me is not about physical abilities, the presence or absence of particular kinds of genitals with specific paper trails, not about dollars and cents, mechanical or critical-thinking skills, meanings, or extrapolations. Having said that, i've nevertheless judged myself pretty harshly around it and suffered external and deeply internalized cissexism and ableism. At times, i've become some arbiter of butch to the point of self-exclusion, self-hatred, and spiritual dishonesty. Ew.

It's like this: i'm a gimp who's seriously uncomfortable in my skin: it itches and aches, needs to move and stretch to get

---

1 i'm speaking only about my own self, not conflating butch folks and trans men. This all-too-common and often non-consensual conflation is based in ciscentrism (centralizing the lives, ideas, experiences of cis [non trans] folks), misses the complexities of both butches and trans men, ignores trans women butches, seeks to find connection where there may well be none, and neglects the experiences of femme and otherwise-identified trans men. i am not a man; i am trans and genderqueer and butch. This is my gender, my experience, and it may not be extrapolated to the wider categories of butches, trans men, or genderqueers.

even temporary relief. i have restless leg syndrome which comes along with the ankylosing spondylitis that's slowly turning my body in and out on itself. As i've transitioned away from a traditionally understood butch, my disabled body has transitioned right alongside. Pain and stiffness has increased, while mobility, strength, power, endurance have been challenged to their cores. Some of the changes are pretty rough, but there's also this learning—including a deepening understanding of what it means, on the ground, to gender physical ability, learning some of what it means for non-butch folks to be constrained simply for being "other." i believed, as did enough influential folks during my formative butch years, that to be butch meant being strong, silent, sexually stone (despite not identifying with that), and able to hide or deny emotions at all cost. Pair those misguided notions with a long history of being on many sides of abuse, alcoholism, unaccountability, and progressive disabilities, and let me tell you: while i deeply regret some of the choices i've made and the impacts they've had on others, the best thing that ever happened to this butch was finally getting sober, getting real, and beginning the process of exposing every inch of my bullshit. i'm honestly unsure the extent to which that would be happening had i not been crushed by a car, had i not begun a gendered transition, had i not gotten sober, had i not been this person i am. Don't get me wrong, none of it is a blessing; if i could be not in so much pain, yes i would take the blue pill. There's no silver lining here, but it's nowhere near the curse i once hoped it was. Being disabled has and will continue to fundamentally impact my relationship to being butch, and i'd like to begin deeply appreciating the lessons instead of only rolling in the hurt parts.

Then there is this: This restlessness. It's a symptom of ADHD and of how i relate to my gender. i think i have "Restless Identity Syndrome." i just invented that because it describes what i feel much of the time: this itchy, achy need to move, change, and stretch it out to get some kind of even temporary relief. How can i locate myself when i am trans and transsexual and a non-genderfucking genderqueer, all at the same time? Why do i not feel "trapped" in someone else's body, and why do i not feel ashamed of this one? How can i be not a woman and not a man, yet still be taken as a dude pretty much 24/7? What does it mean to be this particular butch? And by butch, i mean butch, not butch as in Tom of Finland in assless chaps. How can this be right? How can this feel right? How can this look right to me and be interpreted right by others?

And how can i fully appreciate all of this when no matter how i'm interpreted, i still feel the need to stretch and itch and change? Some folks think this means i'm "not really trans." i often get this from some other trans folks who are understandably invested in not being perceived as anything less or more than who they are. But my and their beautiful selves are not necessarily interconnected through the fact of our trans-ness, and we don't need to consider each other in all our decisions about our own bodies and identities. Or i hear that i am really "just a butch, aha!" Generally, i get this from queer cis folks who aren't honouring these complexities as much as they are just not fucking getting it or who are way too invested in the bodies of trans people to pay much mind to what we have to say about our fetishisation, conflation with identities that are not our own, and our bodily autonomy. i'm unsure why i've believed for so long the cissexist lie that i can't be this kind of trans as well as this kind of butch.

But, y'know, after years of giving up pieces of myself and my only ever for-real home, there remains this itching, and in the space between feeling it and stretching it—for even temporary relief—i begin to remember who and what i am in the deepest down:

Butch. Sweet, protective, hot, needs met, desire contained and loose all at once, conflicted and simple, heart beating, swishing, sweaty, solid, dirty, right there in the tightly knit pocket of my goddamn fluttering gut, my deepest connection, and only home. Where did i start to get over the hotness and start feeling shame for the connection? When did that shame become more important than the truth? Where did my truth go that a person of any bodily configuration can be butch? How have cissexism, transphobia, and ableism caused me to doubt and judge myself as a butch? Butch, which, despite what anyone else may have to say on the matter, if i just gave it half a chance, could certainly contain this fucked up broken-ass disabled trans body, right? This body that feels so much like a campsite or Vancouver: transient, always on the road to some other place and mindset, none of which ever fits right. Yeah, i'm definitely home/sick in body, landmass, and identity, and the one thing that sustains me through all of it has been butch. Perhaps not home anymore, but a sometimes-secret hideaway where i can retreat to remember that the whole of who i am is pretty fucking fabulous. Butch is my Skye boat: that link between the mainland of my homesickness and my mossy island paradise, the most beautiful, honest place i've ever known. It remains intact.

Out of time, home/sick for my birthplace, for my first family, for my body the way it used to be, before abuse, before disability, before injecting testosterone, before ... this, there has always been something i've known: Before i knew i was queer, poor, or Scottish; before i called myself gimp, before i ever picked up a guitar, before i was fat, an immigrant, a drunk, trans, outspoken, kinky, creative, an introvert, sober, or an anarchist; before beginning to scratch the surface of what it meant to be a white person living in a white supremacist state; before honestly, intently learning how to be good to my partners; before recognizing what it meant to prefer for myself a supposedly "masculine" presentation to a "feminine" one in a virulently sexist society, i knew i was butch. In my nerves, the then soft hairs of my hands, lungs and the sway of my tits—tits and a swagger that were/are all at once targets, pride, shame, survival, vulnerability. Heart and gut, i've always been butch, will always be. No matter my nerves now a mess, the hair now coarse and thick and every goddamned where, no matter my now bald head, less tits, swagger now a limp, cancer-scare insides scraped out; no matter the inconsistencies, misinterpretations, ache, or itch.

i shy away from talking about re-framing butch in my communities because to do so opens old wounds; for some, it cauterizes and for others, adds salt, and in this male-passing place i both live and hate, that feels entirely too driver's seat. So instead, i re-frame it for myself so as not to disappear in much more time spent agonizing over how my body doesn't ever seem to fit and in mitigating damage to it. Butch as i remember it no longer exists for me. Parts of it are uncomfortable and sticky—and not in a hot, challenging way. i feel like i don't belong in butch-only space or in butch-and-femme-only space. i feel i am a butch who is somehow not, and am gonna have to be okay with that. Do i look to others for an invitation? The deepest parts of me that seek connection, understanding, and acceptance will likely hear those who want me the most; i will justify turning down the volume on the ones who don't; i will wiggle and shimmy my fat ass into the space and, in the process of possibly shutting down others seeking refuge, will ultimately feel alone there too. i'm now perceived to be a man, by my own hand, and surrendered my claim to butch in the eyes of some folks i love and a whole bunch i don't even know. This breaks my heart, but what's to do? i don't need to take up space at your conference, don't need to be invited or assumed into your gatherings, i just want to be perceived and treated with respect and kindness.

As a disabled trans butch getting more disabled, more read as a man and less perceived as butch, i feel parts of me slipping further away, and some which have disappeared under the surface entirely (drowned or holding breath i couldn't say). How much of this is based in the ableism, transphobia, and cissexism rampant in every goddamn community i've ever known, and how much is just my own heart stretching and changing and trying to find some space to fit, i also couldn't say. But i would very much like to cut this axe into the ground and leave it there forever; let rust or waves or whatever the fuck take it in and do whatever needs doing with it, but get it out of my hands once and for all. What will it take for me to let go of the handle instead of rotting into it, i wonder? Someone else's permission? Support? Inclusion? An expansion in our understanding of what butch can be, can look and sound and feel like? i think it'll take considerably more than that, and yet so much less. This butch plans on sticking around to see what comes of all of this, mossy hands out, heart engaged, sliding off the handle, splinters and all.

romham padraig gallacher is a long time g/imp upstart living on unceded Coast Salish territories (a.k.a. "Vancouver, BC"), a fat, genderqueer, butch, trans, anarchist, accordion-playing-but-barely dancing bear aiming for a whole lot more love, knowledge, resources, and community. They've written plenty of their own stuff and contributed to others' on the topics of gimp love, lust, and community, getting sober, challenges to fatphobic narratives in queer and trans communities, and keeping shit real while navigating some messy territory.

Looking Straight at You

Zena Sharman

I walked out of the Vancouver airport, weary from another business trip, and joined the queue at the taxi stand. I was still wearing the outfit I'd put on early that morning for an all-day meeting in Ottawa, so I blended in with the other trench-coat wearing, briefcase-carrying business travellers. My cherry-red suitcase was the only thing that marked me as different. It contrasted with my fellow travellers' indistinguishable black bags, a sign to those who knew how and where to look that all was not as it seemed.

Shifting impatiently from one high-heeled foot to the other, I inched forward in line and hoped for a taxi driver who didn't want to chat. I was too tired for the captive small talk that's typical of some cab rides. No such luck. My taxi driver was a handsome, dark-haired man in his late twenties, eager for conversation—I could tell from the way he turned the car radio off as I arranged my belongings and myself in the back seat of his tidy cab that smelled of tree-shaped air freshener. We greeted each other, then he asked me where I'd been and whether this was home. After the customary pleasantries, he looked me in the eye in the rear-view mirror and said, "I have to ask ... how old are you?" As a prematurely grey thirty-one-year-old woman who chooses not to dye her hair, I get asked this question a lot. "Thirty-one," I answered and then launched into my usual explanation that I started going grey when I was eighteen, that it runs in the family.

"But your face!" He shook his head, incredulous. "You look so young. And beautiful. Your hair makes you look old. You should dye it blonde like the lady in the picture." He was referring to the red-lipsticked, retro blonde bombshell on my luggage tag who proudly proclaims "I love not camping." I thanked him for his suggestion but said I liked my hair the way it was. Then he asked me a simple question that required a not-so-simple answer: "So, do you have a boyfriend?" Before I answered him, I needed to make the kind of rapid calculations necessary to determine whether it was safe or smart to come out to this stranger, especially since we were still miles (and at least twenty minutes by car) from my house.

That particular evening I decided I was too tired to negotiate the speed bumps of my sexuality with someone I'd only just met, and I didn't have the energy to fend off a straight guy's clumsy advances. All I wanted to do was get home and climb between my lavender-scented pink sheets. So I took the easy way out. I said, "Yes." After all, my butch partner is my boyfriend. Just not the sort of boyfriend the man behind the wheel had in mind.

Decisions like this one are part of my everyday life because I'm a queer femme who passes as straight, at least to the untrained eye. I feel as comfortable with the word "lady" as I do wearing my favourite little black dress. Don't get me wrong—it's not that I try to look straight. Like many femme-identified people, I know exactly whose eye I'm trying to catch when I wear my black leather boots with the four-inch heels or swish my hips just so. The gaze I crave is decidedly queer, and being seen is an integral part of the queer experience. We sometimes want others—our (past, present, and future) lovers, friends, family, fellow queer folks, members of the wider community, the state—to see us the way we see ourselves. There's a validation, a recognition that comes with being seen. It's a way of saying, "I am." As a femme, I'm especially covetous of the "dyke stare," "the eyes held by a stranger fractionally longer than decorously necessary, establishing a deft, brief and secret kinship, a mirroring, which colludes to simultaneously acknowledge and rebut shame."[1]

Then there are the times we don't want to be seen, as when

---

1   Sally R. Munt, "Introduction," in S.R. Munt, ed., *Butch/femme: Inside Lesbian Gender* (London, UK: Cassell, 1998), 6.

riding alone in the back of a cab or walking downtown with a lover after the hockey game. This is often a matter of security. It can sometimes be safer to blend in, which some of us do more easily than others. If you walked past me on the street, you might notice the way my young-looking face contrasts with my silver hair or the way my purse matches my carefully chosen outfit. Men hold the door for me, and women compliment my shoes. The last time a carload of guys shouted at me as they drove by, it was to say, "Hey, lady, you've got great legs!" It's a far cry from the invasive questions, hostile reactions, and violence that my masculine partner is confronted with on a regular basis.

Loving my partner has made me acutely aware of the privilege that comes with my gender identity. I often pass as straight, and it's an especially privileged straightness because I look like your stereotypical white, clean-cut, tax-paying, respectable citizen.[2] I do middle-class femme as only a girl raised on welfare in a small town who busted her ass to jump a class rung or two can.

Middle class didn't come naturally to me. My mother, who is an activist, an artist, a survivor, and a feminist, gave me the best life she could on our fixed income. A single mother, she read to me, sewed costumes for me, and never wavered in her confidence that I could achieve whatever I set out to do. But my upbringing didn't include tutelage in the ways of middle- or upper-class femininity. We were poverty class. There were no vacations or ballet lessons. Car-free before it got trendy, we walked or rode the bus everywhere we went. I remember the shame of having to put back groceries when we got to the checkout counter and realized that the bill exceeded our budget. I haven't been poor for years, but I still feel a little thrill every time I get to choose whatever I want at the grocery store or the mall.

---

2   My appearance affords me many kinds of privilege. This piece is primarily focused on my gendered and classed identities, but it's important to acknowledge that I also experience the privilege that comes with being white, temporarily able-bodied, and cisgendered.

Everything changed when I won a full scholarship to a university about 850 miles from home, in a city three times the size of the place where I grew up. In the city, I got more than just a degree. Like many poverty- and working-class people who attend university, I got an education in class and gradually learned how to pass as something other than poor.[3] Ten years of higher education, hard work and, more recently, a well-paid full-time job, have made me fluent in the language and behaviour of the middle class, while widening the gulf between my life and my mother's. I send her money every month, but she is still poor, still living in the same small northern town. I keep instant coffee in the cupboard for her annual Christmas visit, when our worlds collide in ways that sometimes make me uncomfortable. Last December, as we made our way through a crowded department store, I was mortified to see my mother slip her poorly fitting false teeth—the kind you get when you're on disability and you can't afford to buy them yourself—into her coat pocket. Where I might've felt sympathy for a stranger in similar circumstances, I felt ashamed and vulnerable when my own poverty-class origins were exposed at the mall.

As a femme who can pass, at least on the outside, as both middle-class and straight, my class identity and gender presentation are deeply intertwined. Lisa Ortiz talks about her double passing as an experience of "actively claiming" multiple identities—in her case, as a femme and as a Latina.[4] I don't equate my classed

---

3   For other accounts of this process, see, for example, Michelle M. Tokarczyk and Elizabeth A. Fay's edited collection *Working-Class Women in the Academy: Laborers in the Knowledge Factory* (Amherst, MA: University of Massachusetts Press, 1993), or Kenneth Oldfield and Richard Greggory Johnson III's *Resilience: Queer Professors from the Working Class* (Albany, NY: State University of New York Press, 2008).

4   Lisa Ortiz, "Dresses for My Round Brown Body," in L. Harris and E. Crocker, eds. *Femme: Feminists, Lesbians, and Bad Girls* (New York: Routledge, 1997), 90.

experiences with Ortiz's racialized ones, but her notion of actively claiming identities resonates with me because I actively claim my femme gender and poverty-class origins and will strategically out myself in both areas. But while I valorize femme, I don't try to look or act poor, especially now that I can afford to choose not to. I admire my femme sisters who know how to make torn fishnets look fabulous, but I wouldn't dream of leaving the house with a run in my stockings because I'm afraid it would give the impression that I couldn't afford another pair.

In choosing to look the way I do, I experience a privileged sort of femme invisibility, one that enables me to move through the straight world with relative ease. Invisibility is a common thread in the femme narratives I've read, and it seems to me that how femmes experience and respond to this kind of invisibility is as diverse as the range of femme identities.[5] Pick up any book or anthology by or about femmes and you'll find eloquent descriptions of how it feels to go unrecognized by one's people, or to not be seen by the straight community. The corollary of femme invisibility is what I think of as strategic visibility, those moments in which we choose to out ourselves. Femmes are chameleons, able to blend in or to stand up by standing out. We know when to make our colours burn bright for our chosen mates or as a way to disrupt someone's expectations about what a queer person looks like and when to match the wallpaper.

This strategic visibility is part of how I experience the power of being a femme. While I understand why queer writers and others have criticized "passing" as a way of perpetuating divisions within and among marginalized groups, I'm also wary of setting up a hierarchy of visibility, with "most visible" as the

---

5   Here I am primarily referring to the narratives of, for lack of a better term, female-identified femmes. Like butch women, male-identified femmes (and effeminate men) are often hyper-visible for the obvious ways they challenge binary gender.

most vaunted status. Haven't our people fought long and hard to look and love and fuck who and how we want to?

Invisibility isn't inherently bad. I'm of the opinion that we need to rethink our relationship to femme invisibility and the privilege that's attached to it. As Audre Lorde once said, "To use privilege requires admitting to privilege, requires moving beyond guilt and accusation into creative action. Unused privilege becomes a weapon in the hands of our enemies."[6] There's a difference between invisibility by default and invisibility by choice. I love being a femme and looking the way I do. My gender identity is pleasurable, and it's empowering, even if it means I sometimes get funny looks at the dyke bar. And my shifting class background has given me a unique relationship to the privilege that comes with my appearance, since this middle-class-looking femme was made, not born. I don't always get it right, but I work hard to own my privilege and use it mindfully.

While being a femme sometimes renders me invisible in the eyes of the queer and straight communities, it can also open doors. After all, invisible women can use our stealthy wiles to access spaces that others can't, and while inside we might even be able to hold the door open for others. That might mean I can make it easier for my partner to use the women's washroom by chatting with her or asking to borrow a tampon, or engaging in friendly small talk with the nice middle-aged straight couple at the campsite next to ours, using my girl-next-door charm to distract them from wondering about my partner's gender identity.

It often means being the one to deal with authority figures. My "Type A" personality and ability to shift into business mode means I'm usually the one to negotiate the rental contracts for

---

6   Audre Lorde, Letter to *Gay Community News* 17 (January 21–27, 1990): 5, as quoted in David P. Becker, "Growing Up in Two Closets: Class and Privilege in the Lesbian and Gay Community," in S. Raffo, ed. *Queerly Classed: Gay Men and Lesbians Write About Class* (Boston, MA: South End Press, 1997), 234.

the queer cabarets I co-organize in my spare time. And I was the first choice to explain to two police officers why they didn't need to worry about our raucous Pride party getting out of control, even though the lawn was full of glittery, scantily clad partygoers of all genders and orientations. It worked, and they drove away satisfied. I bring my values into the privileged spaces to which I have access, like the fourteenth-floor boardroom where I politely but firmly explained to the chair of the national health research meeting why it wasn't appropriate to refer to transgendered people as "its." I don't always care whether the people in these situations know that I'm a homo. I just want to use the tools I have at my disposal to do right by my community.

Sometimes being queer while looking straight is about blending in, which has the potential to be a powerful and subversive act. You find out who your allies and your enemies are pretty quickly when they assume you're "one of us" (instead of "one of them"). Whatever you call it, femme invisibility or passing can help keep you and your loved ones safe. At other times, being a femme is about choosing to stand out, which can be synonymous with coming out—something many femmes get a lot of practice at. Think of it as a conscious, strategic use of privilege. Think of yourself as a hidden weapon in the fight for queer liberation.

ZENA SHARMAN is a fierce femme and a radical bureaucrat. She is a researcher by day, specializing in gender and health studies, and a superhero by night. She can rock five-inch heels and your world, all before lunchtime. She has her PhD, so you can call her doctor.

A Butch Roadmap

Ivan E. Coyote

A couple of months back, I came upon an article in the online version of *Xtra*! entitled "Winnipeg Pride Wants Parade to be 'family friendly.'" In the article, the then-chair of last year's parade was quoted as saying, "We have to remember that this is a public event; part of the parade is to show people we're not extremists." When pressed to explain just what she meant by extremists, she responded, "drag queens and butch women." She then added it was important to show the people of Winnipeg that there are "mainstream" queer community members, too, like "lawyers and doctors."

I was so mad I seriously considered a stern letter. The subtext of her words stung my eyes and burned in my throat. Apparently, according to this genius, regardless of my politics or attitude or tactics, I was an extremist, solely by virtue of my appearance. Nothing of who I was or what I might contribute to my community mattered, because of what I looked like. In order to be acceptable to the good citizens of Winnipeg, we needed to put forward a more "mainstream" face to the general public, an array liberally laced with professionals. I wondered how this line of reasoning was going to go over with the many perverted transsexual leatherdyke lawyers from working-class backgrounds I am lucky enough to know. Apparently, this woman hadn't read that part of queer history when drag queens and butches started the whole thing by finally standing up and rioting in response to police persecution and brutality. And now she didn't want us at her parade anymore. We weren't family-friendly enough. Then I wondered what exactly this meant for those of us with families.

Then, just recently, I heard a rumour that the younger queers don't like the word butch. This makes me wonder—if I were twenty years old right now instead of forty, what would I call myself?

I grew up without a roadmap to myself. Nobody taught me how to be a butch; I didn't even hear the word until I was twenty years old. I first became something I had no name for in solitude and only later discovered the word for what I was, and realized there were others like me. So now I am writing myself down, sketching directions so that I can be found, or followed.

If the word for you is butch, then remember this word. It will be used against you.

If the word for you is butch, remember, your history is one of strength and survival, and it is largely silent. Do not hide this word under your tongue. Do not whisper it or sweep it under the basement stairs. Let it fill up your chest and widen your shoulders. Wear it like a sleeve tattoo, like a medal of valour.

Learn to recognize other butches for what they really are: your people. Your brothers or your sisters. Both are just words that mean family. Other butches are not your competition, they are your comrades. Be there when they need you. Go fishing together. Help each other move. Polish your rims or your chrome or your boots together. See these acts for what they really are: solidarity.

Do not give your butch friend a hard time about having a ponytail, a Pekinese/Pomeranian cross, nail polish, or even a Smart Car. Get over yourself. You are a rare species, not a stereotype.

Trim your nails short enough that you could safely insert your fingers into your own vagina, should you ever want to.

Scars and purple thumbnails are a status symbol. When attempting to operate, maintain, or repair anything mechanical, always remember the words of my grandmother: "The vast majority of machines are still designed, built, driven, and fixed by men. Therefore, they cannot be that complicated."

Be exceptionally nice to old ladies. They really need their faith in the youth of today restored, and they might think that you are the youth of today. Let them butt in the line at the Safeway. Slow down and walk with them at crosswalks so they're not the only ones holding up traffic. Drive your grandma to bingo. Shovel her driveway. Let chivalry not be dead.

If you're going to be the kind of butch who is often read as a man or a boy, then be the kind of man or boy you wish you would have slept with in high school. Be a gentleman. Let her finish her sentence. Share the armrest. Do her laundry without shrinking anything. Buy her her very own cordless drill.

Open doors for men, saying, "Let me get that for you."

Carry a pocket knife, a lighter, and a handkerchief on your person at all times. Learn flashy lighter tricks, how to tie a half hitch, a slip knot, and a double Windsor.

Learn how to start a fire with a flint and some dry moss. Then use lighter fluid or gasoline and a blowtorch. Burn most of your eyebrows off lighting the barbecue with a birthday candle, and then tell everybody all about it.

Wear footwear that makes a clomping sound, as opposed to a tick or a swish.

Let the weird hairs on your chin and around your nipples grow unhindered.

Learn how to knit, quilt, crochet, or hook rugs: women appreciate a fellow who isn't afraid of their feminine side.

Practice saying you're sorry. This is one activity where you should not use your father as a role model. Fonzie was an asshole. If you are too young to remember who the Fonz was, then YouTube it.

Locker room talk? A sure-fire way not to get laid a second time.

Learn to recognize other butches for what they really are: your people. Your brothers or your sisters. Both are just words that mean family.

IVAN E. COYOTE is the author of seven books, including the award-winning novel *Bow Grip*, the Lambda Literary Award-nominated *The Slow Fix*, and, most recently, *Missed Her*. Ivan has also released three albums and four short films. A renowned storyteller, Ivan frequently performs for live audiences internationally.

To All the Butches I Loved Between 1995 and 2005

An Open Letter about Selling Sex, Selling Out, and Soldiering On

Amber Dawn

You were a set of sturdy boys in well-worn Carhartt jeans and rock T-shirts. Rough scrubbed, each one of you, from your Brylcreemed hair to your polished black jump boots. You rode bellowing muscle bikes circa 1970s, drove cars with duct-tape interiors, or walked with practiced swaggers. You could hold your own at the pool table and in the kitchen—cooking your mamas' comfort-food recipes. You played "Ace of Spades" on electric guitar and hemmed your own pants. Your days were spent painting six-bedroom houses in Shaughnessy, tending to show-jumping horses, keeping university grounds, or otherwise soiling your fingers. You were evolved renditions of the very boy a small-town slut like me was expected to wind up with. But unlike that probable boyfriend, you were a feminist, you rejected the status quo with much greater consideration than it rejected you, and you didn't leave me a knocked-up single mother-to-be. I couldn't possibly have told you enough how truly remarkable you were.

To all the butches I loved between 1995 and 2005, there is a consequential and heartfelt queue of things I never said to you. Blame booze or youth, frequently practiced self-flagellation, homophobia, or any brew of stinking societal influences for me holding my tongue. What matters now is that I put some honest words to our past and—if the graces allow—that you will hear me.

If the details are a blur (and I don't blame you if they are), let me remind you that I was your girl, your mommy, your headache or your heart song (depending on my mood). On a good day I wrote poetry, walked rescue dogs, or led survivors' support groups at the women's centre. I'd all but quit rush drugs, but on a bad day I drank like a fancy fighting betta fish in a small bowl. I spent my nights gliding around softly lit massage parlours in a pair of glitter-pink stilettos. Personal economics informed my femme identity. My transition took place in prudent increments: I grew my neon-orange dyke hair into a mane of bleach blonde; I shaved my armpits and pussy; I dieted down to 100 pounds, and, in effect, I learned to indulge the tastes of men with money to spend. When the business was good, I made more in an hour than you did all week.

This is where my overdue disclosures begin. Whenever I picked up the dinner tab or put gas in your tank, we'd both swallow a quiet shame. I might have mumbled something aloof like, "Easy come, easy go," handling the neatly folded bills with the same cool discretion as my male customers did when they paid me.

For a good long time, I positioned this shame entirely in a have-and-have-not credo. I believed that all my shame came from the very same stomping grounds as my pride: from my humble class background.

I've since realized that this summation is too easy.

You and I and just about everyone we knew were salt-of-the-earth folk. Salt of the earth meets pervert, that is, on account of us being the kind of kinky, tough-love queers that set us apart from our back-home birth families. Ours was an elbow-grease, adult-children-of-alcoholics, there-ain't-no-such-thing-as-a-free-lunch butch-femme. That's right, let's say it again. Ours was a damaged-goods, bitter-pill, better-luck-next-time butch-femme. We were cut from the same threadbare cloth, and we wore it well. Our world was filled with modest, yet revered, codes and traditions. When guests came over, they were offered mismatched kitchen chairs to sit on. If there was whiskey in the cupboard, it was either Jim or Jack. Clothing was swapped. Tools were shared. There were logging-road camping trips and back-alley bonfires. We danced like crazy in creaky-floored rental rec centres and declining dance halls; we'd make the air hot and muggy, the old wood floors stickier than fly paper. And in the dark safe corners of the night, we fucked with our fists, teeth, and hearts like we were indestructible. This was our behind-the-eight-ball butch-femme. I was never ashamed of it.

The shame I felt came from sex work. There it is, as barefaced as it can be. Don't get me wrong, I still wear my feminist-slut badge. This isn't some dubious argument between the merits of waiting tables for minimum wage versus the formidable money-making of prostitution. Morals are not being re-examined. I'm not moving from "camp empowerment" to "camp victim" (such dichotomies are far too short-sighted to sum up sex workers). What I'm coming out about is that sex work changed my relationship with being a working-class femme and, in turn, my relationship with you, my butch lovers.

Sometimes you tried to talk about it. I want to thank you for being brave enough to speak up, even though you didn't always say the right thing. I remember waking up one morning to your big green eyes. You had been watching me sleep since sunrise, adoringly at first, the way smitten lovers do, then your thoughts took a turn and you began to wonder, "How the heck is this my girlfriend?" Fake tan, synthetic hairweave, fake, long airbrushed fingernails; you said that lying beside me felt "surreal." I suppose I looked like a poster child for the beauty myth we had been warned about in our early '90s feminist education. I looked like the kind of femme who is dubbed "high maintenance" or "princess"—indeed these labels were used to describe me—though the reality was that sex work had only made me tougher and more fiercely independent. Still, there wasn't anything punk rock or edgy, humble, or even queer about my exterior femme persona. I pretty much looked like I belonged in a chat-line or diet-pill commercial. The familiar fit of you and me (your butch and my femme) had been disrupted. Had I sold out our butch-femme codes? Had I snuck the bourgeoisie "other" into our bed?

"I make more money when I look like this." How frequently I used this disclaimer. It was fractured thinking I employed as a sex worker: there was the persona and then there was the real me. But, as I've already mentioned, easy dichotomies fall short. As with my appearance, sex work began to reshape my life. Prostitution money paid for my liberal arts degree, followed by an MFA in creative writing. If I was going to be the college-student-by-day, working-girl-by-night cliché, I was determined to average at least a 4.0—even if it meant turning a date with a dental student during lunch break so I could pay for my biology tutor that same afternoon. I was raised with the principle of sacrifice; if I was going to obtain the things that my class background hadn't afforded me, I figured I was bound to suffer at least a little.

While I'd grown somewhat accustomed to grappling with the personal sacrifices that came with sex work, witnessing your inner conflict was an entirely different challenge. Although we both agreed in theory that my job ought to be treated like any other line of work, if your boss called to offer you an extra shift, the biggest conundrum was whether or not the overtime would cut into our upcoming scheduled dates. "Baby, you don't mind, do you?" was all you needed to say, conversation closed. In contrast, entire nights seemed to be ruined when my madam called to ask me to take a last-minute client. As I'd whisper into my cell phone, I witnessed your face stiffen. Eventually, the sound of my ringtone alone was a cause for pause.

I never had to lie to my friends about what you did for a living. "She's a carpenter" or a "welder-in-training," I boasted. These were strong, rugged, and proudly butch professions. Telling people that your girlfriend was a sex worker was a crapshoot, at best. Of course, there were our close mutual friends who I was out to. Others were told a half-truth: that I was a stripper rather than a full-fledged, blowjob-performing prostitute. This explanation spared you from uttering an outright lie and also from making your buddies uncomfortable or concerned. What kind of man dates a prostitute? He is considered either a tyrant, a pimp, or a broken man who can't take care of his woman. Our radical queer values didn't protect us from these stigmas. "I wish I could protect you" was another brave thing that you frequently said to me. I took what comfort I could in this sentiment and let you wrap your arms around me a little tighter. This tender statement, however, affirmed how truly uncomfortable you were with sex work and, worse still, how uncomfortable you were that my work made you feel powerless. Butches aren't "supposed" to feel powerless. I was inadvertently de-butching you. And, as a femme who believes (and celebrates) that her role as a femme is to make her butch feel like one hell of a butch, I was de-femme-ing myself, too.

Sex work changed the way I fucked. Confessions don't come any harder than this one.

I remember the first time I refused to kneel for you. We were making out at one of our fuck spots, between a row of high-school portables a few blocks from your house. You took out your cock, ran your thumb along my bottom lip, and yanked my hair as you did when you wanted me on the ground. It was Friday night. The next day was my regular Saturday shift, when all the big-tipping clients visited the massage parlour, and I couldn't risk having my knees scraped like a "cheap whore." It might have messed with my money. Moreover, I refused to reveal the real me at work. My work persona didn't have scraped knees (or welts or hickies, etc.).

The simplest, sexiest diversion would have been to spit on your cock and lift my skirt. Instead, I stood there frozen in that inciting moment when I realized that keeping my real life and work neatly separated was impossible; it was failing at every opportunity. Sex work was not simply coating the surface of my body like a topcoat of glitter nail polish. It had sunk in.

We could playfully liken my appearance to a drag queen's. My money financed more than a few good times together. But we met an impasse when the impact of sex work entered our bedroom. Setting boundaries around scraped knees was only a preview to long and reccurring phases where I couldn't be touched at all. Contrary to your fantasies and my own, I wasn't an inexhaustible source of amorous coos and sighs. My pussy was not an eternal femme spring, always wet and ready. These coquettish images may sound overblown, but they were critical to our relationship. They were critical to who I was as a femme. I hadn't chosen the saccharine country classic "Touch Your Woman" by Dolly Parton (my working-class femme role model) as a mantra for nothing! Who was I, as a femme, if I couldn't offer my body to you, my butch lovers, as a touchstone, a safe haven of hotness, a soft-skinned, sweet-mouthed reminder that who we were was right and good?

A bigger question: what the heck did sex between us look like if I wasn't going to spread my legs anymore? Most of you had your own set of complex raw spots—as our generation of butches with hard-knock pasts often do. I'd spent my younger femme years devotedly learning about and responding to the nuanced body language and boundaries of butches. Suddenly, it was all I could do to keep up with my own changing limits and body issues.

For awhile I tried on "stone femme" as an identity. In many ways, this label protected me and made me feel powerful. It also became a regular topic for dissection in our small community. "A stone femme, meaning a femme who loves stone butches?" I was asked repeatedly.

"No, I mean I myself am stone," I'd say. "I don't let lovers touch me."

"Hmm." I got a lot of doubtful "hmms" in response, as if I was speaking in riddles.

Ultimately, changes to the way I fucked meant we both had to reinvent the codes and traditions of the butch-femme bedroom as we knew them, which under different circumstances might have been a fun task, but the possibilities weren't as discernible as the losses. The question "Could we ...?" was not asked as often as "Why can't we ...?"

Let's just skip the berating part, where I say, "I admit I wasn't always an easy woman to stand beside." Let's move right to the part where I simply thank you for doing so. If you've hung on and heard me this far, then please let me finish this letter by explaining exactly what it is I am thanking you for.

You were adaptable. You tried really darn hard to be adaptable. Most of the time this only made you about as flexible as a flagpole, but I noticed you bend and knew that you did it for me. I remember the time you let me strap it on and be the first femme to fuck you. It ranks quite high up in my list of favourite all-time memories. Later, you gloated to your butch buddies, "She's more 'butch' than me between the sheets." To my surprise, comradely arm punching and shared stupid grins followed this admission. It made me wonder if you needed that fuck (and those that followed) as desperately as I did. Maybe you needed a damaged-goods, stone femme like me to ask you to become something besides the ever-infallible butch top you were accustomed to being.

Likewise, maybe you needed to cry with me during those rare times when you resisted the urge to take up the emotional reins and say "Baby, don't cry" or, "It will be okay." This was a delicate and extraordinary space, when we both unabashedly cried together. For me, this was the emotional antithesis of the wordless reactive shame I often felt but lacked the guts or words to talk about. Thank you for sharing this space with me.

There were many moments when I doubted myself during those years—hazardous moments, like brushes with bad clients, when yours were the strong arms in which I sought respite. There were also many instances when I lacked the confidence to walk with dignity into a university classroom or a square job interview, moments when I was tempted to blow my ho money by going on benders because climbing the class ladder was terrifying. Thank you for loving me the way you knew best. Your big calloused hands held me strong to this life. You still took me dancing until our clothes were soaked through with sweat. You popped Heart's *Greatest Hits* in your car stereo, and we drove the back roads singing "Crazy on You" in comically awful disharmony. You called me "old lady" and "beautiful" and "my girl." You taught me that butch-femme wasn't about dress codes, the gendered skills we'd acquired, or jobs we held, or even about who bent over in the bedroom. At the crux of it all, our butch-femme traditions were about creating a place that was distinctly ours. Again and again you brought me to this home, this shelter from external pressures, this asylum from troubled pasts and uncertain futures. Thank you for assuring me that I always had a remarkable, shameless place.

Amber Dawn is a writer, filmmaker, and activist based in Vancouver. She is the author of the novel *Sub Rosa* (Arsenal Pulp Press, 2010), editor of the Lambda Literary Award-nominated *Fist of the Spider Woman* (Arsenal Pulp Press, 2008), and co-editor of *With a Rough Tongue: Femmes Write Porn* (Arsenal Pulp Press, 2005). She has toured four times with the infamous Sex Workers' Art Show. Her three-year-running queer readings series, thrilLITERATE, raises funds for literacy initiatives for survival sex workers. Currently, she is the director of programming for the Vancouver Queer Film Festival.

Brother Dog

S. Bear Bergman

In a dim bar in Atlanta, in the corner, in a conspiratorial tone, she asks me: "So? How's butch-on-butch married life?" I shrug and grin, then reply, "I really wouldn't know."

While it's true that my husband, he of song and story and many wonders indeed, is a masculinely gendered person, it is also true that he's not a butch and never has been. I'm not trying to suggest that he's insufficiently handy with tools or excessively interested in his hair or whatever your personal classifiers of butchness are. It's simply true—he is not a transman of butch experience, as some of us are, but rather a faggot of faggot experience, with a side order of homoflexible interest in a certain type of bossy, brash girl (and really, even the direct of Kinooyo could understand that, no?). He has always danced at the boy bars and joined the men's discussion circles, always had a dragwear section of boas and tutus in his closet. He never was a butch. It's simply not his thing.

The butch-on-butch action in my life, instead, is enjoyed with my boyfriend, one of the aforementioned transmen of butch experience and overall a guy so much like me that we refer to each other with great fondness as being of the same breed, like brother dogs. He's the one with the anachronistically formal manners when ladies (self-identified) are present; he's the one whose nearly stone sexuality was formed at a similar junction of shame and desire; his hands rest on a table exactly the same way mine do. It was a full year of dating before we found any measure of grace on the topic of who would open the door for whom.

Butches are formed in the crucible, is what I say when people ask. Butches—the ones I have known and loved and been protected by—are the ones who find our way through the fire and emerge both singed and hardened but also smelling of a particular experience that cannot be counterfeited. I find that I recognize the whiff of it across lines of race or class, that butch heart, that big and battered tool of so many unexpected reconciliations, unlikely forgivenesses, and full-bore love affairs. I recognize it and love it. I seek it out, sniff it out, because I've learned that it makes my heart melt and also my dick hard.

There's a rogues' gallery of them in my secret heart, the butches I have known up close, in their skin, under whose hands I have eventually and gratefully found a sweaty renewal. Even though my life has improved so much that I rarely see my melting point these days, tenderly cared for as I am by the ministrations of my new small family, I still treasure every experience of butch-on-butch intimacy as a rare and precious thing. I remember the chef whose tattoos I licked my way across while she growled my name, and the postman who let me love him so grudgingly and who I always knew would break my heart, and the activist who cried with relief when I took hold of his cock and called it that, right out loud.

I know what kind of trust it takes when, hardened as we are, we reach out for someone who knows exactly what we've been through and can also see right through our bullshit. There are dodges I would never try with another butch, diversions away from the tender and difficult truth another butch could never sell to me. When my boyfriend and I are together, we have to schedule hours to just sit and talk, smoking a cigar or eating ice cream or people watching, so that we can say as much as we need to—which is always a great deal. We talk, and we rub away at one another's fire-blackened façades, rough edges against rough edges, smoothing one another out and polishing one another up by tiny degrees with each date.

(For me, I mean. I get in trouble here all the time, saying what I think plainly, as though it were the truth. It's my truth. And my butch self has learned that when you betray doubt or uncertainty in your words, sometimes people try to take them away from you or change your mind or make it sound like you said something very else. So I just lay it down as it lives for me, but of course, here and everywhere, I mean—for me. I think. In my experience. Your mileage may vary.)

Husband and I rock each other's worlds, shine each other up, bring new wonders into being every day. Day in and day out, every day and every night. Boyfriend is a hot and painful grind that leaves me improved but sometimes hurting—sweet and grateful, but hurting nonetheless, like the three-day burn you carry home from a hot conference affair. I couldn't live next to it, but I get close and breathe deep as often as I can. As often as I can stand. Not him, I adore him, but the opening up required to get a good dose.

The butch can be a closed ecosystem if she or he or ze isn't careful. It's tempting to simply batten down the hatches and resist any further incursions and any inclusions they may bring. It's why butches can be such sexist asses, and it's why we can be such fiercely loyal friends; whatever gets in gets magnified, built upon, embellished, and amended until it's huge, especially if it's the sort of thing that flourishes in the dark. If we bring in a spore of shame we can grow a garden of it between our knees and our ears. Letting the light and air in is the only way to prevent it, and letting the light and air in is one of the hardest things to do if opening up has already caused a lot of pain. I wouldn't do it myself, but I understand every butch who ever tried to rinse the fucked-up parts away with alcohol and found hirself filled up by it and drowning. I surely do.

And so I follow my good sense and my stiff dick and I walk right up to the butches that welcome me, with heart in one hand and aforementioned dick in the other. I adore their fur and their ink, their scars and their sore spots; I have learned to treasure bad backs blown out on years of moving other people's stuff and busted-up hockey knees that prevent even the briefest kneeling on a hardwood floor. I know to turn out the lights; I know how to make wrestling turn into fucking (and movie-watching turn into wrestling). I know how extraordinary it will feel to take the trust of a warrior on my shoulders and do everything I know to show hir a good time, to have the kind of safe sex that's not about preventing infection but about preventing dis-ease. Touching her just right, firmly enough to make it clear that I'm not doing anyone but myself any kind of a favour here. Murmuring to him in the dark that he's so fucking hot. Letting my sweat drip onto her face as a mark of pride. Letting him want. Letting him need. Or having the same for myself, brutally beautiful and unsustainable, urgently wanted and too difficult to do more than rarely. Closer to never than seldom.

Right now, just now, I am sanding down an old black filing cabinet so my husband can have it in his office, brilliant and functional and fabulous like him. Every touch of the sander makes a fresh spark and a new small patch of gorgeous raw material, and the metaphor is too perfect to ignore. I get better every time I expose myself to another butch in some way, or rather, I am made better and hope I am making that butch better as well, sparks and all, burning smell and all, hot and bright and just a little bit revealed. Just a little bit of revelation.

S. BEAR BERGMAN (*sbearbergman.com*) is an author, a theatre artist, an instigator, a gender-jammer, and a good example of what happens when you overeducate a contrarian. Ze is also the author or editor of three books, most recently (with Kate Bornstein) the anthology *Gender Outlaws: The Next Generation* (Seal Press, 2010). Bear has also created and toured four award-winning solo performances, and is a frequent contributor to anthologies on all manner of topics from the sacred to the extremely profane. A long-time activist, Bear continues to work at the points of intersection between and among gender, sexuality, and culture, and spends a lot of time trying to discourage people from installing traffic signals there. Ze lives in Toronto with hir husband and son.

Butch is How I Feel

Brenda Barnes

Butch is the only word I've ever found that describes how I feel. It has been a long process to find and accept it as the right word. But butch is the word.

For sure I knew since before puberty that I was a different kind of girl—a tomboy, yes, active in sports, yes, and something else different that I could not yet define. I saw other girls wearing dresses, seeking the attention of boys, and wanting to have children. I didn't want any of those things. I wanted the girls wearing dresses.

When I was young, my family shied away from the word "butch" to describe the ways in which I differed from the other girls. There were other words which meant almost the same thing. My father and uncles referred to me as either Brünhilde or Bertha Krause. These names drew attention to my physical resemblance to girls or women, mostly of eastern European descent, who were notable for their largeness and their lack of femininity in our Canadian WASP prairie culture. Initially horrified to think they may have known something about me before I did myself, I've come to realize that those Barnes men instinctively had some things right and surprisingly, they still do.

A few years ago, one of these uncles asked me just before his son's Mexican wedding whether I wanted to attend the stag or doe. I asked whether it would feel weird to the men to have me there, and he told me that they thought I'd probably have more fun and would feel more comfortable hanging out with the guys. I was dumbfounded and validated all in the same moment.

So, instead of getting dolled up and parading out to dinner with all the pretty girls in their little cocktail dresses, up-dos, and heels, I went to a pub crawl through Playa Del Carmen with the guys, and we eventually partook in an annual male Canadian tradition—watching the Vancouver Canucks lose during the NHL playoffs.

I know some of you are thinking, "What, she gave up the chance to be the only 'guy' amongst all those beautiful young women? What a moron." Yes, I chose to be with the guys that night because that's where I wanted to be, but more importantly, I wanted to honour something in my family that understood some essence of me, even if they didn't use the same word I did.

I'm not saying their radar doesn't go on the fritz from time to time. We went to a rooftop-patio bar with a pool and vintage 1940s movies being projected on the wall. Cool place. In that place, however, I was definitely not one of the guys. All the gorgeous young male staff overtly ignored me and fawned over all the men—my father, my uncles, my cousin and his equally gorgeous friends. Off to the side, I smoked and observed in silent bemusement.

I didn't tell them until the next day that we had been at a gay bar.

As a younger adult, I'd often been called "sir" when someone approached me from behind (I have large linebacker shoulders from years of speed swimming), but as soon as I turned around and they saw my tits, there was no mistaking that, biologically speaking, I was a woman.

Once I'd met the word butch, I wanted to claim it and keep it as my place. This was a factor when I was considering breast reduction surgery. Would my second-wave feminist colleagues think I hated my body and had mutilated myself? Because I was having top surgery, would my dyke friends think I was trans? These considerations ultimately were not an impediment to doing what was right for me. It took me twenty years to make the decision to proceed. My nipples had to be completely removed and then grafted back onto my body. I thought about that for a long time. A combination of being diagnosed with a food allergy that caused me to gain a lot of weight and wanting to forestall a future of ever-declining mobility finally motivated me to take action. The tits themselves had been an impediment to being regarded as butch within queer culture. They moored me to the wrong place on the gender spectrum. Those ladies were between a 56 G or 56 H. That's H as in Jesus H fucking Christ, those things were huge. In a two-hour operation, five pounds of each breast were removed to reduce my chest size to a 48 A.

Before my breast reduction, my image of myself was not as a person with large tits, but trying to ignore their size was impossible. They were always there, though they did not feel a part of me, so I gave them their own separate identity and third-party status in conversation. I had a large repertoire of really good boob jokes (thank you, Bette Midler and Bruce Vilanch) to counter and subvert unwanted attention, including teasing, harassment, and bullying. These jokes were also the prime feature in a number of my well-honed public personae, including DJ Double D—my retired deejay handle—and Captain Torpedo Tits, a costumed alter-identity for a breast cancer fundraising event, Mardi Bras.

I'm liberated now. All my adult life, until I was rid of the boobs, I'd felt as though I was in drag in my own skin. Now I don't need to create or play those self-protective characters any longer to guard me from other people's judgments, whether real or imagined. My outer self matches my inner self. That's an even larger weight lifted from my shoulders than the breasts themselves.

I was feeling the most butch I had ever felt in my life at a reception about six months after the operation when a butch pal said I looked like I was "supposed to look." She didn't mean that I needed to alter my body to be my true self, but simply that now I looked like she had always envisioned me. It was a pretty powerful moment of butch brotherhood.

I find it hilarious to observe how fiercely the gender code is enforced through language by a younger generation of gender-queers who may never claim the word butch and who may reject the gender identity with which I continue to wrestle and dance.

Recently, I was telling a story about how my young boyfriend—more than twenty years my junior, woman-born, and male self-identifying—and I felt after working out as butches. My boyfriend, within earshot, corrected me and said that, whereas I'm butch, he's a muscle fag. I looked at his spindly little arms and 1980s-era matching pink singlet and headband and roared with laughter. Isn't it fascinating that we've evolved in our gender definitions to the point where a little girly man is seen to belong to a more masculine part of the spectrum than a large, physically imposing, Buick-bench-pressing dyke does?

When I first told my partner that I wanted to submit a piece to an anthology of butch and femme voices, she told me that the words butch and femme no longer apply. She pointed to all the ways in which we subvert the stereotypes of the butch-femme dichotomy; she likes power tools and fly fishing as well as sweater sets, and generally seeks the company of women. My usual uniform is T-shirt, jeans, and boots, though I have infrequently been known to femme it up in capris, slingbacks, and collared blouses when throwing a government press conference. I generally prefer the company of men. But, after further discussion, she did agree that, despite small deviations, the words butch and femme were the only accurate ones to describe the obvious gender differences between us. That conversation made me think about other times when, as an adult, I've had gender either projected or forced upon me. It made me see that it was necessary to question the basis of people's gender presumptions.

Once, while driving to the Dawson City, Yukon, Music Festival, my partner, a straight girlfriend, and I stopped at a small landing on the Yukon River to shuttle the truck of a friend who was canoeing to the festival. When we arrived, we found the truck had a flat. Our straight friend noticed that my partner did most of the heavy-tool work. She insists to this day that she discovered some hidden truth about our genders. She assumed that, because I wasn't doing the hard physical work, I was the femme and my partner was the butch. All our friend was really doing was projecting archaic notions of gender roles in straight relationships onto a lesbian relationship. Actually, I was just being lazy, and I also knew how competent it makes my partner feel to use mechanic's tools, so I deferred to her in that particular moment and pitched in only when further muscle was required.

Those same dumb stereotypes are the reason why, when femme or straight women do manual labour, they're considered dexterous beyond their gender, but when a butch declines or defers the task, her gender gets called into question.

When our next-door neighbour, a willow-thin yet wiry runner who's young, single, and straight, came over to borrow the lawnmower, I told her about this piece I was writing about being butch. Was that a word I embraced, she asked, and how about "queer" and "dyke"? I wondered if this was a test and whether, because she was a straight woman, she would think these terms derogatory. However, when I said that I liked and embraced all three words, we agreed that some people wouldn't understand the importance of reclaiming these terms (like how Dan Savage wanted to call his syndicated column "Hey Faggot!"). Checkmate on my own assumptions, I thought. But as I was leaning down to pull the mower from its winter spot, I banged my head. My petite neighbour pushed me out of the way and, as she muscled the mower out of the shed, turned to me and said, "Butch, my ass."

I'll admit it's my partner who most often mows our small lawn, though I do the majority of the snow shovelling during our eight-month winter. We both cook. I raise garden vegetables while she's on outside flowers, house plants, and kitty-litter duty. I'm the big softy with our three cats, and anyone who's seen me with them in the home environment could testify that, yes, there are maternal bones in butch bodies.

Our neighbour further remarked that I rarely wear plaid shirts as she offered me one of hers in order to buff up my butch credentials. The problem with a plaid shirt is that, whereas on my partner it would just look cute, on me it would drive things over the top, and I have tempered my embracing of butch so as to resist self-parody.

Ten years ago, while on a camping trip through Alaska, my partner and I treated ourselves to a hotel room and a night in the big city at a gay establishment in Anchorage. Although there was a large integrated bar in the centre, most activity was taking place in sex-segregated dance floors flanking the main space. The "girl" side featured many large, unadorned mannish gals in mullets, work boots, and plaid shirts, two-stepping to the *Grease* soundtrack. Wearing sandals, quick-dry yellow capris, and a red collared shirt, I just wanted to trance-out to some House music. I got a few puzzled stares before we shifted over to the "boy" side, where we were given glow sticks by the over-moussed, bling-adorned, and glittered twinks who discoed with us until dusk (that's about 3:30 a.m. in July).

In retrospect, if that bar's layout had been representative of a linear gender continuum, this chameleon's place might have been in the relatively deserted middle ground. Neither of the extremes that were being expressed that night fit me, though I can appreciate and defend the need my queer brothers and sisters feel to trumpet the extremes in order to claim their existence. It's just not my personal style.

My personal style now is to be even more proud of my body, to be active in my community in order to feel valued, and to work toward a gentler, more equitable society. I already had a high level of self-esteem before the breast reduction; but now, after the operation, I really feel centred and grounded in my body for the first time in my life. My centre of gravity has literally shifted closer to the earth. To me, that's all butch, no matter what anyone else thinks.

And it's just as well. It's too hard to find plaid collared shirts in my size.

BRENDA BARNES is an articulate butch of a distinguished age, who is married and settled in downtown Whitehorse. A former journalist, broadcaster, arts administrator, and naval officer, she now works in communications and violence prevention.

Slide Rules

Nairne Holtz

Who offers a lap and who sits on that lap is one of those slide rules of butch and femme—a useful way to make fast calculations, if not hard-and-fast rules.

The calculation people make about my lover is that she's a man. Generally, the people who make this assumption are straight, but not always. Once, two gay men invited my lover to have sex with them. ("They thought they were getting a papa bear, not a mama bear," a friend joked.) Another time, a lesbian tried to throw my lover out of the women's bathroom at a gay bar. The calculation people make about me is that I'm female and heterosexual. Generally, the people who make this assumption are straight, but not always.

I'm femme and my lover is butch. But I'm the one who kills bugs that get into the house, and I had to snuff out a dying mouse struggling to get out of a trap. My lover, who is good with her hands, does all of the carpentry and house repairs along with the mending and ironing.

So what makes a butch? What makes a femme? Here's another slide rule. Are you attracted to women more feminine than you? Then you're butch. Are you attracted to women more masculine than you? Then you're femme. Simple, except when it's not. Butch plus femme is the most popular equation in the lesbian community but not the only one.

What makes one person butch and another femme in a couple is hard to pin down yet easy to recognize. I remember laughing with another lesbian couple over something the four of us had all experienced: a quarrel while driving during which the femme stormed out of the car at an intersection, and the butch drove along the curb at a crawl, calling, "C'mon, honey, get back into the car."

Being recognized as butch and femme isn't always that comfortable. A few summers ago, I was cutting the front lawn while my next-door neighbour mowed hers. Her husband stood on their porch teasing her that she had missed a spot. When my lover stepped onto our porch, the man looked over at her and said with a grin, "Oh, I see you've put *yours* to work, too." While his remark was somewhere between a joke and a goad, he was also, in some sense, acknowledging and accepting our relationship.

Our neighbour would probably say my lover is the "man" in the relationship, and I'm the "woman." We wouldn't use those words, but the term butch is beginning to seem, well, dated.

Butches had a heyday in North America in the 1950s and '60s only to disappear with the advent of hippie culture and radical feminism. There was a revival in the 1990s, but today in the queer community we are more likely to hear the terms "bois" and "transmen."

But my lover doesn't want to call herself a boi. It seems inappropriate for a middle-aged adult with responsibilities. She'd rather be a man, except she doesn't want to be a man. She has no desire to change her secondary sex characteristics, which are a source of pleasure for both of us. At the same time, she thinks of "women" as "them," as not quite her.

Both my lover and I grew up in quasi-rural areas where we spent a lot of time alone exploring nature. My lover went ice-fishing and hunting with her father, although she refused to kill anything and used guns simply for target practice. Her father, a machinist, also taught her to use power and woodworking tools. From a very young age, my lover had a profound sense of being different from other kids, but she never doubted herself; she merely doubted other people's perceptions of her.

My own experience was in many ways different, but at a more basic level, the same: I never doubted my femininity or femaleness, only other people's limited conceptions of what this identity should mean. As a child, I built camps in the woods with my sister, and then we would put on vintage gowns and traipse around pretending we were at a ball. My mother, a former tomboy, gave my sister and me gender-neutral toys like Lego and Dinky cars—but when she discovered us holding weddings for our toy cars, she threw up her hands. However, neither my sister nor I were as brainwashed into passive sex roles as our poor mother assumed. Our Barbie dolls were bionic and were always rescuing their boyfriends from train wrecks and sinister crooks. I did believe in "women's lib," only my version—influenced by *Charlie's Angels* and *Wonder Woman*—didn't preclude girly fashions.

Like my lover, however, I felt like an outsider, but that was mostly because my parents were hippies. My sense of difference was never tied to my gender until one day in girls' health class in grade eight. Our teacher asked us to write down what we wanted to be when we grew up. My imagined vocations were: a) spy; b) private detective; and c) writer. I jotted them down, adding that I wanted to have adventures and do crazy things like skydiving. We weren't supposed to put our names on our papers, but when the teacher read my list out loud, everyone looked at me and burst out laughing. All the other girls had written down that they wanted to get married and have children. Not only had these goals never occurred to me, but they seemed utterly boring. Yet I felt a sense of isolation, as if the other girls and I were standing on separate ice floes, and mine had drifted out to sea.

Fluid notions of identity are popular, but I'm uncomfortable with such a relative approach. Maybe it's because I used to work as a librarian. Cataloguing a book is often a difficult decision, as much art as it is science, but it is valuable, a way to help people find what they want. Systems of classification are indeed historically contingent: for example, advances in information and communication technologies have led to an exponential increase in the computer section of the US Library of Congress (which issues classification numbers used throughout North America), and at times, this results in somewhat clunky and inexact classifications. But these systems evolve and adapt in much the same way that social systems do; lesbians rejected the rigidity of 1950s role-playing classifications while not dispensing with notions of butch and femme.

"I'm not butch or femme. Don't put me in a box," a woman once told me. Then she asked me my zodiac sign.

Are we comfortable with some systems of classification but not others? When some lesbians say they don't believe in roles, I think what they mean is they can't or don't want to live up to certain expectations. It is easier to say, "I'm not butch," than to say, "I'm butch, but I don't want to be in charge all the time, especially in bed." It is easier to say, "I'm not femme," than "I'm attracted to butches, but I'm too fat and not pretty enough to be considered femme."

When a masculine woman claims she's not butch, what she may be saying is: "I'm not that stereotype; I'm not fat; I'm not ugly; I don't have a blue-collar job; I don't hate men." I could point out that these attributes are nothing to be ashamed of, but a more overlooked point is that you don't have to be a stereotype to be masculine: most middle-class women need look no further than their fathers for alternative examples of masculinity.

When a feminine woman says she's not femme, she may be protecting herself. Despite the imperatives women receive from a sexist society to be thin, pretty, and feminine, there are sensible reasons to resist this. As a slender, conventionally attractive woman, I no doubt reap certain benefits, but I'm also treated like prey. When I was in my early twenties and complained to my lesbian roommates about being sexually harassed, they responded with blank stares. It seemed that if you were female and masculine or simply got a short, punk haircut and started wearing baggy shorts and Doc Martens, you could eliminate a certain kind of hassle.

I say a certain kind a hassle because my lover has experienced the other side of the coin of sexism: harassment for staking out masculinity, which some men think belongs to them. A guy tried to beat her up once for this. On another occasion, some frat boys screamed, "Fucking dyke!" as they drove their jeep onto the sidewalk in an attempt to run her over.

A few friends have wondered if their lives would be easier if they transitioned. Transitioning may mean less danger on the street and more benefits at work, but I don't think my friends would feel safer at, say, a hospital or nursing home.

These days, my lover and I have noticed we attract far less attention than we did in the early days of our relationship. Has our culture become less sexist and homophobic and more tolerant? Or are we, as women who have now reached middle age, perceived as less desirable and therefore less of a threat?

The world now uses calculators instead of slide rules because they are more precise; they can handle more complex equations. But I don't need a calculator to know my lover and I add up to butch and femme.

NAIRNE HOLTZ was described by the *Globe and Mail* as a "writer to watch." She is the author of *This One's Going to Last Forever* (Insomniac, 2009), which was a finalist for a Lambda Literary Award, and *The Skin Beneath* (Insomniac, 2007), which won the Alice B. Reader's Award for Debut Lesbian Fiction and was shortlisted for the Quebec Writers' Federation McAuslan First Book Prize. She lives in Toronto with her lover and miniature dogs and is indubitably femme.

Embodying Hunger and Desire with a Fistful of Bliss

Laiwan

Before I knew that there is a difference between men and women, before I knew, as a girl, that my desire would be considered a particularity particular to women, I saw him fit into a place of desire in my imagination: a lithe, graceful body of movement without excess, feline, suave, and intent.

Lee: he had the same surname as my aunts. Bruce Lee: known throughout the African continent, where my family had settled, as the iconographic Chinaman, a Chinaman with the perfect guerrilla skills for surviving in the colonies—skills ancient and perfected by the infamous Wong Fei-Hung, who fought invading foreigners in China at the turn of the twentieth century. Wong Fei-Hung: heroic solely among the Chinese, signifying the selective heroics of wars, politics, imagination.

At twelve, smuggled into a Rhodesian drive-in, I saw, for the first time, Bruce Lee's precise leaps and philosophy of body existing in a place of perfect timing, perfect choreography, perfect self-defence. Side-stepping assault to re-use the misspent chi of the boring and untrusting. An articulation of body that could be mine.

"Like the only cinematic Chinaman I knew of as an icon, I too wanted to be a streetfighter: a boy with position. I wanted to be the butch philosopher: a fighting drag king. One who knew that the punch came from a place of passion—not anger nor sorrow—'from the heart, with feeling' he had said ..."[1]

---

1   Laiwan, "On Heroics," *Mix Magazine* 22(4) (1997): 56.

I now have a swagger born out of years of facing everything that I wasn't. A profound inner hunger and desire propelling me toward living without excess, living a practicality where stripping down my identity over many years created a tough simplicity embodying energy that could sustain and survive. Born in Rhodesian apartheid, there were few options for excess. You existed and you adapted to stay invisible and out of trouble.

My family modelled free spirit within the privacy of our home—a spirit that could navigate passage with a cloak of invisibility through the unmapped yet expected discriminations and hatefulness of apartheid. My father taught me how to change car tires, fix shorted fuses, and shoot a gun because he was teaching these skills to my brother. It was practical and convenient. He believed I would survive with these skills. I could be boyish, play boys' games, have boys' toys, desire my best friends, and be protected because the discriminations of racism dictated that I not be seen. In this construct of society, I did not exist except in the margins of tolerance, and I did not attempt to be accepted. I did what I pleased, remaining within the borders of my silence and privacy, wearing the cloak.

There is a family story that my surname can be traced to a Buddhist monk named Chu Yuan-Chang. In 1368 he fought against a hundred years of Mongol occupation in China and founded the Ming Dynasty. My blood has claim to fight off invaders, even if the invader is within me. In this Buddhist understanding of the clearing of an inner landscape, this life-long pursuit of peace, I claim my awakening compassion and loving-kindness to now embody a swagger celebrating all my beloved demons.

> now she challenges every ideal you hold about yourself
> and about her
> and you fight back
> you invade her because she is strong and desirable

she will say there is much work to do
she will say she does not want you
that she does not need you
you will realize how foreign you are

and in defense you will say "Your men are the women of
our world"
she will say there is much work to do[2]

Daring to persist with an endurance and tenacity that questions anything that comes too fixed, too easy, too comfortable, and in order to explode external restrictions and stereotypes, I embrace a warrior lineage battling for confidence and trust. I am compelled by a vision of empowerment to overcome what is oppressive, internalized, hateful, and phobic. I move toward liberating what can be invested by bodily being (everything invisible in apartheid); somatic intelligence, a physical intelligence articulate in feeling, with depth, sensing, listening, attentive to bodily awareness and movement, so as to feed and nurture my original hunger and desire with love.

It has taken a long time, and a swagger never comes easily.

Schooled by German nuns, I imagine it as a stereotypical story: them holding me hostage for nine years of my childhood. Here I really adapted invisibility as a means of survival. What held me in that purgatory I can now joke about with humour, appreciating the limitations and boundaries that have shaped my inner rebel without a pause. It pushed my hunger and desire further, like a fetish that no one in the all-girls convent admitted to, but we acted out regardless, like the time a group of us six-year-olds stole out to the laundry to check out the nuns' underwear. I

---

2   Excerpted from Laiwan, "Ubiquitous China," in Laiwan, *distance of distinct vision / point éloigne de vision claire* (Vancouver: Western Front, 1992).

wanted to know what was underneath their cloaks.

Outside of school, I revelled in climbing trees, getting dirty, thinking of nothing in particular, honing skills in daydreaming, embellishing imaginary best friends with benefits, being a free spirit as best I could. I loved my desert "bush-baby" boots, and I wore them all the time. My clothes were practical and, who knows for what reason, I didn't have any skill in accessorizing.

The cloak of invisibility allows one to negate emotional and bodily experiences. This silence could easily be mistaken for butch skill, for the butch strength of quiet fortitude and endurance. My version showed no such skill, but instead was rooted in a trap of silence bullied into an immobilized raced and queered body. Luckily, my profound hunger and desire for freedom—to have voice, to speak up, and to move actively in the world—demanded it differently. I have worked and continue to work toward a physically engaged and articulately present intelligence that can remain without words, improvisational, and often unknown in every moment.

I got interested in becoming articulate, not through words, necessarily, but through feeling and movement—dance, music, sex, running, jumping, walking, and being alive in the world, active and fluid. Becoming articulate in what cannot be put into words, in what is physical, cellular, and bodily. I grew really interested in body tenacity, in acknowledging the persistence and endurance of our flesh, in what our cells know, what we desire and hunger for. I learned patience experiencing duration, sticking it out, following the flow even if it gets uncomfortable, and listening to that discomfort until it passes through into understanding and compassion. Becoming bodily aware within every moment, attendant to feeling and sensation, shifting anything negative to become positive, breathing in dark so as to breathe out bright, dispelling what is haunting and of inner demons so as to sit with this moment with patience, particularly while living in a world of technological instantaneity.

The German nuns did teach me one thing: to persist regardless of the challenge. And within this, to work at achieving a Tai Chi fluidity that can avoid an earnest blow, tripping the opponent with his own force. Arriving in Canada at the age of fifteen, shocked by this cold, wet climate and extremely foreign culture, I began to embrace an intense identity of intellect. A form of protection—armour against the sudden discovery I was no longer invisible. I aimed to be cool, unfeeling, always thinking, striving for a mind of laser precision and economy and, most of all, I learned to channel my isolation, hunger, raging teen hormones, utter confusion, and nagging spiritual hunger into active creativity. A Cartesian trap of mind-body divide, the challenge here was how to bring me out into the world, substantially bodily present, with a swagger of confidence and self-knowledge.

I don't know if I make a good butch. It doesn't really matter. I don't often name myself as butch, yet I accept that I am often identified as one. After forty-nine years of hard work, I am confident in and trusting of my movement without excess, my engaged and articulate cells, my somatic experience in this world. I am comfortable in my skin, in my T-shirt and jeans, in my Chinese appearance, in my savannah heat and spaciousness, in my nerdy delight, at my swagger learned in rebellion and at great cost. This growling, prowling hunger, my tendency toward intimacy, my tendency toward tenderness and embracing of my own vulnerability—loving openly, generously, and non-possessively—awakens me to all that was once numb, dumb, and ignorant, helps me to persist in a continual awakening, with a child's curiosity and imagination, to aspire toward freshness in any given moment, to value an innocence that fixed naming cannot catch, and be present and engaged in every moment.

Being present and engaged shapes one's chemistry. I know what I like ... and what I like often returns what I like. It is the law of attraction. It is the universe who is a lover to be seduced. She is the one who I want to attract. I don't have names for what

I attract, but I often experience goose bumps, electrical touch, a skin shiver, a tremble, weak legs, hard breath, a gasp, thumping heart, throbbing vision, unclear thoughts, inarticulate tongue— all of these I attribute to chemistry, a physically and emotionally informed intelligence, in which I know my persuasion is to love women. I am attracted by a type of woman who embraces attention to how she is fluidly physical, moving, and aware, spiritually and emotionally brilliant and radiant, flaunting innocence with a worldly experience, analytically effective without saying a word—often not needing words—and is similarly hungry and wild in loving women and being a woman.

I love my shape. I didn't always. A few years ago, my massage therapist advised: "Stand naked in the mirror and say, 'I love you.'" A colleague and I laughed about this afterward, but I persisted with this through a series of health-building efforts toward increased somatic intelligence. It worked. The massage therapist recently told me, "I could work on you all day; you know how to receive, and not everyone knows how to receive." I was pleased with this diagnosis. Released from the baggage of apartheid, my cells and muscles are open and light. These are also aspirations of both traditional Chinese medicine and Buddhism.

Bruce Lee believed that in order to be a good fighter in martial arts, you must have loose hips. For this he practised the dance of cha-cha. Loose hips and a swagger can propel a generosity and lightness that is infectious—it can become viral. A femme can swagger much the same way a butch can swagger, but every swagger has a different tenor, a different musicality, and this is rooted in chemistry, cellular memory, and cellular exchange via touch, fluids, sound, taste, sight, intuition, instinct, guts, breath, etc. All expand bodily intelligence, physical and emotional attention, and consciousness.

To balance yin and yang, I work with somatic intelligence performatively; that is, I perform with intentional, conscious of ways of moving in the world. Like an actor, I can choose which pose, which posture to embody, to appropriate to any given moment. At a young age, I saw Clint Eastwood in *A Fistful of Dollars*, and I wanted to wear a blanket in the desert, ride alone on a horse, eat beans from a tin plate. Luckily, I didn't get trapped there. My imagination was demanding and rigorous and, instead, I propelled myself into this soulful trajectory, embodying hunger and desire with a fistful of bliss.

Born in Zimbabwe of Chinese parents, LAIWAN immigrated to Canada in 1977 to leave the war in Rhodesia. She is an artist, writer, and educator who uses poetics, improvisation, and philosophy to work across disciplines. She is interested in things ephemeral, sublime, delicious, relational, and spacious.

She can generate small, near-invisible gestures for viral dissemination, or she can create large multimedia installations such as *Quartet for The Year 4698 or 5760* (2000) and *Duet: Étude for Solitudes* (2006), both of which explore qualities of improvisation with clarinet virtuoso Lori Freedman. Laiwan's current investigations are live improvisational performative work, viral poetics, cacophonous musicality, and tenuous subtleties aimed to em008poweringly rebel against stereotypes and fixed expectations.

Recently, the Vancouver Art Gallery included her work in two group exhibitions, *How Soon is Now* (2009) and *Everything Everyday* (2010). Laiwan was honoured with the 2008 Vancouver Queer Media Artist Award by Out On Screen. She continues to exhibit in various group and solo shows; to curate programs in Canada, the US, and Zimbabwe; to publish work in numerous journals and anthologies; and to be active in feminist, queer and "of-colour" community organizing.

She participates in panel discussions, gives solo readings and lectures, and teaches in the MFA Interdisciplinary Arts Program, Goddard College, Port Townsend, Washington, while living in Vancouver, BC.

Between My Fingers

Stacey Milbern

I grow up hearing that the way I walk is not how "young girls should walk." To move forward, I launch my tottering trunk left to right until my body gets caught in a pendulum-like motion. Ambitious white doctors say I will become a woman after they iron out the crookedness of my body. I don't want to be the woman they want me to be (the gracious, docile type who jumps at the white man's word), but I do want to be a woman, so I do what they tell me to do. When my body grows tired and I start using a power wheelchair, they see it as a failure to reach femininity or womanhood. No matter my age, I am stuck in genderless, asexual, disabled child-land.

Fast-forward fifteen years.

I am pouring all of my time into radical disability organizing. Using potlucks and retreats to create safe spaces for people I love pushes me into a world where I am confident that I know who I am and exactly what needs to be done. One day, a Chicana butch blogger says that when she met me in person, she perceived me as a femme. Even though I am taking pleasure in things that are traditionally connected with queer femme identity, associating that term with me makes me dizzy—dizzyingly and deliriously pleased that someone sees me as something. I immediately look up "femme" to discover what she could possibly be referring to, wondering what I might have in common with the gorgeous queers in my life who call themselves femmes.

I start rolling the word "femme" around on my tongue and then between my fingers to see what I can create. There is no model for what femme could look like for a disabled woman of colour, but as the femme in my hands grows bigger, things start to make more sense. The ability to take public gawking and turn it into an opportunity to command everyone's attention—

femme. Shit-talking from my wheelchair during card games—femme. Being able to tell you the exact level of force or gentleness I want you to use when touching me—femme. Taking care of business—femme. Everything goes back to femme.

Femme is work, though, right? To be femme means to pick up a shovel and constantly hit it against the never-ending mountain of oppression that has snowed down on top of me. It means telling myself, "Yes, the way you love and exist in the world is fuckin' fierce," even when I don't have someone who can help me get dressed in a way that makes me feel fierce. It means letting myself understand that the way I organize and cultivate community is powerful, even if I can't show up to help someone move into their house or make soup when they're sick. (Most of the time this is because I can't actually get inside of their house ... structural ableism sucks.)

The questions still exist: how do I be femme when much of femme culture's deepest fear of disability is who I am? How do I be femme when ableism works hand in hand with heterosexism to create very narrow definitions of how minds and bodies should function?

I am still learning.

STACEY MILBERN is a powerchair-roaring, queer disabled radical woman of colour. Stacey has spent the last twenty-three years living and loving in the American South and is new to the San Francisco Bay Area. She is a youth organizer, media maker, and poet. She blogs at *blog.cripchick.com*.

Masculine of Centre, Seeks Her Refined Femme

B. Cole

In this essay, I explore female masculinities of colour that lie outside of the iconic butch narrative, i.e., womyn[1] like me. I stumbled into academia quite by accident. I cut my teeth on political campaigns and worked with social justice organizations around the country. I'd always felt that the conversations that take place in academic spaces lacked roots in the communities I come from and live in. Sure, there was never a shortage of stories about these places that I call home, but the real stories, told by people who look like me, have more often been told through personal narrative, film, and art. When I found myself sitting in the Gender Institute at the London School of Economics, I struggled with the absence of stories about people like me—queer womyn of colour along a masculine continuum whose lives and loves don't get told, who have to search for reflections of our stories in the margins of butch narratives, the constant sidekicks and stereotyped footnotes of "minority masculinity."

So I set out on a quest that has led me all the way to this book in your hands. I had some amazing conversations along the way. When I set out to write, I realized that I didn't even have the language I needed to reach out to my community, though I'd long known what butch meant, thanks to my butch elders. Even though I called myself butch, all around me there were signals about what that was supposed to look like, and the word never fully reflected who I am. One of my first conversations with Oshen T., an activist and she-pronoun-using stud, echoed this unease with which many of us take up the mantle of butch.

---

1 Womyn here is used to reflect that, for many of us, as masculine of centre, our gendered identity is not accurately reflected in the term women.

I identify as stud but, growing up, I didn't know that
there was a word, "stud." What was more common was
butch, but at some point, like in my mid to late teens, I
noticed that butches were usually white women, and even
though I did see some black butches ... at some point it
got really irritating and didn't fit me. I don't feel butch,
and I don't like that word, even saying it. Stud came out
of me and my peers having a conversation, and I held
onto the word stud. We younger studs from East Oakland started to gravitate toward that. Butch was white
and older, and as young kids, we were studs. There was
some age stuff, race and class. All the books were about
stone cold butches ... just white people. We were like,
nah, that's not us.
—Oshen T.

If butch wasn't the word I was looking for, what was it?
Should I use dom? Stud? AG (aggressive)? None of these quite
worked, and so in 2008 I introduced the term "masculine of
centre" (MoC) as more encompassing and less racially and class-
specific than butch. MoC also speaks to the cultural nuances
of female masculinity, while still recognizing our commonali-
ties—independent of who we partner with. The inclusion of the
language "of centre" sees beyond the traditional binary of male
and female to female masculinity as a continuum. "Of centre" is
a way of acknowledging that the balance each of us determines
around our own masculinity and femininity in the discovery of
our gendered selves is never truly fixed. Masculine of centre recognizes the cultural breadth and depth of identity for lesbian/
queer womyn who tilt toward the masculine side of the gender
scale, and the term includes a wide range of identities such as
butch, stud, aggressive/AG, tom, macha, boi, dom, etc.
    Over the last two decades, queer gender theory, influenced by

Judith Butler's discourse on gender performativity[2] has evolved to incorporate analysis of butch gender and female masculinity.[3] This analysis has produced a range of understandings regarding the social construction of butch consciousness, female masculinity, and sexual expression and identity. The argument suggests that every individual constructs a personal narrative that reflects their gendered self. As these theoretical frameworks around "butch" emerge as areas for critical inquiry and awareness, so do questions addressing their limitations.

Existing work on female masculinity and butch identity has crossed numerous disciplines such as queer theory, masculinity studies, psychology, and ethnic studies. Butch themes have emerged from beyond the academy into poetry, film, biography and autobiography, and fiction. Yet, despite this explosion of work, including the emergence of female masculinity as a theoretical concept, theorizations of "butchness" among womyn of colour are largely absent from the academic canon on gender. Even as authors such as Sherrie Inness in "'G. I. Joes in Barbie Land': Recontextualizing Butch in Twentieth-Century Lesbian Culture" and S. Bear Bergman in *Butch is a Noun* have disrupted the "fixed" understandings of "butch gender" in the master narrative, very little of this work has challenged its construction as a racialized identity.

I think it's possible to tell this story, my story, without changing the rich history and stories of how the mainstream butch narrative has created the social and political space we all live

---

2 See the Sources list at the end of this essay.

3 Sue Ellen Case, "Toward a Butch Femme Aesthetic," in *The Lesbian and Gay Studies Reader*, eds. Henry Ablelove, Michella Aina Barale, and David M. Alperin (New York; London: Routledge, 1993), 295–306; Judith Halberstam, *Female Masculinity* (Durham, NC: Duke University Press, 1998); Sally R. Munt, *Butch/Femme: Inside Lesbian Gender* (Washington: Cassell, 1998); Heidi M. Levitt and Sharon G. Horne, "Exploration of Lesbian-Queer Genders: Butch, Femme, Androgynous or 'Other'" *Journal of Lesbian Studies* 6 (2002), 25–39.

in, and which makes it possible to write this piece. The deep irony is that historically butch identities have been more embraced among MoC womyn of colour than by white queer communities. Despite this rich history and legacy, the image of what butch looks like in popular media and academic writing is still overwhelmingly white. I want to begin creating room within the existing narrative for young womyn of colour to explore the intersections of our gender and race as critical sites that inform our identity. It is in that spirit that I offer "masculine of centre" as a space to unify all of our vibrant transformative, feminist, gender queer ways of knowing so that we can build social and political power together.

RAGING BULLS: ICONS OF A WHITE FEMALE MASCULINITY

Theorists[4] have explored what some have called "lesbian gender" in its many forms, including butch identity, femme identity, and female masculinity. This theorizing has not only validated the lives of masculine-of-centre womyn, but has also been instrumental in framing butch as a construction of gendered identity, rather than as a "role." The construction of butch and its ability to be read requires that certain representations come to reflect its essence as an identity. Such representations have in the past been referred to as "classic" or "classical."[5] The contemporary establishment of a "butch aesthetic," has, by producing representations of itself, "effectively refused the multiplicity of cultural, social, and political intersections in which the concrete

---

4   Case, in *The Lesbian and Gay Studies Reader*, 37; Joan Nestle, *The Persistent Desire: A Femme-Butch Reader* (Boston: Alyson Publications, 1992); Madeline D. Davis and Elizabeth Lapovsky Kennedy, *Boots of Leather, Slippers of Gold: The History of a Lesbian Community* (New York; London: Routledge, 1993); Halberstam, *Female Masculinity*; Munt, *Butch/Femme*.
5   Case, 37.

array"[6] of butch identity is actually constructed.

While focusing on demonstrating butch and female masculinity's epistemological origins, many feminist theorists have interpreted butch as a way of "knowing, interpreting, and doing lesbian gender." Ontologically, these lesbian genders are seen as being "concerned with having an identity, and a kind of true self."[7] Some understand it as both socially constructed "gender performance" and others as representing an essentialized heterosexual, biological, male identity that merely clones the referent. The expressions of one's gendered butch identity are intrinsically linked to culture and race. In Davis and Kennedy's classic *Boots of Leather, Slippers of Gold: The History of a Lesbian Community*, they describe "a new style of butch, a woman who dressed in working-class male clothes for as much of the time as she possibly could, and went to the bar every day, not just on weekends. She was also street wise and fought back physically when provoked by straight society or by other lesbians."[8] The political significance of this emergence lies in the visibility lesbians gained in the 1940s and '50s as World War II reshaped the American landscape, changing women's roles in relationship to work, gender, and family. Butch was a site of resistance to the heteronormative limitations on women. It was a place to embrace one's identity in a public way that allowed for alignment between the public and private self, a way of claiming space with your very presence.

There is a long-standing history of butch representations that have helped solidify the iconic image of today's butch. The icon of butch identity was fashioned through historical narratives,

6 Judith Butler, *Gender Trouble: Feminism and the Subversion of Identity* (New York; London: Routledge, 1990), 83.
7 Munt, *Butch/Femme*, 1.
8 Davis and Kennedy, *Boots of Leather, Slippers of Gold*, 68.

poetry, biography, and classic novels such as Radclyffe Hall's *The Well of Loneliness*, written in 1928 and long considered the most well-known lesbian novel, *The Beebo Brinker Chronicles* from Ann Bannon, which moved butch into mainstream consciousness in the 1950s, and Leslie Feinberg's *Stone Butch Blues,* set in the pre-Stonewall era of the 1960s, which solidified the archetype. This "butch raging bull," as Halberstam argues,[9] is meant to "offer masculinity a new champion" drawing on the iconography of the white male boxer.

These works created a narrative for what and how butch looks and feels that still holds significant cultural power today. The external signifiers—the class and racial location of these historical accounts and cultural references to bars and customs—locate butch identity. This locating of butchness within a specific culture, class, race, and ethnicity makes it difficult for the masculine of centre person of colour to enter into the narrative without their gender presentation, specifically their version of masculinity, being questioned.

Attempts to disrupt this sense of "classical" butch continue to rely on representations and cultural location within whiteness and white notions of masculinity and femininity. As Halberstam points out, there is cultural value in marginalizing masculinities that divert from the master narrative.[10] Even though Halberstam is speaking to heteronormative masculinity here, these diverting narratives have the potential to "dilute" the "authoritative power" of white butchness in the same way. As this narrative is pushed into the mainstream queer consciousness to construct butch identity, many of our experiences are left out. Supporting versions of masculinity that we enjoy and trust, many of these "heroic masculinities" depend absolutely on the subordination

---

9   Halberstam, *Female Masculinity*, 43.
10   ibid, 1.

of alternative masculinities.[11] This role of the dominant narrative being constructed and circulated while simultaneously preventing alternative narratives is an important factor in establishing fixed understandings of female masculinity and butch.

Halberstam[12] goes on to address female masculinity's relation to whiteness and identifies it as a site of inquiry for "cultural studies" yet does not venture down the road of how the relationship to race critically alters female masculinity as a concept. The challenge in theorizing butch gender and identity is that to determine how it operates, you have to locate it within certain bodies and cultural and sexual practices. These various locations, when analyzed, become fixed and static through the work of the writer exploring their creation and development. A central argument in *Female Masculinity* is that masculinity "becomes legible as masculinity where and when it leaves the white male middle-class body."[13] While a considerable amount of the analysis explores when and where the narrative departs from the male body, less attention is given to when and where it departs from whiteness.

Unlike white female masculinity, female masculinity for womyn of colour is based on sites of power *and* systemic oppression—through masculinities of colour. The assumption that they can be resignified with equal subversive and revolutionary actions against white manhood is false. The ability to access masculinity pivots upon the ways in which gender intersects with race, and these gaps have been filled with many new ways of naming ourselves. In the last decade, the explosion of young masculine-of-centre womyn has created a demographic shift on the butch landscape, giving way to terms like "stud," "boi," "tom," and "macha" in California and the South, "dom" within the DC, Maryland, and Virginia region, and "aggressives," or "AGs" in New York.

---

11 ibid.
12 ibid, 2.
13 ibid.

These identities represent a redefined female masculinity that is rooted in the experiences of womyn of colour and is more genderqueer than historical interpretations of butch. For some this raises the question: "What is happening to all of our butches?" I think this evolution highlights the fact that, for many of us who came of age ten or twenty years ago, and even called ourselves butches, we never felt fully rooted in that language and space. As a community, we have the opportunity to respond with an open heart to this evolution, ensuring that the legacy of butch as a social, political, and personal space continues to grow and thrive. But we must also concede its limitations. The title of this piece, "Masculine of Centre, Seeks Her Refined Femme," is a heading from the first dating profile posted using the term "masculine of centre." It speaks to both a historical legacy of butch-femme and a longing for a language different and new.

Masculine of centre is already moving into mainstream consciousness in queer spaces, white as well as of colour. Organizations such as BUTCH Voices, whose mission is to enhance and sustain the well-being of all women, female-bodied, and trans-identified individuals who are masculine of centre, and online communities such as *thedefinition.org* (for masculine-of-centre women, transmen, and our allies) have integrated masculine of centre into their mission statements as a broader calling to our communities.

The emergence of this new language would not have happened were it not for the ways in which masculine-of-centre womyn of colour live their female masculinity through the lens of race. Our identity has socially transformative powers and there are still nuances to our identities—masculine-of-centre mothering, social mobility, and historical racial oppression—which shape masculinity in ways that have yet to be fully explored. What masculine-of-centre womyn of colour do with masculinity, how we interpret it, and how we embody it, contains lessons for other womyn and men, both queer and straight, regardless of race.

This is an invitation for all of us to reshape female masculinity through our experiences so that we may better understand the whole of who we are.

SOURCES

Ardill, Susan and Sue O'Sullivan. "Butch/Femme Obsessions," *Feminist Review* 34 (1990): 79–85.

Bannon, Ann. *The Beebo Brinker Chronicles*. New York: Triangle Classics-Quality Paperback Book Club, 1995.

Bergman, S. Bear. *Butch Is a Noun*. Vancouver: Arsenal Pulp Press, 2010.

Butler, Judith. "Merely Cultural," *Social Text: Queer Transexions on Race, Nation, and Gender* 52/53 (1997): 265–77.

———. *Gender Trouble: Feminism and the Subversion of Identity*. New York: Routledge. 1999.

Case, Sue Ellen, "Toward a Butch Femme Aesthetic." In *The Lesbian and Gay Studies Reader* edited by Henry Ablelove, Michelle Aina Barale, and David M. Halperin, 295–306. New York; London: Routledge, 1993.

Davis, Madeline D. and Elizabeth Lapovsky Kennedy. *Boots of Leather, Slippers of Gold: The History of a Lesbian Community*. New York; London: Routledge, 1993.

Feinberg, Leslie. *Stone Butch Blues: A Novel*. New York: Firebrand Books, 1993.

Halberstam, Judith. "Mackdaddy, Superfly, Rapper: Gender, Race, and Masculinity in the Drag King Scene." *Social Text: Queer Transexions on Race, Nation, and Gender* 52/53 (1997): 104–31.

———. *Female Masculinity*. Durham, NC: Duke University Press, 1998.

Hall, Radclyffe. *The Well of Loneliness*. New York: Anchor Books, 1990.

Inness, Sherrie and Michele Lloyd. "'G. I. Joes in Barbie Land': Recontextualizing Butch in Twentieth-Century Lesbian Culture." *NWSA Journal* 7 no. 3 (1995): 1–23.

Levitt, Heidi M. and Sharon G. Horne. "Exploration of Lesbian-Queer Genders: Butch, Femme, Androgynous or 'Other.'" *Journal of Lesbian Studies* 6 (2002): 25–39.

Levitt, Heidi M. and Katherine R. Hiestand, "A Quest for Authenticity: Contemporary Butch Gender." *Sex Roles* 50 no. 9–10 (2004): 605–21.

Munt, Sally R. *Butch/Femme: Inside Lesbian Gender.* Washington: Cassell, 1998.

Nestle, Joan. "Butch-Fem Relationships: Sexual Courage in the 1950s." *Heresies* 12 no. 22 (1981): 21–24

———. *A Restricted Country.* New York: Firebrand Books, 1987.

———. *The Persistent Desire: A Femme-Butch Reader.* Boston: Alyson Books, 1992.

Oshen T., Interview with author. Oakland, CA. September 1, 2010.

Phelan, Shane. "Public Discourse and the Closeting of Butch Lesbians." In *Butch/Femme: Inside Lesbian Gender,* edited by Sally R. Munt, 191–99. Washington: Cassell, 1998.

Walidah, Hanifah and Olive Demetrius. *U People,* DVD. UPeople LLC, 2007. *www.iLoveUPeople.com*

B. COLE is a PhD student in Sociology at the University of California, Santa Cruz. She received her MSc from the London School of Economics and has worked as a community facilitator, strategist, and consultant for the last ten years. A Rotary International Ambassadorial Scholar, recipient of the Harry S. Truman Scholarship, and the Spirit of Dolores Huerta Award, she has worked across the US and internationally on issues of leadership development and economic justice.

Cole launched the Brown Boi Project *(/brownboiproject.org/)* in 2009, a leadership development program that bridges gender and racial dialogues between masculine of centre womyn, trans men, queer men, and straight men of colour. This work reflects Cole's deep commitment to bridging academic discourse and social movements of change, rooted in communities of colour.

No Butches, No Femmes

The Mainstreaming of Queer Sexuality

Victoria A. Brownworth

Are queers and straights basically the same except for their sexual attractions/orientations, or are there intrinsic differences that create and hence define our separate societies? It is my belief that queer culture is unique, that the distinctions between queer lives and those of heterosexuals are defined in part by the sexual outlaw status that accrues to being queer and in part by the culture—art, literature, music—that has been created to affirm, explore, and explain queer lives. Assimilation threatens not only that carefully constructed queer culture, but it also threatens queer sexuality. Assimilation neuters queers by demanding a narrow, heterosexually normative paradigm that insists on a strict gender-based orientation. This disallows the range of sexual expression in gender attributes that we once considered essential facets of who we were/are as lesbians and gay men. In short, assimilation forces us to pass as straight, even when we are out queers, by denying us the full range of our queer gender expression. To be truly assimilated, we must mimic straight women and men, which means we cannot include, for example, butch lesbians and gay male queens in post-assimilationist culture, because there are no comparable persons in straight society.

As a lesbian who came out while in high school in 1969, I represent the first generation of post-Stonewall out queers. I also represent those who straddle both eras of queer history—bar culture and pride culture.

I came of age in gay bars populated by stone butches and nelly queens, B-girls and Marlboro men. I came of age under the tutelage of women and men who seemed, to my young and untrained eye, to live lives that were only possible after dark, when mystery naturally descends, the impossible seems suddenly possible, and women could be with other women and men with other men.

As a fourteen-year-old high school sophomore who looked several years older than I was, I slipped into bars with a wink and a nod and a fake ID. My age and my naïveté provided a measure of protection from many of the risks attendant in the bars in those days. I often quite literally didn't know what was going on. But what of the others who seemed to walk a much more dangerous line than I did—a line which, of necessity, crossed over from night to day and included jobs and families and possibly even spouses? What did women who dressed like men and men who dressed like women do during the day? Where did they come from and where did they go? How did they survive beyond the safe and rarefied atmosphere of the bars? These women and men inhabited a mysterious world I had limited entrée into but to which I wanted desperately to belong. I needed to know how these women and men lived outside the bars, because theirs was the life I assumed I would be living in just a few more years: The life of a lesbian in America. These were the only lesbians and gay men I knew; they were my ambassadors to queer society. Yet the idea that I would have to choose from the limited identities presented to me in the bars was confounding. I did not fit into any of the available categories. So who would I become? If I didn't fit in, did that mean I wasn't really a lesbian? That seemed to be the one thing of which I was certain.

In 2011, queer bars are wholly different than they were decades ago. The old danger has been replaced by the new edgy. The risks that attended entering a gay bar in the years immediately post-Stonewall no longer exist in most places—certainly not in major cities with thriving queer communities. The mainstreaming of queer culture and straight society's widening tolerance (if not acceptance) of lesbians and gay men has meant that youths like I was now have a myriad of options before them.

Or do they?

The demimonde lure of the bars that existed when I first came

out was intoxicating. Queer society was uniquely different from
the world of my working-class neighbourhood or my public high
school. It was difficult to imagine that everyone who went there
didn't feel as I did—that it was the only place where everything
was as it should be, where we could be ourselves. Making the
shift from the bar to school was difficult and often painful. How
much more so would it be when I got older? How much more
so was it for the women and men who had to pretend they were
something else in complex daytime lives?

In the bars, the dynamics were set; there was a formula to
follow. That intoxicating sense of difference was thrilling even
as it was unnerving, because I was both too young and too un-
schooled to truly navigate the world of butch-femme relationships that formed the foundation of lesbian bar culture. And yet,
this was the formula that introduced me to lesbianism and which
would establish both my lesbian identity and my lesbian desire.
As one young woman told me early on, "I could never go back
to being straight. It's so boring. This is real life."

For the years when all I knew of queer society was the bars,
it was indeed real life for me. I often wonder how those who
didn't grow up in the queer bar culture established their queer
identities. Who did they learn how to be queer from? Who were
their models? These were the years before there was a queer literary canon. The politics of being queer were just being formed. I
learned how to be a lesbian from the butches who ran the bars
I went to, the bouncers and bartenders with short men's hair-
cuts and bound breasts and low voices that were somewhat masculine and seriously sexy. Yet I also learned from the queens
who wore makeup, platform shoes, and hot pants, and fluffed
their hair constantly, their voices as affectedly feminine as the
butches' were masculine. This was my society—everyone had
something to teach me.

The lure of bar culture was magnetic. For me, a high-school
student whom everyone assumed was straight, getting on the

subway and heading for the bars was like stepping through a portal to another world from the one in which I went to classes and church and babysat for neighbours' children. It was a parallel universe where I was myself and yet not myself; a parallel universe in which everyone knew I was a lesbian just by virtue of where I was—the bars—and who I was with—other women.

The excitement I felt in the bars was tempered by knowing that I didn't fit into any existing paradigm of that queer culture I so yearned to be part of. I had no idea what the rules were for behaviour or language or even just standing against a wall versus sitting on a bar stool. The first time I went up to a woman sitting on a bar stool to ask her to dance she looked me up and down and then proclaimed, "You're a femme. You don't ask. You wait to be asked." And then she turned away.

I had no idea what a femme was. The women and men in the bars spoke a language I didn't speak and for which there was no dictionary. It was learn-as-you-go and without a teacher, I was left floundering. This was the country I was adopting, and yet I didn't know all the rules for living within it.

In fact, I was not a femme. But in bar culture terms, I wasn't a butch, either. My blonde hair fell to the middle of my back, and I wore the tight T-shirts, bell-bottom jeans, platform shoes, and earrings that other girls of my hippie era wore. But there were no girls my age in the bars, just as there were no girls who dressed like boys at my all-girls school. The femmes in the bars wore short skirts and stockings and high heels. They wore heavy makeup and false eyelashes and had to keep straight men at bay even as they tried to attract butch women.

The bars were a minefield of unknown etiquette but also a danger zone because of impromptu and harassing police patrols and straight men who wandered in looking for something outré. Some of the femmes were also prostitutes, as were some of the drag queens. Bar society was its own society with its own rules for the sexual outlaws who lived there.

Queer bars today, even in small towns a decade or so behind the times, have an entirely different milieu than was found in those I frequented years ago. All-ages nights now welcome teens and college kids to the club scene. Straights aren't turned away; the best clubs in major cities are almost always the queer ones. Straight women ogle gay men. Ostensibly straight couples cruise lesbians for the possibility of a fantasy threesome hookup.

What you won't find in the bar scene now, however, are the very people who populated the Stonewall Inn on that steamy June night in 1969 or on any of the nights when I was hanging out in bars just like it a few years later. Yes, there's the occasional drag queen or transgendered person, but the stone butches have been replaced by sleek, suburban-style dykes. The B-girls and high femmes have been replaced by the casually feminine lesbians of *The L Word*. Where the bars and clubs of my youth were populated with a clearly defined butch-femme dynamic among both lesbians and gay men, in that same scene today, it's hard to tell the queers from the straights. The people who founded the movement for queer equality—the bull dykes and nelly queens—have been marginalized by the mainstreaming of queer society.

From an assimilationist standpoint, of course, this homogenizing of queer culture is a good thing. It underscores and validates the rhetoric queers get from centrist queer political groups like Human Rights Campaign that we—the LGBTQ contingent—are just like them, the heterosexuals. In the mainstreaming of queer culture, the only initials that really still matter are DADT ("Don't Ask, Don't Tell") and DOMA (Defense of Marriage Act). Being queer is no longer the love that dare not speak its name. Ellen DeGeneres is a spokesmodel for Cover Girl; Neil Patrick Harris is on *TV Guide*'s list of the "The 25 Most Influential People in Television;" Tim Gunn sells housewares for Macy's advertisements; Nate Berkus has his own TV show; and *The Real L Word* reality series has replaced the fictional version.

We've arrived.

Assimilation is a tricky business, however. The demand for equal rights and integration into mainstream society often leads—or forces—minority groups to pattern themselves on the majority, disengaging from the very things that make them who they are as a separate and distinct group.

When I was a teenager in the bars, I wasn't sure I wanted to embrace what seemed to me to be the restrictions of lesbian culture—the butch or femme code. I tried dressing like a boy—it didn't work. It didn't matter that I knew I was butch; I never looked the role as defined in those days. The kind of butch I was had no category in 1970. But in 2011, the kind of butches who tutored me in my teens have no place either; they've been assimilated out of the culture. So too have the nelly gay men that were a fixture of those bars—boys in hot pants and platform shoes with long hair but no breasts.

In Frank Marcus's iconic play (later a film by British director Robert Aldrich) *The Killing of Sister George*, a climactic scene finds Mercy Croft, the woman stealing George's girlfriend Childie from her, telling George that she's an anachronism, that there is no place for her in the new queer world of 1960s London. The soignée Mercy tells George that she's no young girl's dream.

George is an old-school butch. She keeps her femme, Childie, whose real name is Alice, in a sham marriage of her own convenience. Childie is fearful, submissive, and dependent, dressed in baby-doll nightgowns and lots of lipstick. George sports a tweed suit and forty extra pounds of toughness and bravado. It's an isolated world the two live in, which no one else can enter but where, at times, there is bliss—until someone opens the door to alternatives for Childie and the dream is destroyed.

Does the assimilation that came with liberation mean that the dichotomous sides of lesbian sexuality—butch and femme—can no longer exist? Is there room only for lesbians who can flip, like the lesbians on TV shows such as *Grey's Anatomy* or *The*

L Word? Has the mainstreaming of queer society made butch lesbians and femme gay men the anachronism that Mercy Croft intimated in *The Killing of Sister George*?

In 1970, there was no place for a lesbian who looked like I did then. The subtle gradations that would gradually filter into the lesbian community didn't exist yet. In 1970, you were either the top or the bottom, the butch or the femme. And you looked the part: short hair and men's pants, shirts, undershirts (not bras), and men's shoes were de rigueur for butches. The butch dress code could get you arrested if the police raided the bar and took you in—it was illegal for women to dress like men in the US— but that stopped no one. A butch looked the part.

Forty years later, Sarah Jessica Parker wears a man's tuxedo in *Sex and the City 2* to attend a gay wedding, and it's presented as a sexual come-on—to men. The days of police arresting women for dressing like men are long past in America. But has queer culture moved too far in the opposite direction from the butch/ femme dynamic of the years immediately pre- and post-Stonewall? Is it our own community now that disallows the male-centric butch because she fits a stereotype that assimilationists want straight society to either forget or ignore—the bull dyke, the bull dagger butch who doesn't turn straight men on and doesn't have the potential to be heterosexual?

So it would seem. The marginalizing of the butch women and femme men who once comprised a significant and vital demographic of queer society has forced many lesbians and gay men toward an alternative identification as transgender, even when they may not be. Many young butch lesbians, for example, say they feel pressured to claim a transgender identity, rather than what used to be termed a stone butch identity, because of the gender narrowing within the assimilationist queer community. The personal ads that used to read "straight-acting, no femmes" have been acculturated into the queer community: We are no longer willing to accept those who are not normative by assimilationist standards. Severely butch? You must be transgender—born into the wrong body. That's okay, it's not your fault; it's a genetic mismatch. But severely butch and still think you are a lesbian? Rethink that, because we're all just like straight people now and we have to look the parts.

The freakification and marginalization of the butch women and femme gay men of not-that-long ago—the queers who cannot pass for straight—is a disturbing trend. That marginalizing devolves specifically from the presumption that straight approval is the only way to achieve social equity, since that equity is granted by straights to queers on sufferance, whether individually or through the courts or legislation. At some point during the fight for queer equality, it was deemed necessary, and even essential, to present as "just like them." If we wanted equal rights, then we had to prove we were "normal" and not the hyper-sexualized, promiscuous, living-for-sex creatures straight people believed us to be. Women who dressed and acted like men and men who dressed and acted like women advertised an undercurrent of sexual obviousness that was impossible for straight society to ignore. This "flaunting" of queer sexuality was considered socially obscene; it was thought to promote the notion that queers are driven by sex and sex alone. Since gender outrage is the primary imperative behind homophobia—straight people can't cope with (and feel the need to punish) women who clearly aren't interested in men or with men who don't want to be masculine—one step toward ending homophobia has been to neutralize the sexuality of lesbians and gay men. A neutered queer is an acceptable queer.

Lesbians who appear feminine, or at least as feminine as their straight counterparts, are non-threatening to both straight women and men. Gay men who look and act like other men won't bring on an attack of queer fear in the locker room or the office. Assimilation demands that you act like the majority group. Alas, assimilation also destroys the differences that are essential to the subset culture within the larger one. If every Jew converts to

Christianity, who is a Jew? If every bull dyke puts on lipstick or every queen grows a beard, is there a subtextual culture within queer culture or are all queers just like straight people?

Female sexuality is purportedly more fluid than men's. In her 2008 book *Sexual Fluidity: Understanding Women's Love and Desire*, Lisa M. Diamond notes that most women fall somewhere in the centre of the Kinsey scale; there are fewer completely lesbian or completely heterosexual women than there are men who are completely gay or straight. The most common sexual fantasy for straight women is sex with another woman. Portrayals of lesbians on television and in movies not made by lesbians are of women indistinguishable from their straight counterparts. In these couplings, there is no discernable butch-femme dynamic and no discernable butch. The butchest lesbian character on television is Shane on *The L Word*, one of the softest butches ever to strut her stuff. In Diamond's book, there are no butch lesbians, there are only women who weave back and forth between lesbian and heterosexual identities. Is there true female sexual fluidity if only some women's sexuality is charted?

The theory of female sexual fluidity seems invented specifically to deny the depth and intractability of lesbian sexual identity: a truth that depends on an assimilationist view of female sexuality in which men are always at least occasional players in women's sexual lives, even women who identify as lesbians. An alternative perspective is that the acculturated desire for mainstream acceptance and the need for approval by straight society forces women who identify as lesbians to make choices about how they present themselves to the world, opting still to pass for straight, even while claiming a lesbian identity.

Whether pre-Stonewall era queer sexuality differed from post-Stonewall queer sexuality may be a matter of conjecture, but the construction of overt sexual identity has definitely changed in the post-Stonewall era. It's not just the addition of the various letters to the original L and G that has altered the sexual orientation landscape, it's the requirement to fit within the gender and sexual constraints of one of those letters that has changed. Sexuality has, to a certain extent and for assimilationist purposes, become a choice.

Consider the gay man who dresses like a woman once in awhile or even regularly, yet identifies as a gay man, not as transgender, and has sex only with other men: is there a place for him within the realm of "gay," or is he expected to identify as a transgendered person even if he hasn't had hormone treatments or surgeries or ever even wants to?

And what about the butch lesbian who's not a soft, non-threatening butch but a tough, masculine-identified yet wholly lesbian and not transgender butch? Is there a central place for her in assimilationist queer society, or is she relegated forever to the fringe, marginalized in ways that even pre-Stonewall butches were not?

Heterosexual society now seems much more forgiving of men in drag, who can be written off as campy and comedic, than of women who have a clearly defined butch persona that screams sexual independence from men. It's easy to perceive gay men in drag as playing a role that is akin to acting and not sexual in any way. It was straight audiences that kept *La Cage aux Folles* on Broadway for years. But the butch lesbian has none of those camp qualities to make her an accepted or acceptable foil for some heterosexual. Straight men don't want to pal around with bull dykes, and straight women don't want to go shopping for shoes or have a mani-pedi with them. How can they hide their butch identities on the job, whether in an assembly line or an office? These butches are outside the realm of acceptable/accepted straight-seeming behavioural norms and therefore Other and suspect.

All of which begs the question of how far assimilation has really taken the queer community post-Stonewall and if the direction can be viewed as a positive one if whole segments of the queer demographic are left clinging to the fringes. If the focus of straight society is still on the "threat" queers pose to straight society—threats to children in the form of the myth of the gay male pedophile, the myth of the homosexual agenda needing converts, and the myth that queer teachers are recruiting, threats to heterosexual marriage if queers gain marriage equality, threats to service persons if openly gay or lesbian personnel serve in the military—then has any level of assimilation actually been achieved? When queer-fear defences can still be iterated in court by straight men and considered viable, in the trials of the murderers of Matthew Shepard or young butch lesbian Sakia Gunn, then queers are not just unassimilated, they remain second-class citizens. Their outlaw sexual status translates into real outlaw status, when the victim is described as the perpetrator—as members of Congress referred to Matthew Shepard during the federal hate-crimes bill hearings in 2009.

The promises that accompany assimilation are rarely fulfilled; they are the lure to force minorities into being more like the majority—more tolerable, more palatable, less like themselves, less Other. Meanwhile, the detriments to community, to individual self-esteem and, in the case of queers, to personal sexual identity, are manifold.

I think back on the way I felt as a teenager in the bars of my barely post-Stonewall era. While I felt intrinsically safe in those bars and as if I was among my own people for the first time, I also know that I didn't fit the butch-femme pattern that had been in play long before Stonewall. I was butch, but not enough. I looked femme, but I wasn't, really. The construct of that era didn't fit the "new," post-Stonewall, post-liberation lesbian that I was.

That nagging, sometimes gnawing discomfiture left me feeling that I didn't quite fit in with the people who were my only community. When I think back on those feelings, particularly in the context of the deep yearning I had to be part of and accepted by that queer world, it makes me concerned for the teenage butches and queens who don't see a place for themselves within the restrictions and constrictions of assimilationist queer culture. As expansive as queer culture seems to have become, with the growing list of letters following that original G and L, it's still very much about compartmentalizing who we are. How many people will tell the budding butch that she really is transgender, born a man in a woman's body? But what if she's really just butch, that is, content with the confluence of her female body and masculine persona? Will her confusion lead her to hormone treatments and surgeries she will later regret when she realizes what her true identity is?

Queer society and culture continues to evolve, as does queer sexuality. What we need to consider as a community and as individuals, however, is whether the goals of our equality can be met if that equality means we must force members of our community into living in a different closet, one of our creation and devising. If we have to act straight and look straight in order to gain straight acceptance and ultimately equal status as queer citizens in straight society, might the cost of that equality be too steep? The mainstreaming of queer sexuality comes with many caveats. The trick, it would seem, is to keep from losing our unique queer culture, or, more importantly, our unique queer identities, while also gaining equal standing in straight society.

VICTORIA A. BROWNWORTH is the author and editor of more than twenty-four books, including the award-winning *Too Queer: Essays from a Radical Life* and *Coming Out of Cancer: Writings from the Lesbian Cancer Epidemic*. A nationally syndicated columnist and book critic, she is an editor at *Curve* magazine and Lambda Literary. Her work has appeared in more than a hundred newspapers, magazines, and journals worldwide, both mainstream and queer, and in more than fifty anthologies. She is the publisher of Tiny Satchel Press, an independent publisher of young adult and children's books. She lives in Philadelphia with her partner of eleven years, the artist Maddy Gold.

What We Know to Be True

Sasha T. Goldberg

When we wake up together in Brooklyn, we are three thousand miles away from our daily lives on the West Coast, and I already know that I am in love with her. We have slept facing East, and sunrise, Jerusalem, farther; the morning light streams in through the thin curtains, and when I open my eyes I can see her smiling at me. We have grown close to one another, and then closer; I look at this smile of hers, and I think that maybe she has started to see her future in me. That night we celebrate Shabbat with her family, and then we return to bed, to celebrate with each other.

This is a simple Jewish story and a simple love story. A nice Jewish boy meets a nice Jewish girl in the woods, and they start what seems to be a summer camp romance, only it holds, and through the campfire flirtation, they become an us. But the story here is also between two queers, and this infuses each layer: My butch self to her femme self, my tattoos against her bare skin, the glasses that we each have to take off when we kiss, my white T-shirt against her black slip, and my palms, pressed into hers, fingers entwined; all of the ways that love has threaded itself between us, the most simple and complex of revelations.

Before we know each other well, and before we tell each other our stories, and before I am hers, and she is mine, there is the beginning, and in the beginning I walk across the room to talk to her. She is on one side, and I am on the other, and I am immediately drawn to her, compelled. And then there is also the act of standing near her: there is this deep flash of recognition between us, this low hum just below the surface. There is this feeling of familiarity and ease underneath all the words that we are saying, and all the words that we are not saying—and this feeling between us is like speaking a second language, like speaking the language of our homeland, uncovered. Right from the start, this standing near her, it leaves me wanting more.

The desire is pronounced: I realize that I have started looking for her every time I enter a room. That night we share our first Shabbat dinner together, and though we are in a dining hall with a sea of people, I can only see her. I am watching the way she moves, the way she stands, the way she holds herself; it's so familiar that I don't need to say the word *femme*, and watching her feels like watching my history, like I'm watching everything I know in this world. I do not know, yet, that I will start to see my future in her; I do know that I want to be near her, and that is an unmistakable feeling.

When I kiss her for the first time, the air is cold outside, the kind of dark and cold and crisp and clear that only happens at night in the country. We have been sitting together outdoors, finally alone. We stare at the moon, and we have the conversation that takes us from this to that, and before I take her to my room I tell her that we can do whatever she wants, and I mean it. And so we are sitting side by side on the twin bed, facing each other, talking, the left side of my body and the right side of her body touching, and I kiss her, sitting just like that; I touch her face, and I kiss her, and she kisses me back, and she makes a sound. That sound that she makes, that sound is like no other, and it undoes me.

After that first kiss, she asks, "So is this what I missed at summer camp?" and I laugh and tell her, yes, this is what you missed—but I do not say that it's what I missed, too. She is referring, quite literally, to the fact that she never went to summer camp—and I did go to summer camp, but I can also remember the feeling of what it was like to be shamed, afterward, by a letter of proposed dismissal, the punishment for knowing myself so well, so young. And besides, girls like this girl, this girl sitting on my bed now, in the middle of these woods, girls like her didn't exist back then. Instead of explaining all of this, I kiss her again, and we begin to make up for lost time.

I put my arms around her waist and I pull her to me, the thick red wool of my shirt pressed against the thin red cotton of her shirt, my hand on her stockinged thigh, her legs next to my legs, against the denim of my jeans. Though we barely know each other, right then, she puts her hands on the back of my neck, on my arms, against the flat of my chest, and she lets me kiss her until we could be anywhere, or everywhere. I kiss her until I can feel the hands of the clock starting to move backward. Isn't this the way it was always supposed to be?

Later, she tells me that she has spent years looking for this, years spent searching for a butch who could reflect her femme self back to her. Years of going to queer parties where the only celebrated femininity was the femininity attached to male pronouns, years of feeling invisible as a femme. Years of being dismissed because she still didn't want to date men, even if those men were declared female at birth. When she tells me that she is finally getting her heels fixed, the ones that have been sitting broken for so long, I understand. I am lying in the dark, listening, and I can hear the second hand on my watch keeping the time; all those years she wanted someone to stand with her and revel in each perfectly measured high-heeled step to the subway.

On the night that I invite her to my home, I have the distinct feeling that I am done for, but I don't tell her so. As I am falling asleep with her for the first time, I forget that this is new between us; it is suddenly as if she has always been there, right there with me, all along. I do not remember to guard myself against this feeling; caught between being asleep and awake, between then and now, I wrap my arms around her and ask if we can have a really big breakfast in the morning. And that's when I know. The next morning, over breakfast, we stare at each other. After that, we make a habit of this staring.

I tell her that I have spent years looking too, first as a young butch hoping to find people like me, looking for the women like the ones in those books about lesbian "history," then feeling saved by the reflection that femmes offered to me and, finally, finding other butches, generations of bulldaggers who could give me a glimpse of my own existence.

And I tell her that I know about the parties—years of queer parties where the default pronouns have all become male, and that I feel erased and exhausted from having to explain that my butch identity is not for use on a "transmasculine spectrum"; that my butch identity does not have a "slash" or an "and" or an "or" attached; that butch is a valid stand-alone identity with a proud lesbian history—and doesn't anyone know this history anymore? I am really going at it now, but she tells me she understands; all of those years, we have both just been waiting to be seen.

When I look at the photos of our time in Brooklyn, they are gorgeous. We are in the park, and though it is only mid-May, the photos promise the first days of summer: bright, green, endless. The photos show us as we were, beaming, together in the sun, her soft fingertips resting on my shoulder, my arm around her waist. It is a moment in time, captured, and one that makes clear what we know to be true; by the time I look at the photos, we have already spoken of love.

When I see photos of myself lately, especially photos taken in the bright sun, I have started to notice the lines around my eyes. And just last year the grey hair started to come in, and that's when I realized, with certainty, that I really was going to grow up to look like one of those old bulls, and my heart swelled with pride. Looking again at the photos of her and me together, I can see every photo that came before, every black-and-white snapshot, all of the butches and femmes that gave way to this story.

This is a simple Jewish story, and a simple love story. It is a butch-femme story. This is the story of reaching for one another across the bellows of time on an accordion, bending and expanding our history and our present, and our future. In this story, time again becomes a faithful companion; we are sustained and redeemed by the reflection of what we know to be true. And perhaps, most of all, it is an old story: On all counts, the desire persists.

SASHA T. GOLDBERG came of age as a young butch in Chicago and spent her high school years riding the El and reading *The Persistent Desire.* In between the pages and the El stops, she would often look up hoping to find the right girl, the existence of another butch, or the possibility of a future. Today, Sasha is a Jewish scholar, educator, and community organizer living in Oakland, California, where life is very good. Sasha would like to dedicate her story "What We Know to Be True" to her younger self.

Me, Simone, and Dot

Chandra Mayor

I have always been a failure as a woman. All the women in my family have been failed women, at least by the definitions of "womanhood" so valued, admired, cultivated, and praised by this North American society in which I live, and even by the definitions and values still held deep inside the messy marrows of many, many women, dykes and feminists alike.

One is not born a woman, says Simone de Beauvoir. One becomes one. I was born a femme in a long line of angry, fucked-up femmes. I just never really got the hang of being a woman.

I was talking about being a femme with a friend, a lesbian. "Oh, well, of course it's okay to be feminine," she said, as if she was giving me a gift of broad-mindedness and benevolence. I started laughing, remembering again that "femme" is a term that is lost and feared and reworked and mangled and struggled with, over and over, in our (variously defined) women's communities.

"Feminine" is still often understood to be inextricable from "domestic" (as is "womanly"). My domestic skill-set is limited to Febreze and embroidery, one more practical than the other (and if you think you know which is which, you're probably wrong). You think you can take me home and I'll clean your house for you? Think again. My own house is chaos and dust. I'll invite you for dinner only if you're willing to eat grilled cheese sandwiches, meatloaf, or mysterious-yet-delicious creations made with tinned mushroom soup. I'm an utter failure at the still-shockingly popular lesbian potluck.[1] I know as much

---

1   And as a side note: Why *are* the potlucks still such a loved ritual in our feminist and lesbian communities? Didn't our second-wave sisters work so, so hard to extricate us from the realms and strictures of domesticity? Why am I required to spend hours in a kitchen—after, that is, I

about running a household as I do about running a haz-mat lab. It seems to me, looking around my kitchen, that the two are not dissimilar. I don't grow flowers or vegetables or even house-plants, as I'd rather never touch an insect, inadvertently or otherwise. I'm pretty adept at killing mice, but that's an aspect of house-management rarely praised or validated in the mythical Handbook of Housewifely Delights.

I just never learned those things, those womanly, feminine things—how to take down an ironing board, which of the dizzying array of cleaning products to use on which surfaces, how to sew on a button or throw together a salad. There are books, lovers, and friends to (even belatedly) teach me anything I might need to know. I'm reasonably bright and excellent at making it up as I go along. I can figure those things out if I need to.

---

learn how to cook something acceptable to the rigid rules of radical-queer communal food consumption, made with ingredients I can't afford from specialty-food stores not on a bus route, and have no idea what to do with once I get them home and set them on my messy counter—so that I can socialize with other world-shaking barrier-breaking political folk? My mother's answer to potlucks was invariably a giant vat of chili made with a pound of ground beef seasoned with pepper from a shaker, a giant tin of tomatoes, and a couple of tins of pork and beans. Add cayenne, stir, serve. That, however, is the wrong kind of food domesticity for the queer/feminist crowd—failures again, my mother and I. The last time that I attended a Women's Studies department potluck, I lost my mind with anxiety, went into some kind of altered insane state, and spent hours making fortune cookies, one at a time, burning the pads of my fingers pressing the hot edges together to make them stick. I filled them with tiny pieces of paper on which I carefully copied out quotes from feminist artists, poets, and theorists. They were a big hit. One prof held up her little feminist fortune and said, "Chandra, the paper is so beautiful! Is it rice paper?" The answer was that no, it was not rice paper. It was regular old computer paper, taken from my printer tray and cut into strips with my daughter's safety scissors. It only looked like rice paper because the cheap margarine I'd used in the cookies had soaked through everything, making the paper translucent with grease. "Yes, of course," I said, smiling, toying with my blistering fingers, shame and failure rising up inside. "Rice paper. Lovely, isn't it?" And I vowed: never again will I try to be this kind of woman, for anyone.

It's those other womanly skill sets that define femininity at which I balk (often in confusion as much as anything else), the ones involving particular definitions of nurturance, of being powerful only in ways that don't make other people feel badly (side-stepping confrontations or backing down and around them), of not being overtly sexual or angry or ragingly passionate in most ways. It's the unspoken, coded, WASP-y femininity of Jane Austen novels that I can't do. (I don't even understand what's going on in Jane Austen novels—no one ever says what they mean, or means what they say. It's mysterious and boring.)

My grandmother, my mother's mother, Dot, was the ultimate femme-gone-bad. "Femme" did not exist in her world, either as a word or a concept, so she took on the only identity offered up—angry bitch. She met her best friend playing baseball. Dot was good, but she played dirty anyway. (All the women in my family played dirty sports—the only sports advice my former-jock mother ever gave me was how to play dirty basketball, something involving sharp elbows and pivoting on your hips. And even as a vehemently non-sporty kid playing baseball, I was interested only in being the pitcher—the power position on the field—and was known to nail batters in the thigh if I thought they gave me a little too much attitude.) Dot played a dirty game, so sometimes the women on the other team took her on after the game was over—and my grandmother never backed down from a fight. One post-game afternoon, one of those women decided that eight on one wasn't fair, so she jumped ship and aligned her fists with my grandmother's. Black eyes and rage blossomed into a lifelong friendship.

In general, Dot couldn't keep her fists to herself. Ask my mother and my aunt, my cousins. Ask her own elderly mother. Her fists, her words, random household objects—every tool is a weapon if you hold it right, and the arts of war and weaponry were part of my grandmother's skill set.

I tell people about my grandmother and they imagine this very butch woman, a prototype dyke, strong and fierce and angry about not being a boy. The truth is, my grandmother was a beautiful woman who set her dyed-black hair every day of her life. I never saw her without makeup (orange-tinted as it was). She married and divorced the man who I suppose was my grandfather not once but twice (tearing his name out of the family Bible and his head out of the pictures each time), and was rarely without a male companion of some sort. She was a single mother in a time when you weren't supposed to be (and if you were, you were supposed to be ashamed). If she was ashamed of anything, she never let on. She smoked cigarettes and wore bright red lipstick and flirted and charmed and bullied her way through everything and everyone. She wore a tiara to the theatre and played mean head-fuck games with anyone who crossed her path. She constantly rewrote her will, depending on who was her favourite at any given moment, hiding the various copies, spinning webs of intrigue and resentment as a recreational activity. She lied and manipulated and drank at the Legion, and worked her whole life as a grocery-store cashier, saving up enough money for an addition to the house (originally a garage without indoor plumbing) and a cabin at the lake. She wanted the things that boys had that she wasn't allowed (beginning with a university education, better wages, and maybe a union shop job or at least a pro-sports career, and ending with the freedom to do, say, or be anything she wanted without fighting tooth-and-claw for the right to even contemplate those kinds of desires), but I don't think she wanted to be a man. She insisted on her own kind of femininity, and if "bitch" was all that was on offer, then that's what she took. She wasn't much of a traditional woman, but she was one hell of a proud and terrifying bitch.

My mother is her mother's daughter. She shook off the violence of her own childhood, but not the fierceness, not the strength and pride and resiliency, not the rage. And especially, she did not (could not, would not) shake off her innate power.

"Femme" was not a concept available to my mother either, but she fought against the label "bitch." One of the things I learned from watching my mother is that not having a word for who and what you are is a lonely and fucked-up way to live. Are there people who are indeed born as "women" in some way, and then just continue to refine this identity for the rest of their lives?

Maybe. I don't think my mother was one of them. She was (we are) born as something not-woman, and everything she grew up with most intimately taught her ways of womanhood that were not what heteronormative society desired. She tried, though. She got a home economics degree at a time when women weren't allowed to wear pants on campus and were supposed to go on to marry boys from the Agricultural College (she opted for an accountant). She worked hard all through my childhood to fit into the middle-class domestic society of women and mothers in the neighbourhood. (She now refers to that era as "the years when I had more time than brains.") She was, at one point, simultaneously the Block Parent coordinator, the president of the PTA, the Sunday school convener, the baseball coach, the Girl Guide leader and district commissioner, and the Scout treasurer. She took classes at the community centre in the art of paper tole and Chinese cooking. She hand-sewed at least five different Halloween costumes for me every year, from petticoats outward. She drew the line at the Rotary-Anns Ladies Auxiliary, but threw herself full-steam into everything else.

She was deeply unhappy. None of it fit. She didn't quite fit, no matter how hard she tried. She never quite understood most of the other women in the neighbourhood, how they functioned, how they talked around things, how they fussed and worried and never really got anything done.

She was also deeply terrifying to just about everyone. She made my elementary school principal cry in his office. As Brown Owl, the fearsome leader of the local Brownies troop, she was a little like a camp commandant; you've never seen such a well-behaved and frightened group of little girls in your life, churning out crafts and acquiring badges like our very lives depended on it. (As a Girl Guide, I had so many badges that, even three abreast, the sash was full, and I had to start working down the arm of my blue uniform.) All of my childhood friends (and most of their mothers) were a little afraid of her. In my adult life, most of my partners (and many of hers) have been afraid of her as well.

She has never entirely understood this, this respectful fear that she generates, this apprehension, this apartness, and it has made her unhappy and lonely. It has also been a tool that she uses as a weapon (or a weapon that she uses as a tool, depending on what needs to be accomplished).

After she divorced my father, my mother pretty much gave up on traditional domestic middle-class femininity. She bought her own house, started tearing down walls, putting up drywall and needlepoint pictures, and redid the kitchen counters (on her own, because she invariably decided that the various men that she recruited to help weren't doing it right). She bought tiny silver-lamé skirts and shiny gold high-heeled cowboy boots (and truthfully, some of my own best bar clothes have been those I borrowed from my mother) and hung out in the Latin bars, dancing all night long on one glass of red wine and the attention of every man in the room. She is a heart-stoppingly beautiful force of nature with a string of bad boyfriends, difficult relationships with her children, and a deep well of loneliness that will never be filled.

This is part of the legacy of not having a name and a place for what and who you are, in a world that says you're doing it all wrong (how dare you), passed down from mother to daughter.

And I, like it or not, am also my mother's daughter. Except that I am lucky enough to live in a world where, if you scratch and claw hard enough, stand your red-lipsticked ground long enough, you can find a name and a place for who and what you are—who I innately am, and who I continue to become: femme.

It's easy to say that my grandmother was frightening because she was mean and violent and angry. Those things are part of the truth, but not all of it. My mother is neither mean nor violent, and not any more or less angry than most women that I know. And yet people are still afraid of her. (Even my then-three-year-old, high-femme drag-queen daughter, watching my mother drive by and wave her hand at us in a regal salute, said, "Oooh ... scary queen!") What is it that makes my mother (and by extension, so many of us failed-women femmes, named or not) frightening?

My mother is able to make you do things for her before you even really notice you're doing them. I've found a pizza delivery boy fixing her bike on her front lawn with a dazed and confused look on his face. She brought firefighters in full regalia to my apartment when my toddler got a potty seat stuck on her head. (She bumped into them on the way over and said, "C'mon up boys!") My exes have all weeded her gardens, fixed her doorbell, and worn bizarre things that she bought for them. (This power, incidentally, generally works on my brother as well, though not on me or my daughter.) She has an indomitable force of will, an innate sense of her own strength that most women do not carry easily, never mind unthinkingly. People find it mesmerizing, terrifying, and deeply compelling, often all at once.

And this, for me, is part of what's at the sticky, messy heart of femme.

Femme is costume and play, Hello Kitty, red nails and redder lips, hairspray in the bathroom, and heels so high they make your feet hurt. But as my (straight high-femme) friend Christine says, "Femme is more than being a lesbian who looks like she might not be a lesbian." And trust me, I never scan more like a femme than when I'm wearing jeans and my girlfriend's button-up shirt. I'll play with your gaze, but I am not defined by it.

Femme is deeply loving those delicious butches, their good

manners and bravery and hidden vulnerabilities, their hand on the small of my back, their brave and awkward profferings of lights for my cigarettes and drinks with cherries in them. Being a femme is learning and knowing those courtship games like the quickening of your own heartbeat, letting the lovely butches pretend to lead, both of you knowing all the while that you hold all the cards (and their hearts) in your careful hands. But I'm still a femme no matter what manner of girl or boy I'm sleeping or flirting with at any given moment (and no matter who does what once the flirting progresses to other kinds of fun and games). Part of what I hate about "woman" as a gender identity is that it's inevitably defined against "man." I won't be snagged in another dichotomized definition. I love butches with all the pieces of my ragged heart. Then again, I love all sorts of people with all sorts of ragged bits of me, and I don't let any of them define who I am or am not.

Femme is a political stance against the patriarchal strictures of society, a reclamation of "slut" and "whore" and "bitch," and a you-can't-shut-me-up fuck-you attitude. But without something real and genuine and bloody and unshakeable inside, political stances are, ultimately, exhausting and empty. Ask any burnt-out feminist activist. Political stances also rely entirely on context; change the political context, and the stance becomes meaningless. I am not meaningless. I can, will, and do use a femme stance and identity politically, when it seems appropriate or expedient (not limited to creating an unwelcome experiential gender-spectrum education to a downtown Legion, which is how I inadvertently spent last Friday evening). Changing political contexts might affect how I costume femme, how I enact and embody femme, but it doesn't affect the femme in me one way or another. How I act it out doesn't change what it is, deep inside me.

Femme is the gender identity I was born into, as well as my learned birthright from the terrifying women that I am created out of. Every single picture of me as a child, before adolescence descended and sent me reeling into the fear, confusion, and hurt that so many girl-children experience from a world that hates us, captures me staring straight into the camera, hip cocked, chin tilted, eyebrow raised.

Femme is the indomitable will in me, in my mother, in my grandmothers, and in my daughter. Femme is knowing (and knowing that you know) that you can hurt me, but you can't break me. Femme is the deepest part of me, the softest and fiercest, all at once. Women are not supposed to be soft and fierce. We're not supposed to flaunt our vulnerabilities as fully self-possessed tools or weapons, without shame. (Having no shame is not the same as having nothing to hide. Femmes know this intuitively, or we learn it, and we learn how to use it.) All the women in my family had opinions about everything. It didn't occur to us to be otherwise. The only rules were that you either had to back your opinions up or be able to shut down your opponent. It was a survival skill. The trick wasn't learning how to own your own space, or how to break and break and keep standing, or how to play dirty—those were things we already knew. The trick was knowing when to do which, how to stay light on your feet, how to change tactics at lightning speed. The trick was knowing that you can do it all on your own, and that part of doing it all on your own is holding out your hand for help only when you choose to. And that anything and anyone that you hold in that hand is also yours to protect as fiercely as you protect anything inside your own heart (and probably more so).

Women are not supposed to be powerful, and when we are, it's both compelling and scary. Not because we're going to hurt you. But because you fear we might, because you've been taught by everything in this world that a powerful woman just might hurt you in ways that are unfixable. (I think femmes know that while it's true that some hurts are unfixable, it doesn't really matter. Because fixing the hurt isn't always the point.) Conservative religious leaders and certain political queer radicals alike tell you that a woman who uses her sexuality for gain or pleasure (her own or others') is a bad woman. Potluck-loving feminists tell you you're a failed feminist if you can't cook with xanthan gum. Coaches tell you you're not a team-player if you play dirty sports, and teachers tell you you're a bad girl if you talk back, contradict them, or bring your Bible and concordance to religion class with a stubborn look in your eye and a biblical justification for abortion that has as much (or as little) relevance to the issue as the Ten Commandments (true story).

And no one is more suspicious of those kinds of girls than other women. Which makes being a femme lesbian tricky.

I live in a different world than my grandmother's. I will never bully you into anything. (Which works out well, because I loathe bullies and consider it a sacred duty to stand up to them in all guises. You can stand behind me if you need to; nothing upsets a bully more than a woman in lipstick laughing without fear.) I will never fight dirty (unless it's the only way out, and even then I probably won't, because, as I said, I know that you can't break me. So I don't have to). I know that most of the time you're half-fascinated and half-frightened of me. I wish you weren't—I wish that instead of respectfully handing me a drink at the bar and then melting away to the side of the room to watch me from a distance, you'd stick around and talk to me. (I promise—you are much more interesting to me than yet another gin and tonic.) I know that part of your own process of becoming comfortable in your dyke skin was to work hard to find women with bad hair and sensible clothes deeply attractive, and that it fucks you up to find yourself attracted to me. It does not make you a dirty old man to find me sexy. And it does not make you less gorgeous in your own shining self to be whoever you are, standing next to me or not. I don't think less of you for rejecting patriarchal standards of beauty, and I'd appreciate it if you could not think less of me for the amount of hairspray and pins in my hair. I'd appreciate it, but whatever you think won't change who and what I am, and how I wear that in the world. If you're lucky, I'll take the pins out for you later. And truthfully, if you're too afraid to talk to me, you wouldn't know what to do with this particular fierce and ragged femme heart on offer.

When I teach writing workshops, I sometimes tell my students, "Think of the thing that you are most afraid to say out loud. Then say it. Start there. See where you go."

This is what makes me a failed woman, a bad girl, a dangerous entity in the room. The only side-stepping I ever really learned how to do was to step outside of that context, that classroom or paradigm. I never really became a woman. I never particularly wanted to. But I do have a name, a history, a community. And further inside, I have my own self, deep in my own fierce, messy, forever heart. If you want, I have you there too. I'll charm and kiss and fight and fuck and make it all up as I go along. I'll make you believe anything, and then I'll make it happen. Like it or not, I was born a femme. With every fuck-up, I figure it out a little more.

These are my tools, my weapons, my embodiments of what and who I am, what and who I am always becoming: The words in my head and throat and heart, the voices of my mother and grand-mothers—the women that I belong to by blood—and also the voices of all the femmes that I know only through their writings and photographs. This femme language that says, "Go on, try it. See what happens. And fuck the rest of them if they don't like it." My resiliency, my curiosity. This thing that looks like fearlessness, but is really just acknowledging terror—and then touching up my lipstick and doing the terrifying thing anyway, any way I can. And, most importantly and imperfectly, the tattered glittery bits that tie it all together, even (especially) when it's entirely falling apart: this fierce and stubborn love that shines and shines.

CHANDRA MAYOR is a Winnipeg writer and editor. She is the author of *August Witch: Poems*, which was nominated for four Manitoba Book Awards and won the Eileen McTavish Sykes Award for Best First Book. She received the John Hirsch Award for Most Promising Manitoba Author, and her novel *Cherry* was shortlisted for the Margaret Laurence Fiction Award and received the Carol Shields Winnipeg Book Award. The title story from her most recent book, *All the Pretty Girls*, was shortlisted for a CBC Literary Award, and the collection received the Lambda Literary Award for Best Lesbian Fiction. She is a former poetry editor for *Prairie Fire* and *CV2*, and her work has been widely published in journals and anthologies, including *Between Interruptions: 30 Women Tell the Truth About Motherhood*. She performs in festivals and venues around the country, and her work is adapted for the stage for events such as Edmonton's annual Loud & Queer Cabaret.

For Annie B. (1915–81)

Donnelly Black

When I think about butch-femme identities, I remember Annie who came before me.

It was 1962. I was twelve years old. My mother, Sybil, and her friend Myrna are talking when I walk in to the kitchen. Hearing the word "dyke," I lean on the counter and ask, "What does 'dyke' mean?" Sybil looks at Myrna, then turns to me and says, "It's a word that describes women who wear men's clothing and hang around school yards."

Annie—my great aunt—wore men's pants. Annie was born in 1915 in the eastern townships of Quebec. She grew up in a strict, white, Anglo-Saxon Protestant dairy-farming community.

I remember her coming home from work at the plant, walking into the kitchen to talk to Uncle Mike. Mike was often at the sink doing dishes.

Annie wore grey flannel pants to work at the plant. I don't recall her changing when she got home. I do remember her sitting in a La-Z-Boy chair, drinking her beer while watching the hockey game. Uncle Mike would stand in the doorway of the kitchen with his apron on and a tea towel in hand, looking to see what the score was. Mike was not interested in hockey; he mostly was concerned that Annie had not fallen asleep in the chair.

I have no memory of what their sleeping arrangements were.

Sybil had five children with Orville. When I was six years old, Orville passed away from a heart attack brought on by his alcoholism. Sybil sent me to live with her father, Annie's brother. My older sister went to live with Annie and Mike. Later, when I was nine years old, as my grandfather was dying, I too went to live with Annie and Mike in Toronto. My mother kept the two youngest boys, while the oldest boy went to live with cousins.

I have a picture of my grandfather standing next to Annie; I believe he looked out for Annie as he looked out for me when I lived with him. I always wore jeans and let it be known from a young age that I preferred pants to dresses.

In another picture, Sybil has arrived with all my siblings to visit my grandfather. My sister wears a dress and holds a doll. I am in jeans and short sleeves, and my grandfather has his giant arm around my shoulder.

Sybil would scold me terribly for wearing pants. In middle school, I had to wear scratchy wool skirts. Sybil insisted I wear a girdle. I took the girdle off at school, then put it back on before coming home, but as soon as I got home, I changed into my jeans. I feared my mother; she would take her anger out on me physically; you could not cross her.

I played with the boys, climbing trees and playing pirates in a small wooded area near our house in Ottawa. We would make small rafts and paddle down a small creek, collecting pollywogs and tadpoles. I was called a tomboy.

During my adolescence, my sister, who was only sixteen months older than I, would tease me for having no breasts. I didn't really care; I used to stand in the mirror smiling at my boyish chest.

I still own a picture of Annie, taken around 1933, with her arm around a girl close to her age and a younger girl leaning on Annie's leg. The young woman Annie has her arm around is smoking a cigarette. Annie is wearing men's pants; the other girls are in dresses. Annie has her collar turned up. I think this was a happy time for Annie.

My cousin told me a story about Annie that she'd been in a bike accident and had to go away for surgery. What really happened was that she had been raped and become pregnant; she was sent to an unwed mothers' home in Montreal.

Annie married Mike in 1945 when she would have been thirty years old. Mike had been a cook. He used to brag about having cooked for the Queen of England in some famous hotel in

Toronto. Mike had been hit by a bakery truck, which ended his career. Now a homemaker, he would clean and dust and put doilies on the tables.

When I look back at the unique relationship Annie and Mike had, I realize that my sister and I witnessed an unusual exchange of stereotypical engendered behaviours. I think Mike was a queen in his own time. Some members of our family believe that Mike and Annie married during the 1940s in order to pass, due to family and community pressures. It was not unusual for gay people in the '30s and '40s (even today) to marry in order to pass as heterosexual.

Sybil came from the same WASP background as Annie had. When I came out to her, my mother tolerated my choice up to the end of her life. "Just don't tell me about it," she said. She had always disliked Annie. And I wonder now how much of who Annie was had been shaped by the times she lived in and the things that happened to her. Then I ask the same questions of myself. I was molested and raped by several men during my childhood and young adulthood, leaving me with a messed-up sense of my sexual self. My childhood, adolescence, and young adulthood traumatic experiences impacted my ability to recognize my sexual orientation as being gay, loving women. The trauma did not affect my sexuality, it delayed the recognition and acceptance of my preference for loving women. Most young people get to explore their sexual selves during adolescence. I could not do that as my sexual self was being used by an adult male which impacted my sense in the world with my peers.

During the Easter weekend in 1963, my cousins Jan and Kat, along with my aunt and uncle, came to visit. On Sunday they drove from St. Eustache, Quebec, to Ottawa to have dinner at our house. We lived in a housing project of row houses built by the government for families of the armed forces.

Sybil had insisted that we wear our "Sunday best" for the visit, which meant I had to wear a dress. I hated wearing dresses, but Sybil ruled. When the cousins arrived, the adults wanted to talk, so we four girls were told to go for a walk. We hadn't walked more than two blocks when I spied a girl standing on the grass in front of a house. She wore jeans and a T-shirt and stood with her hands on her hips. As we drew closer, she began to taunt us about the way we were dressed. I approached her and let her know that she couldn't get away with talking like that to my cousins.

The next thing I knew, she had pulled me down onto the ground and we began to wrestle; sometimes I was under her and sometimes I was on top. We rolled into the street. She pulled my hair and bit me! I had been taught to fight fairly, meaning you don't pull hair or bite, so I was curious about her behaviour. I found that I liked what was going on between us. As I was becoming more entangled, an adult neighbour reached in and pulled me onto my feet, ending the fight.

I was in big trouble when I got home.

The first day I was back at school, I saw her walking down the hallway toward me. Noticing the water fountain on her side of the hall, I crossed over with the pretense of heading for a drink. The blood rushed to my head; I felt overcome with a desire to be close to her and, as she drew near, we both turned toward the fountain, bent over the water, and whispered to one another, making it known that we wanted to be friends.

It was hard to tear myself away from her. I felt a warm swelling in the area of my vulva. This was the first time I was aware of being aroused by a girl. Intense feelings around that encounter stayed with me for a long time, though I never saw her again. I still wonder where she may be and if she is out there living her life loving women.

When I was fourteen, a friend and I went to a local dance. I noticed some girls milling about and checking us out. One of the girls approached me. She started to ask me to dance, but then a look of horror came over her face. She had thought I was a boy.

In my early teens, I played volleyball and basketball. After the game, we would meet the opposing teams behind the school grounds and fight with each other; it was some kind of collective ritual where we would find ourselves in the embrace of our opponents. I remember not wanting this to end. I often came away with a sprained thumb.

I was on the streets at an early age, part of the hippie movements in Ottawa, Toronto, and eventually, Vancouver. As part of that scene, I managed to survive for a couple of years without having sex, mostly by staving off advances. I believed I would have to learn to like having sex with men. Later, I became the aggressor in my sexual relations with men.

In the late 1960s, a woman named Diane approached me and asked if I was gay; she took me out to Faces, a well-known gay bar in Vancouver. I had a flirtation with a gay man. I tried convincing him he wasn't gay. I met some of his women friends, who began to intrigue me, but I was scared and avoided them.

By the early 1970s, I wanted to get away from the drug scene on the streets; I had become pregnant exploring my sexuality. This produced a son. I knew I wouldn't marry the father.

I left Vancouver to live near a logging town in the interior of the province, in the Kootenays, and settled there for awhile. I got a job at a shake mill. I had an affair with a young woman from the town, Sal, who knew she was gay. She would chase me around the pool table at the local bar. We would go for rides and make out for hours. I would call her a lover now, though we always kept our clothes on. I would write her poetry and she would bring me six-packs of beer.

We were discovered and "outed" by a fellow I knew from the Burrard Indian reserve, now known as the Tsleil-Waututh Nation. He must have heard us talking and threatened to expose me and my "dyke" lover to my "old man," John, who was a draft dodger from California, and the extended hippie community.

During this time, John got himself and a friend into some

trouble bringing back drugs from South America. His friends told me I had to bail him out. I left for Mexico with a straight girlfriend. Before I left, I went looking for my young lover. When I couldn't find her, I left a message for her at the bar. When I returned from Mexico, I learned she had gone to New York and returned with a beautiful woman. One night, Sal's cousin invited John and me for dinner with Sal and her new lover. Over dinner, I announced that John and I were going to marry.

Still not able to exorcise my mother's voice, I heard, "Loving a woman would make you a deviate, at the worst alone." My marriage was doomed. I was running from my childhood and myself, and he wanted to be a rock star and felt burdened by a wife and children. We used drugs and alcohol to cope with our unhappiness. My life was spinning out of control. My husband left me.

I was left alone with three children. Then I lost my youngest child to SIDS. My husband came back; it was his guilt and grief that brought him back. I had not truly grieved. We separated and later divorced.

Sybil sent me tickets so that I could return to Ontario. It was one lonely cold winter. I taught guitar lessons and spent a lot of time at the library.

THE FLIGHT OF THE WOMAN/MAN
In the late '70s, I moved to Edmonton and studied jazz guitar. I went to work as a lounge entertainer—playing guitar and singing—performing all over northern Alberta, Saskatchewan, and BC. My children and I were on the road for more than three years. There were times I would leave them with a friend.

On the road, I often remembered my young lover from the Kootenays, especially when I was drinking. Once in a while, I would pick up women. I argued with bar managers who would try to fix me up with their male customers. Sometimes, I drank so much I blacked out. Once, in some northern town, hanging out with people from a local reserve, waiting for the bootlegger, I found myself making love to a woman in an old abandoned car. This type of behaviour would scare me back into a time of sobriety. I would convince myself that I could not drink and continue to perform, and this lasted sometimes for a few months.

Then I met Joey. I pursued her relentlessly. I had to have her, but she would have nothing to do with me. A year later, I ran into her again in the small-town Alberta farming country where she'd grown up. I was playing in the local bar.

This time she was open to me. I took her to my hotel room. I remember being fearful of performing oral sex on her, worried about what might be down there. No problem!

Joey had known she was gay since she had been nine years old. But she had became pregnant while working as a stripper. Her son lived with her parents. Joey didn't want my children; she put up with them, did not parent them. I wanted them with me, but I was torn. Her parents would sometimes watch them. My son mostly stayed with a friend during this couple of years with Joey.

I remember seeing her dress up for work. Now, I'd say Joey was butch and she was a woman to me. I especially loved to see her in a skirt. She got a kick out of my pleasure. We often would end up down on the floor making love before she could get out the door.

She sold Amway. We both sometimes sold products door to door; I had two kids to support. There was alcohol in the fridge but no food, as Joey liked to eat out. Joey and I lived together for two years.

She came on the road with me when I was performing in bars. Joey was jealous of the attention men gave me; she would argue with the managers. I recall one manager telling me vehemently, "Get rid of the girlfriend." Because of this, I eventually got off the road and went to work in the oil fields with Joey's sister.

I left my children with friends as long as I could; eventually they came to live at Joey's. While living with Joey, I felt strongly that I had to have a sex change. After all, "men make women happy." I was experiencing a sexual-identity crisis (gender dysphoria) and was in great despair over what to do about my feelings for this woman. How could I love her if I was a woman? Women loving women is deviant, is it not? I was losing the ground under me. I really needed to talk with other women.

One night, Joey took me to a bar called Flashdance. It was obvious there was some sort of division among the bar patrons. Some women were dressed like men, others dressed like women. When you went to a bar in the early part of the evening, there was that sense of divide. Later, the butches would sidle up to their chosen femmes and the party would get going. After the folks would mix and be dancing, and everyone was in their proper place (so to speak). I don't recall seeing any gay men there. I went to approach one of the manly women, innocent of the rules; Joey pulled me away and told me that I could not speak to anyone. Joey and I both drank too much and ended the night fighting about how she didn't want me talking to anyone. When we got home, she told me to sleep on the couch.

We started drinking with her sister and mixing alcohol with prescription drugs. Things got physical. Joey even bit me. The sister got into the mix and we were all tumbling around on the floor. Ashamed, I left the next morning.

I made a phone call to my agent and headed back out on the road. My drinking was out of control. Maybe to understand, you could remember that I was not only dealing with my coming out but also the loss of a child I had yet to grieve. And my childhood trauma was also a factor in my drinking to run away, forget, kill the pain. Oh the hell we weave when we shove things down under.

Returning to the Kootenays, I met a gay woman who, along with her partner, took me and my children in. I used this time to stop drinking. Within a year, I entered a recovery home in Victoria, British Columbia.

BUTCH-FEMME: TO THE POWER OF TWO

During my first year of sobriety, I moved to a small city in BC. I discovered a thriving women's community and became involved in the local women's centre.

Discovering other lesbians in the 1980s was exciting for me. They were trying to do something about the violence of the patriarchy. I met other women who had been battered and had a "herstory" of child abuse. I studied childhood trauma and after some years, became a child sexual abuse therapist working in the Aboriginal community.

In the '80s, I was a single lesbian mom. My children were teenagers then and didn't want their mother to have any permanent lovers. Who could blame them? Their experiences had been deplorable. I remained politically active throughout the decade. (Today, I hope that the contemporary queer community won't lose sight of staying politically visible to maintain the freedoms fought for by our elders, the butches and femmes that came before.)

Sexually, I was newly sober. I'd had experiences with loving women, but this was something new and different.

Joey had declared herself to be gay, and by this time I had accepted myself as gay. Lesbians boldly "stepped out of line," and that made us feel powerful. Sometimes when I had sex, it felt lovely, but at other times it was very painful. I have experienced a lover whisper, "You make love like a man," and this confused me. Other lovers whispered, "It must have been the abuse," and I would want to run. Some lovers said, "If you don't orgasm, I will have to leave you." They didn't wait to find out that my orgasms were second only to their pleasure. Desire in itself my intent to please the lover, orgasm not my goal.

Their class spoke loudly of my lack.

Today, I feel quite healthy as a human being. I have faced many of my demons with the help of years of therapy. I no longer have to face my childhood abusers. When I turn to you for physical and emotional solace, I bring my self to you. Treat her gently, this man-woman.

Today, I am a self-identified Pequot-Mohegan-Scots-Irish-English-Gay-Man-Woman-Grandmother. I have practiced serial monogamy, polyandry, and celibacy. I find joy in my life, six out of seven days a week. I love my woman self and my butch self.

I am not drawn to women's things, yet I might dress up for you. I aspire to become a drag king. I am attracted to the fluidity of gender; that's what draws me in. I am attracted to your butchness, your woman-ness. Today, I am a queer sexagenarian. My friends remind me that I am sexy.

DONNELLY BLACK lives in East Vancouver and is a self-identified Pequot Mohegan Scots Irish English Gay Man-Woman Grandmother. I find joy in my life, six out of seven days. Not bad for a disabled sexagenarian with an auto-immune disease and chronic pain. I love my woman self and my butch self. To honour Annie and my grandfather, I have taken their names Donnelly Black is my pen name.

Split Myself Apart

Redwolf Painter

Sometimes I wonder if I can split myself in half or pick the parts I want to be white and the ones I want to be Indian. Can I name my almond-shaped eyes white and my right popping and creaking knee Indian? Can I pick my light skin, name it Indian and call my high cheekbones, which squeeze my eyes shut when I smile wide, white? Can I tear myself apart and put myself back together to name what part of me is butch and what part trans? My right eyebrow butch and my large chest trans. And if I can choose the parts of my body that belong to each identity, can I choose which ones fight each other for the right to be here, take up space, and be recognized?

My grandparents lived across the street from Totem Park, a historical battlefield, thick with Totem poles carved by Native folk to commemorate the deaths that occurred there. Russians, with their Aleut slaves, and Tlingit all died trying to claim their right to be in this particular spot where the Tlingit people had lived for at least 10,000 years. Sometimes I walked alone through the totems, imagining what each pole meant rather then reading the signs underneath them, wondering why I was never taught how to read a totem or speak Tlingit, feeling the weight of each story coursing in my veins.

Grandma and I would occasionally walk through the park together, her telling me stories about growing up on the Native side of town, about living with brown skin, and about the deaths of family members too tired to continue being Native, eventually taking their own lives through alcohol or suicide. She often reminded me to hold my head up high when people made derogatory remarks about my mixed-up, mixed-blood family, made even more complicated by my father's Aleut and Russian blood.

As we walked through the battlefield, searching for arrowheads or remnants of the story, Grandma would say, "Don't you ever forget that our people fought and died here defending our home. Don't you forget your heritage, you hear me? You be proud of our Indian blood: hold your head up high." How could I forget? I was constantly reminded when I looked in the mirror or saw the scars on my family's carapace, marking the passing of another alcoholic.

My move to San Francisco was a conscious choice, one made to help me come out of the closet and own my space in the world. Little did I know how ill-equipped I was, coming from a small Alaskan island with seventeen miles of road. I'd grown up facing the ocean, with mountains at my back. I spent time alone surrounded by trees, with a good book and whatever I could gather for food for the day—sometimes salmonberries, blueberries, red huckleberries, thimbleberries, beach peas, and goose tongue. Every day, I was reminded that my tiny life was nothing to a land so vast and unforgiving.

The constant influx and outflow of people, cars, and things to do in San Francisco left me somewhat breathless with excitement and fear at first. In time, though, culture shock wore off and I took root. I found myself searching every crowd for a glimpse of a familiar set of jowls and almond-shaped eyes, wondering why white folks seemed to think they could ask me things like, "What are you?" I wondered if they knew whether they were asking about my race or gender—or both?

One day, I got a newsletter that mentioned a gathering of a group of Bay Area Tlingits. I was ecstatic at the thought of seeing familiar features, of being seen as Native, the way I was back home. So I called and introduced myself as a recently relocated two-spirit looking for other Tlingits. Only to not be called back. My hurt and anger surprised me, even though a part of me knew that being queer and open about it might be a problem.

There is a roar inside me I have choked off more times than I care to count. A place of duality that I neither fully understand nor want to claim because it seems easier to blend in. This place is so deeply rooted inside me; sometimes I wonder at the Creator's sense of humour. I'm both Indian and white, man and woman. My light skin, hair, and eyes may have made it easy to blend into the crowds in San Francisco—at least until I got in the sun—so it must have been my punk gender ambiguity that caused some people to cross the street to avoid me.

One day, flanked by rows of condoms, harnesses, dildos, lube, porn, *SM 101*, *The Topping Book*, and the slew of other sex toys and goodies that the Good Vibrations store where I worked had to offer, a few of my co-workers tried to get me to accept the identity "butch," pointing at the way I'm often mistaken for a boy. Maybe it's a result of growing up with strong women of colour, or maybe it's that Alaska doesn't have a defined set of rules for what you are allowed to wear or do based on your gender, or maybe it was the fact that the men in my family would never, ever talk to a woman the way I saw butches talking to or about femmes, it didn't matter; if being butch meant I had to treat women or anyone as callously as I'd seen butches treat women, I wanted nothing to do with it.

After a friend/co-worker and I unboxed a new shipment of porn and toys, we headed outside to smoke and chat. Over the last couple of weeks, she had been telling me about a two-spirit community she did ceremonies with and formally invited me to my first sweat. As we two punks—sporting different coloured Mohawks and ragged, worn-out clothes that showed our tattoos and piercings—sat on the sidewalk discussing spirituality, my friend suddenly brought up my unwillingness to claim the term "butch." I asked her why she wanted to be identified with folks who wore misogyny on their sleeves, with an identity that was quantified into comparative statements of worth, as in, "You aren't as butch as so-and-so."

She sighed, told me to read *Stone Butch Blues*, and then got up and left me sitting alone on the sidewalk.

I had identified with very few books, up to this point in my life. *Stone Butch Blues* was the second such book. While it is the not the sum total of who I am, butch is a place inside me, it's part of the whole. The battle of quantification still haunts me in various forms, as I try to define what part is white (the deep red-brown my skin gets in the sun), what part is butch (my large hips), what part is Indian (my blue eyes), and what part is two-spirit (my birth name).

I feel like I am just beginning to understand the place inside me that slides back and forth from man to woman, as two-spirit implies. As a child, I wandered Totem Park making up stories to go with the totem poles. I had no foundation; my family was too tired from surviving colonialism to tell me the stories I needed to hear. Since then, I have been seeking the stories out one by one, listening to them, and creating my own history (Tlingit, Aleut, Russian) and definitions (two-spirit, trans, butch) upon which to stand.

REDWOLF PAINTER is a two-spirit, trans, mixed-blood, Heyoka writer from Alaska. Wolf grew up in a poor American Indian/white family with deep Alaskan roots, which reverberates throughout his writing and social justice work. For the last twenty years, Wolf has been writing, performing, organizing, volunteering, and producing events for various non-profit organizations.

With Both Fists

Conscious Gender Building through the Butch and Femme Identities

Sinclair Sexsmith

"I think you're butch."

The first girl I fell in love with actually leaned in and whispered it right into my ear so I could feel her hot breath on my neck. I was twenty-two, newly out, and considering in casual conversation the popular concept that lesbians were either butch or femme. If that was true, which one was I?

And when she answered, my heart pounded, my throat closed, my stomach knotted, my palms began to sweat. How did she know? A shiver went through me; I'd never been seen to my depths like that before.

I wasn't butch yet, perhaps—but in that moment I knew what I was; I knew that's what I wanted to be; I knew that, someday, I would be. That was nearly ten years ago.

In the swirling communities of gender identities·surrounding butch and femme, I found myself. I came home to my body and to my desires in a way I had never yet experienced. It took me nearly five years after that first jolt, associating myself with that word and identity, before I started dating femmes, and suddenly my butchness had new levels of meaning. I was twenty-seven, but I felt like I was thirteen, discovering my body for the first time, discovering what my body does when someone touches here, caresses there, kisses that little curve. The intoxication of the butch-femme dynamic made me lightheaded, loopy, high. I feared I was "losing it," whatever I thought that meant, and I was, I did: I was losing that old me who didn't know I was this bright new thing. I was embodying another whole spectrum of energy, being pulled into a bigger and better version of me that made me reach out of my own skin into something—someone—new.

Although I knew before then that I was butch, I'd never quite manifested it as I wanted to. I'd never been with a femme; I'd never been with a lover who liked me not despite my masculinity but because of it, because her desires ran the same meridians as mine, opposite and complementary.

The first girl I fell in love with was femme. She and her femme roommate taught me how to help them pluck their eyebrows and appreciate Dolly Parton and showed me how they washed their silicone collection in the top rack of their dishwasher. Together, they were full technicolour, shiny and sparkly, and I was enraptured with them. I would sit on their cute white couch, sipping a beer, and watching them with wide, puppy-dog eyes as they danced or told jokes or tossed their hair as they laughed. I felt out of place, cautious, unaware of how I should be, of who I should be, of who I was in their context, yet thrilled—as though if I moved too quickly, the mirage would burst.

She's the one who first told me, "I think you're butch." It took nearly five more years to get confident enough in myself to manifest that wish, to figure out that I wanted to date femmes and not andro dykes or genderqueer folks or butches or trans men (I guess I had to try a lot of other gender expressions as lovers first, just to make sure), to know how to recognize when the girl I was flirting with wasn't as femme as I thought, and wasn't femme enough for me.

Now, five years into confidently grabbing the butch identity with both fists, declaring it on business cards, and shouting it from rooftops, and ten years since I felt my relationship with that word first open, I know that lesbians and dykes and queer folks are not just one or the other. It seems so obvious now, but when I was an outsider to queer culture, that was one of the first stereotypes I had to break down. There is a huge 3-D gender galaxy out there for us to pick and choose from; aspects of identity out of which to make our own identities and expressions. And

when I came across the masculine quadrant in that galaxy and
the butch solar systems, it was an identity that I felt instantly
in everything: my femurs, my diaphragm, my toenails. It was
through the introduction to this identity, and then the introduction to the communities around this identity, that I discovered
how my relational orientations run. Although I still get occasional boy crushes on my butch and boi and masculine-of-centre
friends, I know if we go to bed together, it won't do that much
for me—not like the femmes do. After years of dating femmes,
I know they can be scary, not because they actually are scary
but because that's who I date. What I mean is that femmes are
scary to me the way that straight girls think guys are scary, the
way men who only date blondes think blondes are scary, because they're the only ones who have broken their hearts. That
is where my attraction runs the deepest: with reclaimed femininity, with heels and lipstick and dangly earrings, with hair long
enough to grab, and that sweet-girl exterior that gives way to
a dirty girl in bed, with a girl who is less afraid than I am of
confrontation who is scrappy and fierce and stands firmly by
her convictions and integrity. Femmes have broken my heart the
hardest, smashed it, made me declare I would never love like
that again, because I had never loved like that before, had never
been able to give myself—my entire self, my deep-down delicious
self—so fully to another, so fully to a relationship.

Being inside of these butch and femme worlds has broken me,
and broken me open. That has been terrifying, but it has also
been liberating. Sometimes the breaking has made me want to
turn away from these circles and never look back. Sometimes I
cannot stand how goddamn small it is, or how many of my exes
know each other, or how I keep running into the same people
over and over. When I feel that way, I begin to cultivate one
of my other (often neglected) hobbies, like stargazing or book-
making or colouring mandalas or drinking quality bourbon or
camping, and I feel better, remembering that butch is just one

part of who I am—a key part, an important part, sometimes my most visible part—but not the whole.

In June 2009, New York City's alt-weekly newspaper, the *Village Voice*, declared on their cover, "The Butch Is Back!" I wondered, as did many: did we ever leave? Maybe we did in some people's minds, but I am sure we've been here all along. Perhaps we went underground, perhaps we weren't in vogue, but this particular manifestation of gender and sexuality has a long history and continues to thrive and survive. Perhaps it's because of the nature of my job running a butch website and writing about sex and gender theory, but I know more butches now than I've ever known in my life. Are we in a butch renaissance? Maybe. I'd like to think so. It seems to me that there are more butch and femme events and parties and communities and dialogues than ever. The two-volume collection of writing *Visible: A Femmethology* was published in 2008 and the BUTCH Voices conference, which started in 2009, is going strong with satellite conferences in four cities around the country in 2010. Blogs written by butches and femmes about navigating their complicated lives are more numerous than ever, exploring both the intimate details of our own lives as well as lofty concepts of gender theory, semantics, and identity construction.

For example, those deceptively simple classic questions remain: What is butch? What is femme? Even after nearly ten years of actively exploring these identities, I don't know if I am any closer to an accurate, singular definition. I could write down a list of qualities and say "check all that apply," but maybe you'd have none of them and still be butch. I know these identities have something to do with masculinity and femininity, something to do with taking a societally prescribed gender role and intentionally or unintentionally turning it into a new gender identity that is not either painful or regulated. It has something to do with queerness, usually, and something to do with human archetypal energies.

For me, it also has to do with picking and choosing which qualities I want to embody in relationship to masculinity, with studying different genres and eras of masculine style (ascots and pocket watches make me swoon) and not having to prove that I'm "one of the guys" by downing a beer or watching "the game." When I was first exploring butch and masculinity, studying it externally to see how I could possibly manifest it in my own life as a feminist and as an aspiring gender theorist, I was appalled at most of the displays of masculinity in other butches and boi dyke friends of mine. We were young, and much of it was in jest, but witnessing the excessive stereotyping of gender by not-yet-adults made me all the more cautious when choosing the traits I wanted to adopt—not the negative parts of gender stereotyping, not the sexism, and not the displays of social hierarchies or commodification of bodies.

Even now, I am still appalled at the gender policing, stereotyping, and blatant sexism that I have witnessed between butch and femme couples, both friends and even, sometimes, in complete strangers. For example, I went into my favorite dyke bar a while back and ordered a vodka cranberry from the stud bartender. I'd ordered plenty of whiskeys from her in the past; she knew something red and fruity was not my regular drink. She leaned over the counter and asked in a low voice: "Are you sure? That drink is really ... sweet."

Yes, I know what's in that drink; I just ordered it. But that comment wasn't about the drink, was it? It was about my gender—about my masculinity. Butches don't order vodka cranberries, her subtext told me. It wasn't a manly enough drink.

I tend to call people out when they pull this kind of stuff. "You're wearing a ... pink ... shirt?" It doesn't happen often. But I can always half-joke about how I'm "secure enough in my masculinity" to order and drink a vodka cranberry or wear a pink shirt.

But I wasn't always. I spent a lot of time choosing how I want-

ed to be before I manifested this identity comfortably: unlearn
ing, untangling, and deconstructing gender roles into gender
components that could be put on or taken off as needed and desired. I don't know if any particular traditionally gendered traits
are "required" for someone to identify as butch or femme—I'd
argue not. With so many options to pick and choose from, how
can we determine the prerequisites? How can we break down
gender into components that are not stereotypical?

I will never say to anyone, especially a friend or a lover, that
what they are doing is "not butch" or "not femme." I don't believe it is possible for a butch to do something not butch or a
femme to do something not femme. For most of us who claim
these words, we become them, and they become us, and thus
everything we do is inside of them. It is perhaps akin to telling an American that she is "not American" because she eats
Mexican food. I may not like that a person, who happens to be
butch or femme, is doing a particular thing, but the actions of
an individual do not necessarily reflect upon their gender identity or expression, nor would they necessarily be considered examples of their race, nationality, religion, ethnicity, relational
status, sexual orientation, shoe size, or hair colour. There is no
singular standard of conduct for all butches everywhere. We all
pick and choose different parts of masculinity, different parts
of humanity, to make up our individual characters. Some of us
may align with more traditional, stereotypical masculinity than
others. Some of us embody a great many supposed contradictions—and like it that way.

Perhaps it is the only logical progression for someone as ob-
sessed with gender as I am to go from growing up believing the
second-wave feminist adage that "gender causes oppression" to
exploding those gender expressions to the point of fetish. What
turns my stomach and makes me queasy in the world at large is
what does it for me the most in my intimate play. Perhaps these
opposites go hand-in-hand, are flip sides of the same coin, and

the disgust and the fascination all lead to a sort of obsession. Perhaps if gender wasn't such a fucked-up, painful, rudimentary system in which we are all indoctrinated and socialized from before we are even born, and perhaps if I didn't see examples of that system so strongly and frequently in all the people I know, in all the dynamics I witness, in all the relationships I've been in, even in so many of the problems of the world, I would not have this particular wound on which to pull. I would not have this particular sore spot to poke at, play with, enlighten, and reclaim when I am my most naked, my most vulnerable, my most small and open self.

So I work for more acceptance. I think, I re-think, I over-think. I write, I record, I analyze. I work toward more consciousness, so that we can all choose to discard the things that harm us, especially the ones we wrap our bodies in daily that have thorns sewn into the seams from the inside. I work to dismantle basic, blatant sexism that everywhere says women are less than men and femininity is less real than masculinity. I challenge the idea of what masculinity might be, for myself and for others. I question my friends and lovers, and I request, encourage, or sometimes demand articulation about their own gender identities, histories, expressions, and intentions. I believe we must be able to make the expression of gender conscious, otherwise we will not know what we are taking on that is not necessary, harmful, or even toxic.

Not everyone feels this way. I hear a lot of "But I just want to be me" and "You really over-think this stuff," and "It's just natural for me to do X or be Y." Conscious gender-building is a lot of work sometimes, yes. And some people are not as analytically inclined as I am, I know. Still, I deeply believe everyone could benefit from more fluidity, less rigidity, and more choice when it comes to gender. For me, much of that has been found in my own butch identity and in the butch-femme relationship dynamic. Butch and femme are controversial: I have stepped in it more than once, accidentally shoved my foot down my throat with the best of intentions, using language to describe people who were terribly offended by any association with them. I have been guilty of proselytizing my opinions about gender.

There are as many ways of performing, embodying, and discussing butch and femme as there are butches and femmes. Not everyone thinks about these identities the same way I do, and not everybody identifies with the ways that I understand my own identity. In the past, it mattered to me that I communicated my own understanding of what my gendered identity meant, but I have now settled into this gender, and come to know myself better, know myself more fully.

Now, if someone came up to me and said, "I don't think you're butch; you're femme," it would just be absurd. I might even laugh. Sorry, but that's just not true. I have studied this lineage of butchness, and I firmly plant my freshly polished cityboy loafers and motorcycle boots in that path. That grand revelatory moment of falling in love with a femme for the first time, and those words dripping from her mouth, "I think you're butch," have brought me to a new understanding of how gender works, how I work, and even how love and desire work.

Butch and femme have opened up an inner world inside me that I had no idea even existed, a self-awareness of how I work, and a context in which I make so much more sense. I had no idea of the breadth or depth of my own inner world, and I had never wandered the streets or websites or thrift stores so eager to buy key accessories necessary for my growing identity until I met that fierce femme writer, that butch plumber, the butch trans guy in training to be a therapist, the femme life coach, the faggy boi dyke and her dog, the butch biker, the femme bass player. It wasn't until I encountered these butch and femme worlds that I truly began the work of exploring, repairing, and playing with gender in this particular dynamic, which ultimately brought me here, finally, to myself.

SINCLAIR SEXSMITH runs the award-winning personal online writing project *Sugarbutch Chronicles: The Sex, Gender, and Relationship Adventures of a Kinky Queer Butch Top* at *sugarbutch.net*. With work published in various anthologies, including the *Best Lesbian Erotica* series, *Sometimes She Lets Me: Butch/Femme Erotica*, and *Visible: A Femmethology, Volume Two*, Mr. Sexsmith also writes columns for online publications and facilitates workshops on sex, gender, and relationships. Find her full portfolio and schedule at *mrsexsmith.com*.

A Guide to Getting Laid by a Girl in Lipstick and High Heels

Belinda Carroll

As a certain kind of girl (no, not that kind), I realize that I'm treated like a wandering and confused straight girl at even the gayest of events. A gaggle of butches try to help me: "Ma'am, are you lost? Do you know where your fag is?" The only recourse is to throw the cutest one up against the wall and show them how it's done. Of course, by "it," I mean a taekwondo takedown. I show them my *kata* in all of its glory. What did you think I meant? We already covered that I'm not that kind of girl. Keep up.

See, my issue, lover pants, isn't the term "femme invisibility." It's the fact that we queers have a visual "Is she or isn't she?" that rivals the US Army's. Without the haircut, no one knows you're a soldier. And, sweetcheeks, I tried the haircut. I looked like a quasi-butch reject from *Miami Vice*. I just couldn't stay away from pastels. Don't judge me.

What we need, my little tattletale, is a kick in the gaydar. Just because I wear a dress and more makeup than Hedda Lettuce doesn't mean I can't throw you around and make you call me Daddy. I have references. The question becomes, "Is she looking you up and down because she likes your shoes, or is she checking your credit to make sure you can afford her goods?"

Now, my dykeness, the inclination is to assume that if she's in a gay bar or at a gay event then, at least, she's probably looking to expand her horizons or, even better, she's about to expand yours. I've had many people say that they don't want to approach the devastatingly beautiful siren (DBS) in the corner because they don't want to offend. Well, it's better to ask forgiveness than permission, I always say. Plus, your DBS probably spent an hour to look like that, and her feet are killing her. If you don't approach her, she's going to try the haircut. You don't want that kind of guilt.

But, you say, "I don't go to gay bars, Momma, I'm a Buddhist monk." Well, even if you are trying to let your DBS know that she's the love of your life at an AA meeting or a bookstore (if you're into that sort of thing), there are certain clues you can look for to reduce the chances of a restraining order.

We queers are like snowflakes; no two are exactly alike. Well, unless they are on the same softball team, but let's not muddy the waters. But just as all snowflakes are white when they fall, there are traits that we have in common. The ability to mate for life on the second date, you say? Well, yes, that is a commonality. Now stop interrupting, twinkle-toes.

When looking for your very own DBS, I suggest you begin at the skin. No, don't touch her without permission. Does she have any tell-tale signs: a rainbow-flag pin, a pink triangle patch, a tattoo that says "I [heart symbol] sex with female-bodied people and sometimes male bodied people if they identify as female"? That last one was a little long perhaps, but you get the point. For example, Yours Truly has two women symbols joined on her upper arm to let people know what team I'm batting for. Who could have foreseen, in the early 1990s, that my sex life was going to get so convoluted that my pickup line would become "What pronoun do you prefer, kumquat"? Now, I just keep it as a Queer Warning Signal. Thank God I didn't get something horrifying, like a labrys or a homage to Melissa Etheridge.

If she's not providing you with oh-so-subtle clues (like a drawing of Sappho on her forehead) you could do something revolutionary by not assuming anything. Go talk to her. Even if she's as straight as Donna Reed (although that theory is contested), she may appreciate the company. If she drops no hint as to her libidinous tendencies, take the plunge and ask. If she's offended, then good. She needs the gay in her life. You may make her think, and then there's a toaster oven in it for you. Who doesn't like door prizes?

So, my little perishable, please take a chance that the girl in the high heels and eyeliner is queer. Even at the grocery store. She's not only being friendly, she's checking out your produce.

BELINDA CARROLL is a Portland, Oregon-based stand-up comic. She caught the comedy bug circa 1986 when she was asked to not only play "Aunt Sally" in the school comedic masterpiece *Tom Sawyer*, but was also asked to sing the national anthem in front of the entire school wearing a grey-haired wig, floral muumuu dress, and her mom's orthopedic stockings. With her pride firmly in the gutter, her road had begun. In an over-the-top, observational style, she tackles everything from her missionary Southern Baptist mother, her life as a teenage Lesbian Avenger, to her current incarnation as a fabulous femme lesbian who missed her calling as RuPaul. A contributing writer for *Curve* magazine, she produces and performs stand-up in shows all over the Pacific Northwest, where she resides with her partner Joe Leblanc and their dog Oliver, who gets treated like a small fuzzy child. See more at *belindacarrollcomedy.com*.

A Patch of Bright Flowers

Zoe Whittall

> *In the movies, authors and screenwriters are often por-*
> *trayed as saintly paupers. Angels in masks. Men with*
> *paunches, taking punches. Sweet, neurotic freaks ...*
> *Patient and loyal and wise. Writers are much dumber and*
> *much meaner than they get credit for.*
> —Brad Listi

Julia is in a hotel room in Vancouver trying on a short black dress. She brought the wrong one, and it's creased from her carry-on luggage. Still, she hopes the dress will get the attention of Karen Heller. She will be attending a welcome dinner for all of the authors participating in the literary festival, and Julia has set Karen Heller as her book-tour distraction. Karen is going to be a challenge. Julia files her nails and paints them, watching a cable show about jungle cats.

For Karen-related courage, Julia empties a tiny bottle of mini-bar scotch into a plastic hotel cup still encased with the cellophane wrapper because her nails are too wet to rip it open. Julia likes immediacy. It burns going down. She coughs.

The dress is too big in the tits and shows a little too much back; that wouldn't be a problem if she hadn't sat still and glowing while Andre tattooed the words from a Nirvana song between her shoulder blades in 1992. Julia has been thinking about covering it up with a patch of bright flowers, but noted during the previous year's Pride festivities that every femme over thirty-two has some '90s tribal Celtic arm band or women's symbols covered up by patches of pansies. She didn't want to stand amidst this unified flowerbed, slowly wrinkling under inky gardens.

Julia isn't sure what to do about aging. She loves that queers are granted an extended adolescence and don't really expect to marry, have babies, or own property until they are well into their thirties, if at all. She used to see ugly babies or annoying children and think, *Oh, thank god I'm not a parent. Thank god I can do whatever I want, whenever I want.* Recently, when she sees ugly babies, she thinks, *I would love that little monster SO HARD.*

Julia presses two pearls of moisturizing cream under each eye and smoothes them out. She forgot to bring mascara. How did that happen? She packed in a hurry, with a hangover, after a marathon fight with her girlfriend. Julia has just turned thirty-five and is now certain, without a doubt, that she wants to have a baby. Her girlfriend, also thirty-five, is suddenly certain she does not. They are at a standstill. So they fight about who cleaned the toaster crumb tray and why they watch so much TV, and things they can see and quantify. The tour of hotels and random chitchat with fans and other writers could not have come at a better time.

The last time Julia toured, her girlfriend came along and it was a disaster. Julia's girlfriend is very attractive, androgynous, on the fey side of the butch spectrum. All the older straight women authors who'd had bisexual phases in college were pinned to her girlfriend's side, flirting like awkward actresses, bumming cigarettes from her when they swore they'd quit years ago, and saying, *Your hands, they're so rough.* One of Julia's favourite authors was the worst at this. When Julia got home she took her entire collection of the author's works that she'd collected for over a decade and dropped them off in the box outside the Value Village. Her girlfriend ate these women up—who wouldn't? Julia was trying to stop drinking on that tour, so often spent nights in the hotel room watching cable while her girlfriend got loaded with the bi-curious wives of Can Lit. This time, when she received the itinerary from her publicist, she didn't invite her girlfriend, and she didn't ask to come along, either. It seemed better this way.

Julia and her girlfriend have an arrangement for travel. When you are on the road, your body is your own, is the basic rule, although they are not permitted to fuck anyone who currently lives in their city or is planning to relocate there any time soon.

When she checked into the hotel an hour earlier, she'd glanced around the author hospitality room and confirmed that all of her attempts to dress the part of a classy novelist were going to fail. She felt jam-handed, a walking visual flaw perennially covered in cat hair. Scrawling her signature on the sign-in list, she noted coffee stains on the front of her blue cotton spring coat. She bought the coat herself with her Public Lending Right cheque, after deciding she wanted to look her age and cover up the many other tattoos that betrayed her love of immediacy and lack of respect for hindsight.

Her feet were soaking wet from the rain she always thought was a regional exaggeration. A girl with shiny red hair handed her a package with the festival guide and an envelope of per diem cash and mumbled, "I really loved your book. Really. I could really see my world in it." Julia felt a rush of gratitude toward this young woman and stopped herself from complaining about the review she'd read on the plane that called said book "a tawdry, sex-crazed tale of marginalization with emotionally shallow, drug-addicted, gender-confused lowlifes no one could ever love enough to care about seeing through to the end of the book." Julia noted the reviewer's name and knew said critic had had a novel rejected by her publisher. The world was full of petty assholes, she'd thought, ordering a glass of red wine from a stewardess.

Julia just said thank you, and the girl smiled, handing her a festival tote bag. Julia had decided to sit in one of the comfy chairs until her hotel room was ready.

The Famous One was in a corner signing copies of her new science fiction book, which she refused to call science fiction. A fawning festival organizer picked up each copy after she signed it, and placed it on the table in a stack, running her palm over the covers as if to soothe them from nerves.

Julia studiously avoided the Famous One's eyes, trying to project an air of who-cares-about-you? You're just a person! But Julia's hands shook when the Famous One stood beside her as she was pouring milk into her coffee from the tiny white dispenser at the food table. Julia's plasticized nametag dipped into the sugar bowl. The Famous One stirred her coffee, looking down into the cup.

Some women just looked classy all the time, like the Famous One with the fifteen best sellers. It was all about her shoes, Julia decided, and the way she never hurried to answer questions. Julia is the type of person who is always getting into accidents. Her new theory was that accidents happen most often when you start to do something and then remember you wanted to do something else so you stop in mid-action to start another action, and then you fall or trip or stumble. Julia was trying to follow through more, in life and relationships and sentences and up and down stairs. She had fewer scrapes and bruises, fewer broken heels.

She thought about telling the Famous One how much she loved her books, but though it would have been a way in, it wouldn't have been true. Instead, she took a hurried gulp of her coffee and wished her room was ready. Julia loves hotels. It's her favourite part of a book tour, that feeling like you are eight and living within a fort of couch and curtains, a tiny little world away from routine.

It was then, as she stood awkwardly beside her carry-on suitcase, that she saw Karen Heller for the very first time. Well, she had no idea she was *the* Karen Heller. Karen had the telltale swagger of an old-school butch, moving gently about the room filled with sixty-something boomer writers, twenty-something assistants, forty-something publicists, and Julia, the lone thirty-five-year-old invited to the festival for a "voice of the young" panel discussion. The other two "young" ones, who Julia knew to be thirty-nine and forty-one, respectively, were arriving tomorrow.

Julia loved that she was still considered young in this milieu. The week before, she'd stood in line at a bar in the west end of Toronto for their weekly lesbian night. A twenty-two-year-old hipster in front of her had said to her friend, "If I'm still standing in lines like this when I'm thirty, just shoot me." A friend three years younger than Julia complained about needing to have a baby before she was thirty-five, when her chances would drop significantly. Julia is in denial about being thirty-five. She doesn't want to hear about fertility treatments. She just wishes time had paused when she was twenty-eight, and she could give her girlfriend more time to think about it. She could have a savings account and own furniture that wasn't second-hand.

At home, Julia tended bar on the weekends and wrote on weekdays. At festivals, she often felt like she'd be more comfortable hanging with the catering staff than making polite chitchat with the recent Giller Prize winner.

Karen walked by Julia, who was still standing by the refreshments table sipping her coffee, leaning on her suitcase trolley, trying to stop thinking about her issues at home, and convey with every muscle in her body and expression on her face *hello hello, you're not the only queer in the room, hi hi hi hi hi hi*. She cursed her decision not to change out of the comfortable slouchy jeans she'd worn on the plane.

Julia tried to get Karen to look at her, but she didn't. Julia exaggeratedly noticed Karen's nametag, pinned above her shirt pocket where she kept a neatly folded handkerchief. Julia loved that hankie immediately.

"Karen," she said, after she read it. Karen looked up from her small white plate of melon chunks and said "Hello," giving that smile that people use when they assume you've met before but they clearly can't place you.

"I love your work. I'm Julia Chapman." This was a lie. Karen wrote the kind of novels that Julia often gave to her mother for Christmas. Generational sagas about torn-apart families, often involving a nineteenth-century across-the-ocean move and some sort of tragic secret. Nothing set before the 1960s or involving even the most minimal of gay side characters. Nary a matronly spinster auntie or a flamboyant and "single" hairdresser. That Karen Heller was actually a savvy butch you'd expect to see at the local lez bar playing pool with some gender-studies femme professor for a wife was totally confounding.

"Thank you," said Karen, who pointed toward the corkboard behind Julia that featured media clippings about authors attending the festival. "You've certainly been getting some great press," she said, pointing to a giant photo of Julia from the *Vancouver Sun* whose headline read "Young Author Is Unafraid to Write of Queer Worlds." Karen smirked at the headline, seemed embarrassed. She didn't say anything nice like "I hope to read it soon" or any of the other potential half-truths authors tell each other. Her eyes seemed to imply an almost mocking feeling, perhaps that Julia is not a real author, writing about real things. This is a common attitude that Julia encounters, that not only is she young, she's also writing about things only a few select people care about, books that won't get shortlisted or be considered important literature. Julia tried not to care about those things, but to think instead about her readers, and the writers who inspired her to keep going.

Karen's publicist arrived with her schedule and said, "Your room is ready." Karen seemed pleased to have a reason to leave.

Julia said, "Nice to meet you, Karen," as the duo walked away, and neither responded.

In the hotel room, Julia tries to safety-pin the dress under her right armpit. Eventually her breasts look even. She remembers a time when she used to be called perky, when her tits pointed skyward all on their own at twenty-one. When she leans into the mirror to line her eyes, the pin stabs her. "Fuck!" she sits back on the bed, marvelling that she wrote something that actually allowed her to be sitting in this hotel room free of charge. Success was still a great big shock and she didn't always trust it.

By the third book, she had her rituals; wrap the remote control in a Ziploc bag, pocket the shampoos if they were nice, and ask for more. Always fill out the little thing on the door that allowed you to get breakfast delivered in the morning. Pack granola bars and dried fruit and try to Google a drugstore in the neighbourhood beforehand. Keep receipts for tax time. Hotels still felt like a new thing, an exciting thing, a symbol.

When she was younger, her parents took the family on camping trips—national parks, canoeing, hiking. An old canary-yellow tent. They stayed in a hotel only once, on the side of a highway, because it was storming too hard to pitch the tent in a nearby campground. Her mother made them eat hot dogs cooked in the hotel coffee maker and then wrapped in white bread.

Until she published her first book, Julia had never taken a trip, really. The odd jaunt to Montreal or Ottawa, places she could go to for a weekend. She'd never been on a plane until her publicist said, "Okay, so here's your ticket, and someone named Gail will meet you at the airport."

When she'd met Gail, a woman in her sixties holding a sign with her name, Julia couldn't stop talking about the flight. "I thought I might throw up, I was so scared!" The woman looked a little pained after a while, driving fast in her blue Subaru toward the hotel. "You look so young," Gail said to her, over and over. "I can't believe you've written a book."

"Thanks," Julia said. She had no idea then that she was going to have to get used to this kind of remark, and that it wasn't always a compliment.

Back in her hometown, when her cousin Anna found out she'd published a book of poetry, she assumed Julia had immediately become rich. Anna stole two sweaters from Julia's suitcase, later telling her mother, *Well, she can afford to buy new ones, right?* Julia's life hadn't changed at all; in fact, she had even less money. She stopped going home so much.

At the dinner, Julia is seated between her publicist and a gay poet from Alberta she very much admires. A seat across from her is empty until the end of the appetizer course, when she looks up from her plate of asparagus to see Karen Heller.

Karen Heller is no longer someone she might flirt with to pass the time, to make her feel better about her failing relationship at home. No. Karen Heller is a seduction challenge. Because Karen Heller—Julia referred to her by first and last name always in her interior monologue—is charming and interested in chatting with everyone except Julia. And the only thing Julia likes more than immediate gratification is the kind that comes after a very serious challenge, requiring cunning and hair-twirling and her very best efforts.

During dinner, the Famous One talks about the 1970s and how poets would spend months in France writing on the Canada Council's dime or living together in a cabin outside of Toronto, and about all the ones who'd become famous and died. There were colourful anecdotes, and Julia wanted to be able to go back in time and watch the poets scrapping drunkenly. "But you know what he was like," said the Famous One, and everyone laughed, and Karen nodded.

Dinner is over in a snap. Julia follows the crowd to the reading where Karen is a featured guest. She reads in a slow, low monotone, and if Julia hadn't established said personal challenge, she would've drifted off or gone for a cigarette midway through. Like the straight women who try to bed lesbians on their book tours, Julia regarded book-tour cigarettes as fictional; she was still a non-smoker, had quit two years earlier, and wouldn't touch one when she got home. Certain things just don't count in this context. She hangs on every one of Karen's words and buys a hardcover copy of the book to get signed.

At the signing table, Julia leans over and proffers the creamy off-white title page. Karen scrawls Best Wishes, Karen Heller. Cheap, thinks Julia. When Karen looks up at Julia's raised eyebrows, she winks. *Thanks for buying the book.*

Later, in the hospitality suite, after Julia had read over Karen's biography and Googled her homepage on her laptop, Karen matches her drink for drink. She has taken notice of Julia's obvious intentions and seems bored enough to play along. Eventually, when the rest of the table is immersed in a never-ending, soul-deadening debate about the advent of e-books and death of the publishing industry, Karen says, "Do you smoke?"

And Julia replies, "Yes, because it doesn't count on a book tour. They're fictional."

"What?"

"The cigarettes. They're imagined. I quit two years ago. I make exceptions for … tour."

Karen doesn't think this is clever or interesting, just pulls out a pack of smokes from her front pocket and walks down the hallway ahead of Julia, as Julia struggles to keep up in her too-tall heels.

Karen pauses at the door and holds it open for Julia. They stand near two oversized potted plants and stare out at the ocean. The sun is going down, and the water is dotted with taxi boats going over to downtown. They make some small talk, where is home, how many other cities are you going to, who is your agent, did you hear about so-and-so's six-figure advance, etc.

There is a pause, and Julia thinks things are going well until Karen says, "So, what is your deal?"

"My deal?"

"Yes."

"I dunno, I think you're interesting."

"You do?"

"Yes." Then Julia, feeling the free champagne crowd her better judgment says, "I love your writing." She rationalizes this could be true eventually.

"Do you remember writing a review about ten years ago of my first book, *The Ghost's Garden*?"

Julia's cheeks redden. Her safety pin jabs her left breast. She remembers it vaguely, from an arts weekly. A short review and, from the look on Karen's face, she gathers not very positive.

"Should I apologize?"

"No, I believe in critical reviews. But I think yours was lazy."

"Probably; I got paid about three cents an hour to write those."

Julia and Karen stand staring at each other, as though in a standoff. All around them other hotel patrons mill about, checking their phones and lighting cigarettes, getting in and out of taxis. People nod at Karen. She nods back.

"So, do you have a wife?" asks Julia.

"Not really."

"What does that mean?"

"We are still living together. But we are not really together anymore. But we had been for thirteen years."

Julia smirks.

"You smirk a lot," says Karen.

Julia stops smirking. "I smile sometimes when I'm uncomfortable."

"It comes off as snobby."

"Well, that's certainly not my intention."

"You're so sarcastic, it's hard to know when you're being real. Like, following me around all night, is that real?"

"Sure," says Julia.

"Your generation—"

"Oh, I always love sentences that begin with 'your generation.'"

"—is so cynical; it's like there's no beauty to anything you can't mock. It's like there are quotation marks around every action you make."

"That's a ridiculous reduction. How do you even know my age?"

"What, you're twenty-six?"

"Thirty-five."

Karen raises her eyebrows. "Really? I'd assumed, because ..."

"You'd never heard of me until this book, so you think I'm twenty-two?"

"Well, yes"

"It's my seventh ..."

"I didn't know you had other books."

"It's my first published by a ..."

"A multinational, yes. Your main character is twenty-one, it's written in first person, and I'd assumed it was—"

"Autobiographical?"

Karen blushes, shrugs. "I guess *I* should apologize now."

"And you are, what? Forty?"

"Forty-two."

"A hot forty-two."

Karen smiles. Her shoulders relax, a blush creeps into her face.

Bingo, thinks Julia. "So, what is it really that you're criticizing, Obi-Wan?"

Karen smirks this time. Inhales her cigarette, not breaking eye contact.

"Your characters are younger."

"I like writing about young people. Your characters are all, what, 236 years old?"

"I'm an historian. We're already saturated in the present. I like to write stories that escape the tyranny of this day and age."

"The tyranny of ... being un-closeted?"

"I love that you assume I'm closeted."

"Aren't you? You never write about it. You never mention your wife in the media. I bet your publicists make reporters promise not to ask about it."

"Look at me, Julia, do you think I have that option? I'm a very private person. My personal life is my own."

"So is mine. Doesn't mean I have to be dishonest."

"Your life might be honest, but it's incredibly public. I Googled you and found out you ate pretzels on the plane yesterday, had a hangover, and are currently writing a script version of your first novel. Your cat's name is Binkie, you really like Mary Gaitskill, and you live with your long-term girlfriend in Parkdale."

"But you didn't catch my age? Not very thorough of you. Plus, I wrote that review you recall so vividly ten years ago, so obviously I wasn't sixteen at the time…"

Karen smirks again. "It's obvious to anyone with sight that I am … who I am."

"Who you are?"

"Yes. You could easily blend in."

"Yes, the femme blend, such credible social commentary." Julia roles her eyes at that one. "Anyway, it's not obvious to your readers. It's important for people to have role models and—"

"Oh god, if you give me the think-about-the-gay-children-in-Idaho speech, I take back my generational cynicism comment."

"But it's true; I rarely see my queer worlds represented in art."

"Do you always have to see yourself? It's art. We don't write to make a political point. Didactic art reeks of inauthenticity; you can detect it from miles away."

"Is that what you think of my work?"

"I didn't say that. I actually think your work is good. You have a way with humour."

"Do I?"

"Oh, the writer ego. You're gonna keep pressing for compliments, aren't you?"

"Maybe."

"In that case … your dress is … very distracting—in a good way."

Julia thinks about leaning in to kiss her, but Karen is stubbing her cigarette in the ashtray and walking back inside. They return to the hospitality room, finish up their drinks, and take the elevator to their floor.

When the elevator door opens, Karen walks Julia to her door and they stand awkwardly in front of it for a moment. Karen leans in and kisses Julia gently, and pulls away.

"You happy you caught me?"

"Yeah."

"I suppose, because of your girlfriend, you're not going to invite me in ..."

"We have an arrangement for these kinds of things, for when we travel."

"Uh-huh. Well, good night, Julia Chapman, voice of a generation of narcissists."

"Good night, Karen Heller, closet case for the Oprah book club set."

Karen leans in and kisses Julia.

"You can't write about this," jokes Julia, once they are inside the room.

"I wouldn't dream of it."

ZOE WHITTALL is the author of two literary novels, *Holding Still for as Long as Possible* (House of Anansi Press) and *Bottle Rocket Hearts* (Cormorant Books). *Bottle Rocket Hearts* was a *Globe and Mail* best book of the year and was shortlisted for CBC's Canada Reads. She has also published three books of poetry, most recently *Precordial Thump* (Exile, 2008). Originally from South Durham, Quebec, she has lived in Toronto since 1997.

Rogue Femininity

Elizabeth Marston

When I arrived in dykespace after twelve years as a femme gay guy, I was welcomed into a sisterhood that took itself to be *the* sisterhood, that still understood femme as the opposite of butch and thought that both these terms were lesbian intellectual property.

I love my new sisters, but I often wonder how I could convince them to see femme as I do—as a sisterhood and brotherhood stretching well beyond the borders of dykespace, as a community that can include men, women, and intersex, cis, trans, and genderqueer, gay, straight, and bi. The word might have been coined by twentieth-century lesbians, but it has travelled widely and has been bent and unbent and hammered smooth by many tongues and many uses. It has changed with time and distance. Let me fold it back on itself.

Let me tell you what femme has meant for me and what it could mean for everyone. Let me stretch the word.

Let's say that femme is dispossessed femininity. It's the femininity of those who aren't allowed to be real women and who have to roll their own feminine gender.

Rolling their own is what cis-femme lesbians did in the fifties. By class and by sexual preference, they were dispossessed of real womanhood. For what woman is complete without money or a man? So they learned how to improvise, how to sew; how to turn a thrift-store sow's ear into a vintage silk purse.

Rolling their own is what contemporary femme dykes do. Invisible in straight spaces and frequently trivialized in queer ones, they must voice their femininity in a way that does not get shouted down or ignored. No easy task.

Rolling their own is what drag queens and trannies do and have always done. For what woman is complete without hairless skin and a cunt? We too learned how to improvise, and when we were mocked as caricatures of real women, we often became skilled caricaturists, owning the insult, engulfing it.

And this is what femme gay men do, too. Dangerously visible in straight space and often ridiculed in gay male space, femme gay men take shit from all sides. The straights dish it to them because they're visible. Second-wave feminists dish it to them because they're both feminine and male, and have thus sinned twice. Other gay men dish it to them for acting like, well, chicks.

What these groups share, aside from a fondness for eyeliner, is the illegitimacy of their femininity. That's how I understand femme: badass, rogue, illegitimate femininity. It's the femininity of those who aren't supposed to be feminine, who aren't allowed to be, but are anyway.

Second-wave feminists used to slander both feminine dykes and transsexual women as "female impersonators." And this is true. What they missed is that female impersonation is what femme is. Femmes can only impersonate real women because we are, by rules beyond our control, not real women. But broke-ass homos, trannies, and drag queens won't be real women until patriarchy is smashed, heterosexism is on its knees, and class counts for nothing. Until then, we are other. Our cleavage is an uncanny valley. And the more passable and invisible we are—the more like real women we find ourselves seeming—the greater our supposed deception.

This sucks. We don't mean to be deceptive. But, like Jessica Rabbit, we're just drawn this way.

I'm saying that conventional femininity not only involves a performance, as Judith Butler pointed out, but also a couple of membership rules. These say that the only people who are allowed to do the feminine performance are straight and have girl bits. No boyfriend, no cunt, no service. If you're ruled out, then no matter how heartfelt your femininity, it will be understood as fake, as something you're choosing to do to have us all on. Bleat all you like; to the world, you're no sheep. To the world, you're a wolf.

I'm proposing that from now on, we all use the word femme to describe every wolf, every feminine rogue. No one is born a rogue; you become one by learning to break the rules. Femme is a move from dispossession to self-possession. We're not allowed to be real, so we've figured out something else to be, something new—and that something is femme.

"Something new" isn't the way femme has always been seen. Both feminine cis dykes and transsexual women have often been accused of trying to disappear. But often, the femme has no interest in disappearing. All that's happened is that straights and lazy-minded queers have mistaken her femme-ness for conventional femininity. She becomes invisible not because she's trying to be wallpaper, but because no one's looking for her difference.

This is not the fault of the femme. But let's say, for the sake of argument, that some or even most femmes do want to pass as conventionally feminine, and therefore as cis and straight. Why the hate?

In the first place, trying to pass as cis or straight is perfectly reasonable if you think you can pull it off without feeling gross. Passing makes life a lot easier. If you have the option, why not take it? And why hate those who have the option and take it? Does it really help the cause if you can tell at a hundred yards that I like women and was born with balls?

Besides, it's not as if passing gets you off every hook. You still carry your difference with you. In queer spaces, you risk marginalization. Straightside, you're always evaluating when it's safe to reveal, always doing the social math. Passing is a privilege, but it still sucks, even when it saves you from oppression.

I'd also argue that passing is still femme—still radical, still political. If a femme is someone who has been forbidden to be feminine, then any time a femme does femininity, it's an unauthorized copy. Passing is as radical as printing money, as downloading music. We femmes are gender pirates. Arrr.

And let's not forget that dudes can be pirates too. Nelly men, cis and trans, gay and straight, who prance alongside us. Twinks, bitches, chickens. Nancy-boys. Traps. Middle-aged weekend crossdressers, for whom femme invisibility is lamentably unattainable. Lisping, delicate little trans fags, perched on their daddies' laps. We're all in this together. We have the same problem by different names. We all get shit for living the feminine, and for getting it wrong, wrong by definition.

ELIZABETH MARSTON is a once-and-future academic marooned in the real world. She identifies as a writer-activist, a permaqueer trannydyke, and an Alberta survivor. Current projects include *The Switch*, a trans-feminist web-sitcom, and *Transist.ca*, a trans-activist e-mag. Hobbies include cycling, piano, and Fluevog.

Changed Sex. Grew Boobs. Started Wearing a Tie.

Amy Fox

Remade by biochemistry, surgery, cultural study, and ribbed tank-tops, I now look pretty much like any other freckled butch. Most dykes accept me without question. But sometimes they discover that I'm MtF, that I transitioned to butch by escaping manhood, and then they brand me as an immigrant, an outsider, a threat—or a confidante.

Dykes find me familiar in that I am butch, yet refreshingly alien in that I am transsexual. So they give me the public tour and show me their hidden demons. From what I've seen, I know that butch is not male-lite™, but dyke culture fears it is. And this fear shapes the butch femme spectrum.

BOLD TOMBOY VERSUS BEWILDERED BOY

Born in 1980, I was fortunate that my mum was a feminist. Toy robots, baby dolls, one book on emotional communication, another on dinosaurs; she inspired me to ignore gender stereotypes.

1986: When they say "those tinfoil wrist-wraps look like Wonder Woman," they mean that this is bad. But they block bullets. I thought that would be cool.

The struggle between butch versus man started when Mum gave me a book for boys entering puberty. It was like a horror novel, like David Cronenberg was directing my body. I was left with a problem: if biology isn't destiny, why would any feminist regret zer sex, let alone change it? Why would a boy pine to be a tomboy? Do I just need a father? And why don't I smile anymore?

1990: Yes, I think we should draw a girl wizard too.

In interests, manner, and politics, I held to subtle acts of gender-defiance, though I was increasingly alone. Does this prove I was a tomboi trapped in a boy's body or just an androgynous kid who flipped the bird to sexism? I don't know. But I scour my childhood for evidence that I always was a butch. I do this because one of the problems with being MtF and butchy is that people may question whether you're genuine or just a man playing a prank. And your harshest accuser may be yourself. So I dig out examples, arguments, and try to look fearless, even when I'm looking in the mirror.

1995: Ripley from *Alien* is the most awesome sci-fi hero ever. She's not like most women, but she's not like most men either ... What's the word for that?

It took me a decade and a half to beat puberty's isolation and depression and make the following distinctions between butch and male:

Playing with the boys doesn't mean I want to be one.

If I see myself as a ladette who gets misread as a lad, my life makes sense.

It is valid, both personally and politically, to change your sex, especially if you then screw with a whole new set of gender norms.

Transition followed. And once safely away from being labelled a "man," I learned to tie a Windsor knot.

I NEVER SAY "I AM A BUTCH" TO A DOCTOR

Doctors can grant or deny you access to safe transgender healthcare. They often do this based on their own prejudices, among which may be the belief that butches are malfunctioning women. So when I see a doctor, I leave the necktie at home and say, "I'm ... tomboyish."

I have said this with a shaved head and singed cargo pants, so the trick may have been transparent. I'm fortunate to have lived in Vancouver since 2006, where practitioners of trans medicine were more interested in helping patients live honestly than exist conventionally. I thought of transition before then, but most other places and times would shun anyone who aimed to transition into a queer identity. Sometimes I hear dykes rail against transgender pediatrics. They fear it will force ("our") young butches into mannish roles and bodies.[1] I very much agree with objections to forcibly virilizing girls, but it's not FtMs we should worry about. They aren't forced to transition, they want to. And most of them aren't girls. Where trans medicine does force manhood onto girls is when it stalls or rejects young MtFs, leaving them to go through the wrong puberty, while being bullied into the wrong gender-identity.

FEMME TRAIL GUIDES

Eight months into transitioning as far as I could get from male, I developed a strange interest in power tools and short hair. But I was too scared to say I was butch. I learned otherwise by dating a femme.

We'd met years before in student organizing, but only shared tea after I'd started transition. She was a big bi femme; a broad who fucks who and how she wants. Her mum and dad thought that it would be kind and freeing to raise her as they would a son. She disagreed and out-femmed this attempt. But even though her femininity was, from the start, a rebellion, in queer spaces, it started the process of her erasure; the men she dated finished it. Consigned to the "quiet ally" seat, she was left dating bi-curious women, whose curiosity she offered to satisfy, sans underwear. Her dates declined, remaining bi-curious rather than bi-informed. She remained frustrated.

Dating a tranny—a girlfriend with stubble and a necktie—made her smirk. She clarified my doubts and explained to me that I fuck "like a girl." She was my anchor in women's circles where I would not be welcome were she not beside me, calling

---

1   Never mind that most trans pediatricians don't give sex changes to kids. They *forestall* puberty so the growing teenager has several years to think over where ze wants to take zer body.

bullshit. Dancing with her, fisting in washrooms, it felt right, intimate, honest. Together, we were bold. We were femme and butch.

Still, I was scared to call myself "butch." Wouldn't that be a contradiction? An Eddie Izzard joke? But she saw the butch and named it. I owe her.

I encounter femmes who shepherd friends and lovers through the FtM spectrum. When they see the butch and smell the trans on me, they discreetly offer a rolodex of gentlemen and gender-queers, friends and exes, to whom I can talk if I, y'know, need to talk. I explain that I am changing the other way. They are happy to hear this, to know that I can honestly be myself right now.

I see how many butches lean on femmes, whether we know them romantically or platonically. I feel like a bulldagger Lois Lane to their Superwomen. Escorting us through everything from washrooms to transition, I wonder and marvel at how femmes save us over and over and what they get in return. Visibility? Help moving boxes? Someone who is not femme who will say, "People see butch and expect male, but I am not. People see you and expect conventional, and you are anything but."

I wonder what we can do so that they could openly lend their help at dyke gatherings, rather than catching our ears in private.

BORDER CONTROL AND FRAGILE FLOWERS

If I get read as trans at a "queer women's event," dykes assume I'm a straight transsexual guy. Ironically, this grants me free access. I bear no resentment toward my FtM brothers, but I do grind my teeth over women's spaces and dyke circles that welcome them yet which exclude my transsexual sisters. I am infuriated by the underlying assumption: my brave FtM brothers, who have sacrificed to become men, are just conformist women, and my bold MtF sisters who have fought to be women, are really men with a fetish for being marginalized. Are we dykes so fragile, so afraid, that we cannot allow anyone to enter, leave, or even explore? When we imply that FtM men are still gay women, how can we also fear that "we are losing our butches"?

Our butches? Whose butches? Does the dyke community own its members? Our sex lives? Our genders? Does it control us for our own good?

Dykes are not fragile flowers. Many femmes wear the flaming rose. It's a flower, but it'll fight back if you try to crush it. What tough flower would symbolize us butches? Or do we fear that butches are the fragile ones, anxious to leave dykespace?

We fear men will undo us, erase us; that we must guard against their entrance into our spaces, or our sister's pants. But men have been part of butch-femme for as long as I can remember. Pre-electrical lesbian spaces contained trans-spectrum men who feared presenting as male in public, and butches who feared looking mannish because of laws, written and unwritten, that prohibited putting a vagina in a pair of pants. Medical transition has been around since the 1930s, and it has not destroyed us. There were gay men who shared our bar scene, and their business kept many of "our" bars afloat. The lesbian communities that most feared men were those that also feared femmes, butches, transsexuals, and every other stripe of gender freedom.

Butch-femme is tough. We are tough. Our culture has survived alcoholism, homophobia, beatings, corrupt vice squads, poverty, and the sex wars—plus all the other problems of living. I think we can survive transgender medicine.

The happiest butch-femme spaces I've seen are those that embrace the gender spectrum. There we find butches and femmes who go by "she" and love their unmodified bodies. We have FtMs who've done the works—T, top, and crotch—who may be men or butch or femme or more. They include me and others who transitioned into being butches. They include femmes without questioning their taste in lovers. And it works.

Men will not undo us. But an unchecked fear of men—of becoming a man, dating a man, having been forced to be one, looking too much like one, being too attractive to men in general, or aiding and abetting any of the above—can and will make our community unliveable if we let it. But we should not fear or police ourselves. If we did that, there'd be no butch or femme in the first place.

SIPPING GENDER WITH BUTCHES

When I meet with butches, there is often herbal tea. Some of the butches are happy; some are not. The distinction between the two is based in their struggle between self-honesty and the fear of ostracism.

The Happy Butch is tickled to hear that I transitioned into butchhood. Happy Butch chuckles to learn that I too explain to straight friends and family, *I know people mistake me for a teenage fag, and I'm okay with that.*

The Unhappy Butch is relieved that "my transition" referred to how I joined, rather than abandoned, her and her gender.

Both Happy and Unhappy Butches know a compatriot. He was younger and genderqueer. Now he's on T and has a new name.

Happy Butch and I will grin, knock cups, and speculate as to just what and who will emerge from transition.

Unhappy Butch sinks into her chair: "There goes another one," she utters, hollow like a cavern. Silent over a steaming cup, her eyes say, "At least I know you're here for the long haul."

In my experience, the difference in attitude runs as follows:

Unhappy Butch wants to mend the holes in her gender, but won't. Whether it's new pronouns, T, or surgery, she'd feel more honestly herself in some other body or identity. She denies herself this out of a sense of duty that is really just fear—the fear of losing friends who accepted her as who she tries to be but who won't accept her as who she needs to be, because that would be accepting a man or something similar enough to a man. She tries to turn her fear of isolation into a virtue. Noble and alone, she will stick it out, the last surviving butch ambassador to the world. But she knows it's a lie, and she mourns her lost brother because she mourns her lost self. I know this gender-martyrdom. I lived in it. And I threw it out when I transitioned into being happy and butch.

The Happy Butch? This butch doesn't mourn our brother's transition but celebrates it. Happy Butch is present in body and pronouns as-is, be they modified, unmodified, or under renovation. Happy Butch knows that any "friend" or "community" who rejects her/zer/him/them/it isn't a real friend or community. Happy Butch crackles with an honest, brave joy that extends to seeing someone else come into zer own.

MY HOME IS NOT AN AIRPORT

The fears that haunt us stem from mistakenly equating female with femininity and male with masculinity. When we do this, we see butch misdefined as a waiting lounge for the next flight to manhood. If butch is just pre-male, then all cissexed butches are looking for a way out. And MtF butches? We don't exist—we can't exist. So we're invisible, even to ourselves. It's stupid and it's silencing.[2] Yet many people live in butchspace happily; some growing into it, others arriving after a long journey through other genders.

Do butches go male out of a thirst for privilege? No. T and "he" might get you a little extra room on the sidewalk, but will probably also get you called "fag," with words or fists. Every trans guy knows that when he gets read, whatever male privilege he has can vaporize quickly and violently.

Alternatively, some people cunningly fake one gender in public, then are themselves where it's safe to be honest. But this is desperation, not transition. I know from experience that if you're

---

2   But it can be damned convenient. As a transsexual, I appreciate a gender that *expects* stone genitals, a packer bulge, and stubble.

not really a guy, trying to live as one 24/7, let alone forcing your body into the "M" box, will make you so sick in the heart that anything else seems worth the risk.

Society doesn't pressure butches to transition any more than it pressures gender-odd kids to be gay. What's changed is that "transition" is now a household word. Friends and family may confide that they'll understand if that's a road you need to take. If they think you're in the closet, they may call you on it. That's not pressure. That's acceptance. Or love.

If I have not already ruffled enough feathers, then let me start plucking: there is no such thing as butch flight. There are transsexual dudes who cheat themselves out of a full life for fear of being ostracized. There are butches who fear to live beyond male and female because dykes might assume they are guys. There are FtM-spectrum folk who have never been butch in their lives. And there are genderqueers who want nothing to do with our decades-old identity wars. But there is no butch flight.

There is, however, butch arrival: people who have tried other genders, most often femme and/or guy, who made the switch and joined the ranks.

So if more butches is what you want, I can get you butches.

Is your community short on butches? First, we need to re-member economic class. Most of the butchless lesbian spaces I've seen, at least the ones strangely lacking harder butches, are also moneyed spaces. Butches, being gender-variant, tend to be broke.

Second, we need to help butches transition in. We must cel-ebrate former femmes who want to dance the boi's part. Like any dancer who switches roles, she'll probably be more graceful than those who haven't.

We also need to help MtF butches make the trip. Their road-blocks are (1) an underfunded, ageist, and rigorously heteronor-mative transgender medical system and (2) a lack of accessible radical gender education. You need to be a gender radical to grasp that it's possible to transition into gender variance and come out as an unconventional kind of trans and/or woman, but most radical gender education is aimed only at those who already are out as trans and/or who the educators read as female. Why are there so many more flaming FtM dudes than butchy MtF women? Most of the trans-flamers started their critical feminist education among women who read them as gender-bending butches. And while they were included, this education did not welcome my untransitioned MtF sisters. So the swishy FtMs transitioned and most of the boyish MtFs assumed they couldn't. But this is changing; every year, I see more MtFs in boy-drag, neckties, and mullets than ever before.

So what we do now is keep fighting gender-normativity in the medical system and orient feminist education to grasp that many "boys" are actually girls who are stuck in the closet. We do this, and the world will not only be a friendlier place for all genders, it will also have more butches. They'll even be tall and stubbly if that's what you're into. And they won't re-transition to male. Probably.

Like freak weather, AMY FOX blows through Vancouver every few months. The proprietor of Tricky Vixen Metal and More, she crafts toys and sculpture in steel and bronze. She is also a co-writer and producer on *The Switch*, a kinky, genderbent Canadian sitcom produced by Fire Thief Studios. At present she is working with Trans Connect in Nelson, BC, to produce a documentary on health and social service access for rural trans people.

The New Politics of Butch

Jeanne Córdova

> *We did not come to fear the future. We came here to shape it.*
> —*Barack Obama, fall 2009*

Why do butches not fear the future but fight to shape it? Why do butches embrace the responsibility of living in a binary-rigid world? Being taken seriously as a butch means you need to be a person of substance—a doer rather than just a talker. Because we are born butch, we don't know how to live in fear; we would rather die fighting for our freedom. Many a butch has indeed died fighting to hold her head up high, and thousands of butches around the planet continue to live and dress openly as masculine women rather than merely exist as defeated, broken people.

My earliest memory of and proof that I was born butch comes from watching a black-and-white eight-mm reel my parents brought with us to North America from post-war Germany in 1952. I am daughter number two. The camera lens narrows to focus on three children playing on a Christmas morning. The two girls, ages four and five, are dressed in identical red pol-ka-dot flannel pyjamas. Their brother, age two, wears a striped sleepwear jumpsuit. But the camera is already lying; the truth is far from its gender-biased gaze. An adult hand reaches into the scene and places two identically wrapped Christmas presents into the hands of the waiting girl children. The older black-haired one delicately unwraps the edges of her package and pulls out a doll whose eyes open and close.

"It's a dolly!" Francie's eyes light up her freckled pale skin as she jumps up and down in slippered feet. She looks at her sister and waits for her to unwrap her present. Number two daughter tears the wrapping apart from the middle to reveal a simi-lar doll, this one with light-brown hair and eyes that pop open.

But no smile or happy-jumping follows; instead, we see number two's face fade into a sad, faraway look, and disappointment shroud her eyes. Wordlessly, she drops the doll to the ground. It clunks to the floor as the camera quickly pulls back from the unexpected.

Suddenly, number two springs into action, and her head of curls turns to the right, where the camera shows us the small brother about to mount his shiny new tricycle. Number two pushes her brother off his bike, grabs it from him, and wheels off—not into the sunset, but away from the camera and away from the whole, wide gender-conforming world.[1]

Decades later, we are experiencing a unique butch renaissance. The term "butch" is now out of the closet, evolving. Feminism, queer theory, and gender theory, together with transgender politics, are bringing new definitions to the concept of butch. We must redefine "butch" in a post-trans world, one in which we now also question and look for redefinition of the concepts of "male" and "female," the masculine and the feminine.

In the 1998 classic, *Female Masculinity*, Judith "Jack" Halberstam posits the very simple yet breakthrough assertion that behaviours called "masculine" don't belong exclusively to men. The British-born Halberstam calls herself a "trans-butch," and theorizes that the purview called masculine can also apply to women. The patriarchal coupling of "masculine" to "male" has long kept the butch trapped in a heteronormative contradiction. By decoupling this fundamental contradiction and claiming "masculine" for women also, we solve the ancient and misguided notion that a "mannish" woman is somehow wrong. In this post-feminist age, reclaiming the masculine liberates all women, especially butch women.

---

1   Excerpt from my work-in-progress memoir, *Lesbian Nation: The Rise of the Tribe.*

Having solved this sexist riddle, butches began to grow more internally comfortable with ourselves. But more recently, the advent of transgender possibilities challenges the definition of butch once again. Karl Marx said that technology defines the direction of social change. For example, the medical technology known as the birth control pill was not available to the first wave of the Women's Suffrage movement in the US (1848–1920). So the right of women to "control our own bodies" by using birth control or abortion had to wait until the second wave of feminism, the Women's Liberation Movement (1966–present). Those of us who study social change in historical frameworks recognize that political movement-building needs to articulate technologically possible goals. And so it was that the Transgender Movement had to wait for the medical technology of sexual re-assignment surgery to drive a social-change struggle around gender. Technology precedes social change.

THE TRANS CHALLENGE

The ability to physiologically change one's gender has been an option readily available as of the mid-1990s. Modern transgender literature and culture is, in 2010, barely one generation old. The possibility of transitioning from one's given-at-birth gender to the opposite gender calls for a fundamental reinterpretation of previous lesbian butch identity. The possibility of transitioning forces us into a deeper exploration of the intersection of butch and transgender and calls forth the question of alliance. Although political activists might be temporarily disturbed—given that their task is to define and format our civil rights agenda—transitioning as a nuanced recognition of the human condition is something to celebrate, not fear.

TOWARD A FEMINIST UNDERSTANDING OF BUTCH

Because of these new understandings, a segment of the younger generation now call themselves butch but might not identify as lesbian or even female. Many of them are changing their female first names to more androgynous or male first names. Name-changing is not new—butches of the 1950s frequently changed their first names, but today we see the younger butches often identifying with male pronouns, having chest surgery, living as men, and taking medical testosterone. So what does butch mean today that it could not mean before feminism and before the option to transition?

For feminists and womanists who grew up in the Women's Liberation Movement, and for young women today who identify as feminist, this radical expansion of butch necessitates new thinking. In attempting to build a political movement, a dominant strain of 1970s lesbian feminism defined all things male and masculine as the root of patriarchal society and therefore oppressive. Lesbian feminism's great ideological gifts—the ideation of woman-power, of women living in a world without male privilege and heterosexual assumption and the creation of a separate lesbian counter-culture—remain strong and viable. But lesbian feminism's short-sightedness in writing off butch and femme as an "aping" of heterosexuality was a narrow and falsely constructed error. Lesbian feminism did not recognize butch-femme as an indigenous lesbian balancing of the yin and yang principle within the pair. A philosophical worldview as significant as lesbian feminism should not continue to perpetuate this heterosexist mistake. Every few generations, important ideologies—such as Marxism, capitalism, or feminism—need to brush off the cobwebs of short-sighted imagination and update themselves or run the risk of becoming irrelevant. Radical feminism must be open to new interpretations of masculine women, butches, and transgendered people. Feminism needs to recognize that not all of humanity neatly fits into the male-female binary, especially since radical lesbian feminism calls for the erasure of the gender binary as a construct built to preserve male power. Feminism should reassess the butch as a genderqueer radical.

Queer theory and transgender politics call upon us to reevaluate yesterday's limited ideology. Are all things masculine really anti-woman? The Millennium Generation answers this feminist denunciation with a clear "no." The existence of tens of thousands of biologically born women and trans-women who walk between the genders proves this.

I am in a doctor's office in 1983, in West Hollywood, California, with Dr Bruce Cohen, an openly gay man who would be dead the following year from AIDS. We are both thirty-four.

> *Cohen*: "I was running some tests, and guess what I found? Do you know you have an unusually high level of testosterone?"
>
> *Me*: "No, I didn't. Maybe that's why I've had to shave since I was twenty-three."
>
> *Cohen*: "Yes, that's why. Do you want me to change it, lower it?"
>
> *Me*: "What would that mean?"
>
> *Cohen*: "That you wouldn't have to shave anymore. And a lot of other more subtle sexual changes."
>
> *Me*: "I like my sexuality exactly like it is. Would I still be gay and butch?"
>
> *Cohen*: "Yes, I would think so! But it changes sexual aggression and receptivity and ..."
>
> *Me*: "My relations with women?"
>
> *Cohen*: "Yes ..."
>
> *Me*: "Oh, no! I'm doing just fine in that department."
>
> *Cohen*: "Okay. Leave everything as is?"
>
> *Me*: "Yes, leave it. I am who I am."

THE FORMER MEANING OF BUTCH

Among the foundational issues of the new butch renaissance is an inter-generationally driven disagreement over what it means to be butch. Butch used to be understood as one among several lesbian-specific identities, a phenomenon within lesbian culture, and a concept that refers to a code of masculine behaviours and gender performativity among gay women. A butch is born as a female, but a female who bridges the feminine and the masculine in that she genetically and later culturally acquires body language and clothing presentation, thought processes, and behaviours, sexistly categorized as "masculine." A butch is a woman who looks at femme women with what the queer black British filmmaker Campbell X erotically calls "the butch gaze." A butch genetically retains a great many of the emotional characteristics of a woman, and therefore a butch was sometimes called a "she/he" or a shaman—"one who walks between the genders." A butch is a human being who is both female and male. As I said almost two decades ago in *The Persistent Desire: A Femme-Butch Reader*, a butch is a "recombinant mixture of yin and yang energy. Like recombinant DNA, a butch is an elusive, ever-resynthesizing energy field, a lesbian laser that re-knits the universes of male and female." A woman could be butch without ever having slept with another woman. Growing up identifying with Rhett Butler instead of Scarlett O'Hara or Iron Man rather than Wonder Woman, butches are socialized from childhood to see ourselves as equal to men in terms of power. We later learn that the real world doesn't agree with us. This disparity causes "butch rage," which functions as both armour and an emotional disability that most teen butches grow up with. Butch rage is instilled in us out of the dissonance of having been born masculine females in a sexist world. As pre-pubescent children, butches feel we are the equals of our sibling brothers and fathers, but in high school we receive cinematic, literary, and social messages from our peers and families that this is not true. We are told that men and women are different, that the difference is power, and that women are inherently less powerful. Because of these messages, many butches internalize a false and sexist sense of shame about being female. As sexist messages decrease (at least in the western world), young masculine-of-centre women today grow up with less butch rage and the ability to dually validate *both* their masculine and female-bodied selves.

By high school, trouble was brewing in my life. Girlfriends at school had boyfriends they "flirted" with, and I hadn't a clue what the big deal was. Teachers started calling me "a ruffian" and telling my mom that I ought to learn "grooming."

"I feel naked with my socks down to my ankles!" and "Grooming is for dogs!" I wailed as Mom stopped me before I could escape the house. High school is hell for tomboys. Tomboys under thirteen are "cute." Those who are still tomboys after thirteen are labelled "weird."

In high school, the best-friend vacancy my brother Billy had left was filled by a series of prom-queens-in-training. To these girls, I represented safety, someone who would always listen and never compete. The role of prom-queen's-best friend provided good cover from the exigencies of dating. Sharon, Margaret, Cathy—they all simply arranged dates for me with the buddies of their boyfriends. It never mattered to me who my guy or her guy was: that I got to double-date with my prom queen on Saturday nights was enough.

I suppose I went underground in high school, as I would again later, in my lefty days when we warred against the military-industrial Establishment. In high school, I was fighting the religious establishment of nuns who seemed to be screaming "Girl! Girl! Girl!" at me.

I learned to fake it long before I learned to enjoy it with women. I faked writing notes to boys, because Margaret did. I faked losing Ping-Pong to Mike, because Sharon said, "That's what girls do." I buried my grief and myself—everywhere but on the baseball field.[2]

---

2 Jeanne Córdova, "A Tale of Two Brothers" in *Tomboys! Tales of Dyke Derring-Do*, eds, Lynne Yamaguchi and Karen Barber. (New York: Alyson Books, 1995).

THE NEW MEANING OF BUTCH

Butch is no longer an exclusively lesbian identity. Butch has grown to include various non-gender-based identities. As S. Bear Bergman says, "Butch is a noun," no longer merely an adjective.

Attending the first all-butch political event of my life, the BUTCH Voices inaugural Conference in Oakland, California, in August 2009, I witnessed a new masculine continuum of butch identity, a broadcloth of butchdom I had never seen before. The conference attracted 400 butch-identified souls (and their allies, both femme and transmen). The occasion was a unique mix in terms of both race and class and brought together three generations of lesbian, queer, and trans-masculine identified butch people. One workshop, "Bulldaggers: A Discussion for Woman-identified, Female-Pronoun-Using Butches," excluded butches who didn't identify as women. (And yes, there were a lot of noun butches, mostly between the ages of eighteen and thirty-five, who didn't identify as women or relate to the word "lesbian.") Another workshop, "The Possibilities and Pleasures of Faggot Play," spoke to butches who sleep with other butches and "faggot butches" who see themselves as similar to gay men. "Butch Survival: Mentoring Gender" was pitched toward trans-masculine butches. By the second day, I realized I was part of a new historic realignment; I saw that the word "butch" can be removed from the male-female binary and exist as its own gender.

This expanded definition of butch now places us on a continuum of masculinity that begins with female-identified tombois at one end, and ends with trans-male identified people at the other. In the spirit of discussion, I offer a chart that visually explains the new politics of butch.

A POST-TRANS BUTCH CONTINUUM

straight women		
lesbians		Female Gender
some gay men		
burlesque lesbians	Femme	
lipstick lesbians		
divas		Feminine Spectrum
power femmes		
tomboys		
androgynous butch w/a twist		
jock butch		Butch Gender
soft ('yin') butch		(lesbian)
genderqueer		
boi		
female pronoun using butch	Butch	
macha or butcha		Masculine Spectrum
trans-butch		
stud		
classic butch ('yang')		Trans-masculine
aggressive		Gender
daddy/papacita		
trans-masculine butch	Transmasculine	
male-pronoun using butch	people	
drag king		
T-taking butches		
Trans Men		Male Gender
metrosexual men	FtM (female to male)	
straight men (some of)		

What are the implications of such a chart?

This continuum does not position "the female" as necessarily feminine, nor "the male" as necessarily masculine. Membership in today's LGBTQ community teaches us that this heterosexual concept is false.

Furthermore, one of the positive, although politically messy, implications is that "butch" is more accurately placed within the spectrum of genderized human behaviour, instead of marginalized as a hidden wing of lesbianism. Psycho-behavioural "accuracy" is always good, even though this new definition might cause some apoplexy in the women's and LGBTQ movements.

It's critical not to project onto this linear chart a value system which glorifies masculinity. We instinctively read from left to right, but one could just as accurately view this continuum flipped from right to left with the feminine spectrum on the far right, seemingly positioned as the most positive. (There remain many things wrong with men and the patriarchal construct which has so wrecked the world and the lives of women around the planet.)

One of the many new attempts at definition I hear is a phrase which groups all "masculine of centre people"—butch women and non-gender identified butches—together. (The phrase "masculine of centre people" was coined by B. Cole, founder of San Francisco's Brown Boi Project, a social justice organization which seeks to bring together all masculine-of-centre people, including men of colour, and recently adopted and popularized by BUTCH Voices.) Dozens of young butch organizations in America are in the process of grappling with and trying to find appropriate language for the thorny new politics of butch. And nowhere were the new politics of butch more discussed and played out than at the four regional conferences sponsored by the organization BUTCH Voices in 2010.[3] These gatherings of over a thousand

---

3 "The mission of BUTCH Voices is to enhance and sustain the well-being of all women, female-bodied, and trans-identified individuals who

butch women and masculine-of-centre people in Dallas, New York City, Portland, and Los Angeles signalled the national infancy of the new butch movement. Many attendees resonated with the words "masculine of centre" and used it with joy, as if to say, "Finally, a new way to say butch!" After all, most butches have always known we are masculine of something! (Since "butch" has had historical association with white women, the term "masculine of centre" is also meant to appeal to women of colour.) Yet an equal number of other butches asked, "Masculine of what centre? Are we referring to the 'centre' of the gender binary that we are trying to erase, not support?!"

And so we continue to debate and move forward.

HOLDING THE BUTCH LINE

Today's butch is being called upon to re-define her-, or himself to allow an alliance with trans-masculine people. On one hand, we see some butch women respond to this call with a strong rejection to any such alliance. But many butches, especially those younger than forty, don't feel the luxury to say "no" when so many of their friends and peers are transitioning. At the Oakland BUTCH Voices Conference, the workshop "Bulldaggers" led by Sasha T. Goldberg, was packed with female-affirming butches. When planning her workshop Goldberg told us that she wondered if there were any woman-identified butches other than herself left in the world. The impassioned discussion that

---

are masculine of center. We achieve this by providing programs that build community, positive visibility and empower us to advocate for our whole selves inclusive of and beyond our gender identity and sexual orientation. Our community is vast and growing and we have many identifications that resemble what the world knows as our 'butchness.' We recognize our diversity as having a foundation rooted in butch heritage. We welcome the ongoing development of movements intentionally and critically inclusive of our gender variant community. BUTCH Voices is a social justice organization that is race and gender inclusive, pro-womanist and feminist."

followed centred on butch women's confusion and fear that so many peers were transitioning. Young dykes from the Bay Area said, "I'm the only one from my crowd who hasn't transitioned!" Some expressed fear that butch was "becoming a truncated species," that there would there be no such thing as a butch in future generations. Others, like the co-editor of this book, Ivan E. Coyote, said her personal solution was not to transition but hit the gym and build up her chest and biceps. Lonely butches, particularly from Los Angeles—the lipstick-lesbian capital of the US—said they couldn't find other butches. I said we had to embrace our transitioning brothers as allies, but that butch women are firmly in the genetic pool as a balancing tool within lesbian couples. Butch-identified lesbians have always existed, and we will always exist.

In attempting to lay out some of the groundwork for a new politics of butch, I want to say where I, as a life-long butch, lesbian author, and queer organizer, stand on these issues. In these complex times, I've recently felt compelled to go within once more and look at whether or not I see myself as male, female, or trans. As a college kid in the early 1970s, I never had choices, never heard about "sexual reassignment surgery." If I got to chose again, would I transition—adopt a male pronoun, have chest surgery, live as a man? Tortured by doubt, I felt dislocation and confusion. But I had to look; I had to re-decide. These months were a painful, but interesting, process. I thought back to the time when I took testosterone for seven months during menopause as an alternative hormone replacement therapy, one with less risk for breast cancer (which my mother had). For a month, I'd lived with the near-manic rush of testosterone in my veins. I thought about living a life without my lesbian feminist community. What did I want? Who was I at my core?

During my search, I came to feel, in my body and mind— and with lots of input from my best transman friend and his friends—that butch women like me and trans-masculine people are different at our core. Our perceptions of ourselves and our psychological relationships to maleness and femaleness are not the same. While some of this difference may be generational or culturally acquired, I've come to believe that this core difference is a genetic difference—that is, it is of the body. I know of no scientific evidence that precisely pinpoints this different core, but I believe someday there will be evidence; we will know the exact how-and-why of gender-based identity.

In the meantime, my body, heart, and soul choose to hold the traditional butch line. I am a masculine, cross-gendered, lesbian-identified, feminist butch. To me, choosing to join the male gender would be a downwardly mobile abortion of my psyche. Yet, as a self-actualized butch woman, I greet trans-butches with an open heart and mind. Butch women were once treated as the cross-dressing lepers of the lesbian community. It's simply not politically or personally moral to treat our transitioning sisters or brothers in the discriminatory way we ourselves were once treated.

I believe that the Genderqueer Movement offers the LGBTQ Movement a more radical future than the Transgender Movement. The Genderqueer Movement asks us to imagine a world without the binary of male and female. Every woman or man is invited to find her or his own messy, but honest, identity. In a truly genderqueer society, where do we locate gayness, lesbianism, and the butch? Already we can see, on prime-time television, that the relationship between straight men and women has totally changed since the sexist *Mad Men* 1950s and '60s. In our exploration of gender, queer people have forced the heterosexual and homosexual worlds to re-think their male-female gender binary.

The butch renaissance of the twenty-first century means liberation for me. I now have the freedom to experience a new lesbian brotherhood among my masculine-of-centre butch peers, FtM, and young trans-masculine friends. After years of living in the butch-femme underground-bar closet of the late 1960s, followed by a decade of quasi-pretending to be androgynous in the lesbian-feminist 1970s, yet another ten years of oppression in the lipstick-lesbian 1980s, and, in the 1990s, trying to sort out the meaning of the trans revolution—I am finally free to return to the four year old who threw away the doll and jumped on the tricycle. I choose again to hold the butch line.

JEANNE CÓRDOVA's life and writings can be found at *jeannecordova.com*. She has been an open butch for forty-two years and is the elder board member of BUTCH Voices. Córdova served as Conference Chair of BUTCH Voices, Los Angeles. Her second memoir, *When We Were Outlaws; Love & Revolution in the 1970s*, is forthcoming from Alyson Books in 2011. Previous books, *Kicking the Habit; A Lesbian Nun Story*, and *Sexism; It's a Nasty Affair* are available thru Amazon. Her butch/femme essays appear in *Persistent Desire: A Femme-Butch Reader, Lesbian Nuns: Breaking the Silence*, and *Dagger: On Butch Women*, and numerous other LGBTQ anthologies. Her work as a pioneer political activist and lesbian publisher appears in gay history books such as *Gay L.A.: A History of Sexual Outlaws, Power Politics, & Lipstick Lesbians, Out for Good: The Struggle to Build a Gay Rights Movement in America*, and *Unspeakable: The Rise of the Gay and Lesbian Press in America*. Córdova lives and writes beneath the shadows of the Sierra Nevada mountains, northeast of her beloved Los Angeles, with six Mexican pets and one South African femme spouse of twenty years.

Femme Cowboy

Rae Spoon

It wasn't until I had brought the axe down a few times on the
log without splitting it that I realized that the people in a circle
around me were laughing. I had been told that we needed more
firewood for the cabin stove that night, so I plodded eagerly outside into the wet Gulf Island air, happy to feel needed. It took
the effort of my entire body to raise the full-sized axe above my
head, but the inertia of its fall seemed to have no impact on the
wood. Noticing them smirking at my failure, I realized that my
friends didn't need the wood as much as they wanted to see me
try to chop it. One of them had witnessed my previous attempts
and wanted to share the visual image with the group. I was once
told that I look like a "petite logger" by a stranger, and I can't
find a better way to describe my appearance in that moment. It
was another benchmark in a long list of grievances I have committed against the stereotypes of masculinity and butchness—
despite my best attempts.

Raised as a girl in a fundamentalist Christian home in Alberta, I was not allowed to play hockey, wear pants to church, or
take shop class. I remember longing for a hockey stick, angrily
scratching at my leotards in the church choir, and illicitly ham-
mering nails into objects behind our garage. If I had been born
male in Alberta, I would have been subject to a hyper-masculine
regimen of welding, truck-fixing, and patriarchal dominance. I
can infer by my preferences, in my state of relative freedom now,
that I would have hated that as well. On either side, the strictly
enforced binary leaves me bereft of a comfortable role. I can't
even say as a transgendered man that I regret not being assigned
male in that environment; that would have come with its own
flavour of violence. I could look back and blame my awkwardness with being raised female on the detail that I was, in fact,

male and should have been treated as such. However, I believe it was the strictness of the constraints and lack of options that pushed my desire to engage in some of those so-called masculine activities. Now that I am fully allowed to do all of those things, but rarely bother, is proof of that.

Last year, on a whim, I took an online test that purported to situate me on the butch-femme spectrum and received the result of "high femme." I was expecting to land somewhere in the middle, but there was some truth to the result. I find that I am more often read as a butch/masculine person in the community than a femme. My grooming is fastidious, but I lean toward male clothes in the binary of fashion. I travel with a mini iron and a blow drier, but I am often placed in the male line by security people at airports, grinning down my pink dress shirt at whatever poor man has to pat me down. Last summer my shorts were dangerously short, but in Montreal, I saw many other men with the bottom of their pockets showing. I am a high-maintenance date. I remember once convincing one of my girlfriends to carry me in her arms over a mud puddle because I was wearing my good shoes, and another time to pull a kayak onto the land before I would get out (for the same reason). The surprising results of the online test helped me put the words together for what I have been trying to reconcile for years: that I am both femme and a trans man.

When I came out as trans in Vancouver in 2001, I had been a part of a lesbian scene (or, more accurately, a self-identified dyke community). There was not a lot of room for trans men because most people identified as women who only dated other women. Bisexuals faced stigmatization when they strayed from the perceived homosexual side of things. When I started to bind my chest, I was confronted about disliking my female body. Did this mean I hated being female? I had no answers; I experienced a considerable amount of discomfort in my body, but was confused about what that meant. It was hard to get people to remember to call me by the male pronoun within the community, and I didn't feel confident enough to request it in any other situation. Overwhelmed, I leaned more heavily on the only thing that had always been consistent in my life, which was music. I decided that my musical identity was something I was more adept at than being male or female. I focused all of my efforts on that, and it became what I mainly sought out in a community.

In 2001, friends of mine were going to the Jazz program at Malaspina College in Nanaimo, on Vancouver Island in British Columbia. I barely had enough money to take the ferry there from Vancouver. So, once there, I would stay for relatively long stretches. I spent my days practising guitar and eating peanut butter sandwiches while the others went to classes. In the evenings, they would teach me the theory they were learning. They identified as straight men, but I encountered very little resistance from them when it came to sharing their side of the binary (because I had mainly dated women at that point, I slipped into a straight identity easily). They respected that I identified as male and called me by the male pronoun. I melded into the group despite our disparate histories and, because they were introducing me with male pronouns, a lot of their friends perceived me as a male without too many questions. This was the longest amount of time I ever spent passing outside of the queer community and, at that point and without many allies, I felt a lot more comfortable hiding my history than defending my choices. Passing came with its own set of stressors. I changed the way I dressed, talked, and walked to increase my chances of being perceived as male.

One of my friends from the group of boys was another country singer named Rueben. One night, we decided to hitchhike back to Nanaimo from a show we'd played in Courtenay (about an hour-and-a-half away) and got a ride from the bar to the highway. I was wearing tight Wrangler jeans, a blue plaid work jacket, and a red-and-white trucker cap. I had shaved my hair down to a quarter-inch long a few days earlier. Rueben was almost a foot taller than me and had on almost the same outfit, except that he had shoulder length brown hair. As we waited in the dark for a ride, it got colder. We drew symbols in the dirt on the side of the road for good luck, scuffing the dewy ground with our boots, acting brave for each other and fighting off the quiet.

A maroon truck shone headlights in our eyes and was going so fast that it looked like it was going to pass us. It stopped suddenly and sent us running up to it with our guitars, fifty feet further along the highway. Rueben opened the passenger door and climbed in. I clambered up and onto the far end of the long bench seat. A trucker in his forties, dressed oddly similarly to us, was seated with both hands on the wheel. The usual hitch-hiking small talk ensued. Rueben told him we were musicians and that we had just played a show. The trucker said he had a son who played music in Vancouver. When he asked our names, I instinctually lowered my voice and grunted "Rae." Rueben sensed my anxiety and told the trucker that I was his little brother, just to solidify my position. The trucker shot a look over at me and said, "I had a baby face when I was young too."

We stopped about half an hour later at an unattended weigh station, and the driver pulled the truck onto the scale and got out. We waited inside silently. When he got back, he put the truck into gear and reached under his seat, pulling out a can of Molson Canadian beer. I am not an advocate for drinking and driving by any means, but I had seen my uncles pull out cans of beer while driving down the highway, so I wasn't totally unnerved. We were close to Nanaimo, so I pushed these thoughts out of my mind and focused on the road. Thickening patches of street lamps were beginning to cast lines of light across our faces. The trucker looked over at me again, and I sensed there would be more questions. I was twenty, but I didn't look much older than fourteen. I knew it was suspicious that I was out playing music in bars and hitchhiking in the middle of the night. But Rueben kept him talking about trucking and music. In Nanaimo, I jumped out of the truck exhilarated, feeling like we'd gotten away with something. But the story we told the trucker wasn't entirely untrue. That night, I felt like I was Rueben's brother; he had gone out of his way to make me feel safe just as I would have done for my own brothers.

Yet my new acceptance as male among my Nanaimo musician friends was contentious. I began to notice the gap that my friends perceived between themselves and women. Cringing when the bravado grew high, I felt like they were putting women down to look better than them. More and more, I would get swept into performing narratives of separation. My acceptance as a male was contingent on my performance as a normative male. I felt conflicted about occupying this role when sexism became an obvious part of fulfilling it. My heart broke when the conditions for my acceptance became apparent. I made a conscious decision to leave and move back to Vancouver.

Over the next eight years, a lot of people came out as trans. Parts of the community in Vancouver became more open to trans people and allies who accepted them. I experienced acceptance as a male without hiding my history. People would often get my pronoun right without an effort on my part to convince them I was male. I slowly shifted my gender presentation. I knew I identified as male, but I rebelled against upholding stereotypes. I stopped controlling my speaking voice, which has a tendency to go very high when I'm excited. Pink became my new favourite colour, and I was known to put on makeup while at parties. I met a lot more trans people on my travels and found that there were indeed other male-identified trans people who also wanted to dance around to ABBA wearing spandex. My sexuality became more fluid. Feeling my gender identity to be respected, I became more confident and grew interested in genderqueer relationships that weren't based on the binary.

I love the butches and the femmes of all gender identities in my life. My butch female-assigned friends let me tag along like a gay little brother even if I don't like getting grease on my hands or know how to drive. We face a lot of the same challenges and can bond over our experiences in women's washrooms and how hard it is to find men's clothes that fit us. I admire their toughness with a soft edge and how strong they are. A special part of my heart goes out to butch women who are older than me; they have made it possible for me to express my gender as I do by standing up to discrimination through being themselves during far more challenging times.

My femme friends let me be one of "the girls." I love screeching around the women's change rooms with them or trying on lip gloss and talking about relationships. Being a femme woman means you are on the radar for a lot of attention that I have never experienced. I have never been yelled at so much walking down the road as I have when one of my friends is dressed up in high femme attire. I am proud to trundle along beside them in my oxfords, blazer, and tie, our heels tapping together while we fill the night with sassy comments. Femmes are sometimes made to feel invisible as queers, but that allows them to change people's notions about what queer is and gives them a platform to show the world how strong women can be. Some of the toughest, most femme women I know are transgendered, and I feel a special bond with them.

When I reflect on what has made it possible for me to be fluid with my gender presentation and sexuality, I know that a lot of it is social support. I could have never imagined the options that have opened up for me since I left Alberta. Ideally, the queer community formed to make space for as many combinations of gender and sexuality as exist. I hope that the space for diversity will continue to open up. I am proud to be known as a femme trans person who engages in genderqueer relationships, but when I find myself crying with a butch friend or watching a femme parallel park on top of a snow bank, I know that we are all changing combinations of many things, with a fluidity that is very human.

RAE SPOON is a transgendered indie-folk musician living in Montreal. He tours in Canada, the USA, Europe, and Australia. Rae has released five solo albums and was nominated for the Polaris Prize in 2009. He is currently working on a book of short stories about growing up in Alberta.

Futch

Thoughts from the Borderlands

Elaine Miller

I have been identifying as a futch for about seventeen years now, and the most frequent question I get asked is not how it feels to actively play with the basic tenets of the butch-femme dynamic, nor do I receive queries on how I choose footwear before I leave the house. I never hear the blunt questions I expect, like: Boxers or panties? Chapstick or lipstick? No, despite how long the term has been in circulation, what I get is the simple request for definition. What the hell is a futch?

Futch: A lesbian, dyke, or other variety of queer woman who possesses or displays qualities and social identifiers of both butch and femme.

That doesn't really cover it, though. Imagine a new ground-breaking indie film, entitled *A Day in the Life of a Futch*. Our protagonist, "Chris," showers, dithers over pomade or hairspray for her 'do, puts on a sundress, takes her best suit to the cleaners, buys a new toolbox, shops for high heels, goes home, changes into a T-shirt and pants, watches some sports, and then calls her best friend to chat. Just before her hot butch lover arrives for a date, Chris reveals to the audience that she's packing her dick and harness under her jeans. As the door opens, the film does a tasteful slow fade into the credits while the happy couple discovers they wore matching briefs yet again. And, okay, maybe Chris is hamming it up for the cameras by playing to both butch and femme stereotypes, but only a bit, and her flux of gendered intent is quite real.

When it comes to dyke gender, I'm like a kid on a swingset, yelling with glee as I swoop from one extreme to the other, passing through every point in-between as quickly as I can, so I can linger breathlessly at the apogee of femme or butch, back and forth. One of the butchiest butches I know describes me as "some sort of bizarre hybrid," and I take that as the compliment (I think) it is meant to be.

Before we go on, a disclaimer is important, as the reader will be able to concentrate on the concepts presented herein more easily if she's not distracted by political ire:

In explaining futch as existing between the gendered extremes of the butch-femme dynamic, I am not discussing gender in terms of medical or social gender transitioning or traditional male-female roles. I am not attempting to speak for any of our queer sisters who choose not to identify anywhere on that butch–femme spectrum. And in reducing dyke gender expression to a single line with a butch end and a femme end, I realize I'm sketching crudely indeed, but I beg the reader's patience with my intentionally narrow focus. A full and respectful treatment of modern gender politics is beyond the scope of this essay.

To sidestep issues of gender identity, I could turn my back on butch-femme, drop the label "futch," and just use "woman"—or, to remove gender entirely, "person." But that wouldn't describe the joy I find in gendered play and presentation. For me, being futch is not about living in a single spot, in a precise middle ground, wherein I can be androgynous and ambiguous and ambivalent. It's about exploring all the ground I can cover, and embodying every point on the line that feels good to me.

Gendered presentation is socially and sexually triggered, recognised, and supported by other people. When I pet my cat, I possess no particular gender, and if I were the last human alive on a post-apocalyptic world, picking through the rubble of despair, my sexuality would be irrelevant. But when I take a lover, or when I arrive at a queer event and enter my people's social sphere, gender matters.

I'm not on any soapbox, except that I am. Every performative aspect of my futch gender feels political; it's a statement. That's because I field quite a bit of nonsense based on the assumed binary system where one can be either butch or femme, can occupy no place in between, and expectations for how each is permitted to act are fixed in 1950s-style male-female gender roles.

"I hung the door myself. I feel so butch."

"You throw like a girl."

"Don't carry that. Let the butches do it."

"I'm not a femme. I can use tools."

"C'mon, it doesn't hurt that much. Butch up."

My feminist futch self finds journeying through these expectations unpleasant. A moment's thought tells us that a futch, femme, or butch can't be spotted by behaviour alone because there are no solely butch or solely femme activities. Assigning a gender to a behaviour opens up a kettle of logical fallacy, which can be illustrated by the following questions:

If a femme displays a stereotypical butch behaviour, does she gain a butch point while losing a femme point? If she gets a butch-full job, like as a greasemonkey at the local garage, is there a point where she'll be seen as butch? What if she *feels* femme, wears silk stockings on dates with her girlfriend, and refuses to equate possessing mechanical competency with being any gender at all? And what if a butch were to do stereotypical femme behaviours? Suppose a butch in low-slung Levis and cowboy boots and a sharp-barbered haircut were to grow flowers for her own pleasure? What if she liked cooking better than home renovations? Does she gain femme points or lose butch points? At what point does she magically turn into a femme?

If it helps to reframe, please think of the iconic Rosie the Riveter. At what point in her heavy-machinery-making career does she turn into a man? Or is she simply a woman who can do anything she puts her mind and body to?

I respectfully submit that although we (who live in a gender-obsessed world) often ascribe such meanings to them, human behaviours are inherently ungendered. Even penetrative fucking. Even watching sensitive movies. Even, yes, opening doors for other people.

There's a flip side to my don't-you-engender-me politics. For a futch, the things we do that so odiously mark us as masculine or feminine to the outside world become not just stepping stones along the continuum, and not just a system of identifying desire, but also a way to open dialogue about those restrictive expectations. Any social framework, if sufficiently rigid, can be viewed as a cage. It is not my intention to live in a cage or share it with others, but rather to loosen the framework and create room to move, to slide, to swing—to play. But mostly, I don't ever want to hear another poor femme-looking dyke forced to haltingly explain her desire to pitch during sex, as if she were as rare as a unicorn rather than only *slightly* less common than femmes who like to catch instead.

Maybe a futch can be spotted by her clothes. If Tom of Finland had Bettie Page as a roommate, their closets would look like they contained my collection of party outfits, although I'll hasten to add that I bear a physical resemblance to neither. I've often jokingly complained that the biggest problem with being futch is not the blank looks coming my way, the accusations of being unable to make up my mind, or the stubborn pigeonholing as femme if the observer has seen me *even once* in lipstick. It's about finding the right storage options for my less-than-modest collection of steel-toed boots and fancy-ass high heels.

That my wardrobe leans toward sexualized gender archetypes is no accident; the clothes we decide to buy and wear fit our inner selves. From the black leather shell of a silver-toothed biker jacket to the simple sheath of glamour we call an evening gown, our clothes are meant to trap the dyke gaze and send a message. From the exquisite romance of a tight white T-shirt with sleeves rolled up James Dean-style to a tight corset with multiple delicate fastenings indicative of control, we reveal ourselves through our choice of costume. A futch like me has to traverse a complex landscape of gender and keeps a foot in both high camps.

Butch and femme should not be boxes we feel we must stuff

our complex selves into, but rather labels we can choose to slip on like our favourite pair of shit-kickin' boots or our best push-up bra.

This I have in common with other futch women I've spoken to—spending time as my femme self feels right and good, and I revel in the power and pleasure of pushing the expression of my femininity to the extreme, even in those aspects which are physically uncomfortable. High heels, constrictive underwear, and false eyelashes—they're not for the faint of heart. But after a visit with high femme, I find myself thinking wistfully of my butch persona, and after a while in that, I'm ready to mix and match again.

Being futch is about becoming comfortable with dichotomy, both the simple dichotomy of cherry-picking my favourite symbols of sartorial presentation from my Tom-and-Bettie wardrobe and the deeper confusion of upholding the butch-femme dynamic while deconstructing it, of embodying gendered behaviours while denying they exist, of refuting the idea that gender matters while metaphorically stitching oneself a hyper-gendered skin to wear for fun and entertainment. What I'm doing is dipping into a well of oft-poisonous stereotypes about masculinity and femininity that have been used to hold women back and hold them down for centuries, and pulling out the bits from each end that I consider palatable, washable, and exciting. These I transform into fuel for my identity, activity and, most specifically, my sexuality.

The practice of BDSM consists of knowledgeably playing consensual games using highly charged themes such as intense pain, misuse of power, captivity, denial, and shame. These experiences are genuinely awful if encountered in a real-life sense, and anyone deliberately inflicting these things on another is behaving reprehensibly. However, for those so inclined, playing with those powerful emotions and sensations within the safety of a BDSM scene can be likened to taking a satisfying ride on a roller coaster, rather than experiencing the real-life horror of being in a terrible traffic accident and driving over a cliff.

Similarly, when we take a dysfunctional set of social morés and expectations about gender and transform them using a powerful sexual and social alchemy, we queer the hell out of the ancient pull between masculine and feminine. Mindfully played, using the butch-femme continuum to increase the apparent distance between our genders can create a fascinating tension and sense of potential movement, while proximity on the gender continuum (butch-butch and femme-femme pairings) creates a thrilling collision of roles and feelings. On the butch-femme continuum, genderfuck is the game of love that no one needs to lose. And a futch like me is in a perfect position to appreciate the game, since I so eagerly play both sides of the net.

ELAINE MILLER is a writer, sex/kink educator, performer, and professional techdonkey. She's also a femme-futch, dyke-daddy, leatherfreak, drag king spokesqueer with a penchant for being a tea-drinking philosophisin' geek.

Butch-Femme as Spiritual Practice

Thea Hillman

If you know me at all, you know I hate butch-femme. When I was coming up and out as a young queer in San Francisco in the 1990s, butch-femme culture here was so restrictive/prescriptive/constricting, it felt like thinly veiled (by black leather and red lace) internalized oppression. In fact, I called San Francisco's scene a butch-femme prison. Even though I looked girly and my lovers were butchly, I refused to identify as femme. I guess that was a long time ago, because today, at least right now, I'm thinking butch-femme might be the answer to my prayers.

It used to be that I just couldn't get recognized in the community here. I mean, in the 1990s, if you were a femme (or in my case, tended toward girly), and you didn't leave the house looking completely undressed, no one recognized you. Your underclothes needed to be on the outside and there needed to be not much or, better yet, nothing underneath. I'm not saying I didn't play along sometimes, it just felt like I was a little kid playing dress-up with professionals. (In a way I was, since a lot of the hottest girls were dancers and sex workers.) They knew how to work what they had. I didn't totally know what I had, didn't quite have long hair, couldn't quite go all-the-way girl, just couldn't commit. It felt too simple. I wanted complex, and wanted my look to communicate that—and to invite that.

I wanted complexity in my lovers. I didn't want a stone butch. (Yes, I even once said that stone was boring. This is before I'd had it, and long before I knew I was a little stony myself.) I wanted a pretty andro-butch who looked mostly like a boy but would don girl underwear once in a while for kicks. I wanted boys in an occasional tutu. I didn't want them to pay for dinner, didn't want them to open the door for me, and didn't want them to not let me fuck them. They were few and far between, and I was always thankful when they appreciated me and my version of adamantly not-femme queer girl.

Years later, I see that maybe the issue wasn't I that I was hard to recognize, but rather that maybe I was just too hard.

What I didn't realize at the time is that while I was looking for someone who was a lot masculine and a little feminine, I myself was a little feminine and a lot masculine, even if that's not how I looked on the outside. Over the past few years, I've begun to think that this masculinity, which I was so proud of then, might have been getting in the way of me getting what I wanted. Because even though I didn't want my lovers to open the car door for me every time we went somewhere, I did want them to drive sometimes. But I never handed over the keys.

Truth is, when I dated men (people assigned male at birth who accept that gender assignment), I dated soft, soft men. And things usually went nowhere, slowly. And when I dated women (people assigned female at birth who did not accept that gender assignment), I dated the hard ones. And since I was hard, even though I looked soft, it was a lot of rocky stone surfaces striking against one another, which makes for a lot of sparks, but there's not much there to kindle.

Perhaps, just perhaps, butch-femme could come out of retirement, and could perform together, in concert, reunited, in me. Perhaps making everything happen makes nothing happen, because if I really like masculine people, and I think I really do, sometimes I have to let them be masculine.

Maybe butch-femme is about tension, the good kind, the kind sexual tension is made of, where there's space for surprise, where you are not like me, and I am not like you. Maybe it's about push, pull, and balance, within me and between us. I think each person and every relationship needs this, be they boy-girl of any stripe, or boy-boy, girl-girl, or even butch-butch and femme-femme. This is the spiritual part, because it's about dynamic, shifting energies and, ultimately, about power. These days, for me, balance of power isn't about topping and bottoming and what kind of marks to leave; it's about leaving no marks at all.

I guess the reason I'm willing to even think about butch-femme, really consider what it has to offer, is that my relationships have been so far out of balance that I've started looking inward instead of looking across the table. I want balance, first and foremost in myself. I think the feminine—not even the girl, but the feminine and perhaps, dare I say it, the femme in me—needs to fluff her feathers a bit. I'm not just saying this; I want it. I think I need it. I'm writing about it, visualizing it, doing rituals for it. Because maybe the answer to my prayers was right there, staring me in the face and not asking me out the whole time.

THEA HILLMAN is an activist and author of *Depending on the Light* and *Intersex (For Lack of a Better Word)*. For more information, visit *theahillman.com*.

Rethinking High Maintenance

The Queer Fat Femme Guide to Not
Blaming It on the Fact That You Don't
Like High Femmes

Bevin Branlandingham

Backstage at a show I was hosting, burlesque legend World Famous *BOB* told me a story about how a (now former) beau had called her high maintenance.

"I called my drag mom and asked if she thought I was high maintenance. She said 'Of course you are, but you maintain yourself. You're like a classic car; if someone is going to drive a '66 Caddy, they will. If they want a Honda, they should drive a Honda.'"

The rhetoric of what is considered "high maintenance" in our community is judgmental and unfairly targets femmes.

The definition of high maintenance I am working from is something, much like the aforementioned classic car, that takes a lot of work to keep in running order. This can be aesthetic work—makeup, hair care, attention to fashion—or emotional, physical, or intellectual expectations that need to be met in order for the person who is high maintenance to be running in top condition.

In the queer community, there seems to be a very negative value judgment on the so-called high-maintenance feminine aesthetic. There are hundreds of stories of femmes coming out of the closet only to be shamed into an androgynous or butch appearance because they wanted to fit into the lesbian or queer community, but femmephobic people called them not queer enough. There is nothing in my lipstick case that prevents me from being queer, and realizing that took an entirely separate coming-out process.

We should remove the value judgment from the phrase high

maintenance, since it should have nothing to do with anyone other than the person being maintained. Everyone can be high maintenance in their own ways; it's all just a matter of whether or not one person's maintenance is compatible with another person's.

While I acknowledge that I am high maintenance, I don't expect my partners, lovers, or anyone else to bear the brunt of my maintenance. The things that make me high maintenance are often the things that make me a compelling person to be with. I hope that anyone who wanted to date me or be my friend would be excited about the shows I put on, the art that I create, and the other amazing whirlwinds that happen around me—not to mention how fabulous I look while doing these things. The most work that manifests for lovers of mine is a high-impact social schedule.

I do admit to often running late, but that has more to do with my propensity for online social networking applications and my lack of time-consciousness than how high maintenance I am. If someone is a stickler for being on time, has to wait for me, and considers my lateness too high maintenance, we are probably not maintenance-compatible.

As a woman with high self-esteem and a lot of confidence, I probably require a lot less emotional work and support than a typical partner. I am really low maintenance in a lot of ways. Since I am in touch with my emotions and my body, I need less reassurance, and I know what I want. Having to play a guessing game about what someone wants or needs can take a lot of time and be extremely high maintenance. Most of the powerhouse femmes I know are, in fact, pretty self-sustaining. The most high-maintenance thing about going out with us is scheduling dates!

In the queer community, femmes are often stereotyped as high maintenance, but let's not forget that butches/boys/bois/men can also require just as much if not more preening and primping as femmes. My ex, a genderqueer named Seth, required forty-five minutes *after* her shower on her hair and fashion choices each day. She looked good, though, and I always appreciated it.

Countless femmes have been told by prospective dates that they "just don't date femmes." Often this is accompanied by an explanation that femmes are too high maintenance, and they don't have the kinds of resources required to date a femme. In the past, I accepted this excuse. While you cannot change someone's preference for or against femmes (and I am certainly not going to argue myself into someone's bed—I don't chase once I hear, "no"), frankly, "I don't date femmes" is a flimsy excuse and used far too often as something to hide behind when the true reasons for breaking things off have nothing to do with femme identity.

Femme, after all, comes in a myriad of forms. Femme is fat, skinny, born boy, born girl, born whatever, wears high heels, stompy boots, flats, sneakers, and boots at a construction site. Femme always wears makeup. Femme never wears makeup. Femme surprises you. Femme is emotionally giving, and femme is emotionally needy. Femme is emotionally stone. Femme is pretty middle-of-the-road, actually, but sometimes has Seasonal Affective Disorder (SAD).

In the same way that I believe there is no one right way to be femme, I refuse to further support anyone's blanket assertion that they "don't like femmes." I've met enough different kinds of femmes to know that there is undoubtedly a femme out there for everyone.

There are those who say "I just don't do the butch-femme *thing.*" Oh, honey, me neither. I cannot stand anything compulsory, and if someone is doing chivalry out of a sense of *role* or some antiquated obligation, I can smell it a mile away. I like people who treat me right because they like to make other people feel good. Chivalry is not exclusive to boys or butches; I know plenty of chivalrous femmes who are sweet, caring, and nurturing, regardless of gender presentation.

It is not the 1950s anymore. While butch-femme couplings

are, of course, alive and well, there is no governing body telling you how you have to be if you are in a butch-femme partnership. (If there is, please direct them to me, as I'd like to have a lively debate on my podcast).

Femme, for me, is stand-alone. It does not rely on my partnership with anyone—butch, genderqueer, trans, or other gender permutations. Identity should not rely on who you happen to be engaging in sexual relations with at any particular moment. If it did, far more people would be "Hitachi-Magic-Wand Sexual" than anything else.

I date a lot of different kinds of people, and that occasionally includes femmes. While I have a few preferred "types," there are plenty of people I have been attracted to who embodied the characteristics I find attractive in extremely different ways. A bad experience with one femme, after all, does not mean that the way she/he acted can be used to predict how another femme will act in a relationship. If we used that same filter on lesbians as a whole, no lesbian would ever date again!

I encourage people who are using the generalized "I don't date femmes" excuse to consider the following (and I say this to every queer in the dating pool with all the gentle, loving, kind, I-know-this-work-is-hard sweetness I can muster):

1. If you are not into someone, try just saying, "I'm not feeling chemistry for you."
2. If you are not feeling emotionally available, try doing the work you need to do on yourself before you start dating.
3. Recognize that dating someone who is much like you—a doppelbanger—(for example, when you are a genderqueer who only dates genderqueers) is sometimes a way to default to what is easy and familiar.
4. Redefine what you mean by "high maintenance" and articulate the ways in which you find someone's

relationship needs hard for you to meet.

5. Think about the ways in which femme-phobia and anti-femme bias might have more to do with internalized misogyny, fear of loss of power, loss of visibility, and other issues of marginalization in the queer community than being just a "preference."

6. Remember that being queer is about having choices and a non-default sexuality (as opposed to the hetero-sexual paradigm).

7. If you have never dated a femme before, challenge yourself to look past your perception of a person's identity and at their characteristics as a human being instead. See if you have a "road block" to being attracted to femmes, persons of certain races, ages, body types/ weights, or transition status, persons with dis/abilities, or any other characteristic that might have to do with your own unexamined biases.

I understand that some people genuinely aren't into certain gender presentations or body types. But don't forget that broad-ening your horizons beyond compulsory ideas of gender roles is arguably the best part about being a queer!

BEVIN BRANLANDINGHAM is "an ultra-rad warrior for self-acceptance" (*Autostraddle.com*). She is the host and producer of *FemmeCast: The Queer Fat Femme Podcast Guide to Life*. She is a flamboyant femmecee, writer, drag king, and burlesque and comedy performer. She is Co-Head Madam of the Femme Family (the New York chapter of the Femme Mafia), on the steering committee for the Fat and Queer conference, and the media committee for the Femme Conference. In 2008, Bevin received a commen-dation from the Mayor of Jersey City for her work with the LGBT commu-nity. Her writing has been published in numerous periodicals, and she has performed throughout North America. Her mission is to make the world a safe place for people to love themselves, regardless of their marginaliza-tions. Her website (including blog, calendar of events, and workshops) is found at *queerfatfemme.com*.

38 B

Sailor Holladay

I haven't always hated my tits. Before they grew in, I sometimes pretended the corners of skin between the top of my chest and the crease of my armpits were my breasts. Soon they were tiny and they itched. I was five years old, and on an exercise bike in the church basement when I squeezed my nipples while pedalling back and forth to Kermit the Frog's "The Rainbow Connection." My chest belonged to me, then. By the age of ten, the boys were telling me what to do with it: "You really should wear a bra."

"Why?"

"Because if you don't start wearing one I'm gonna have to hold 'em myself."

Even my mother speculated with a leer: "Our family's boobs must skip a generation."

"What do you mean, Mom?"

"Well, my granny was flat, my mom was buxom, I'm flat, and you're stacked."

Looking down, I saw Mom was right. Below my chin, my doom was budding.

I turned thirteen, and Mom said, "As long as your breasts are bigger than your belly, you won't look fat."

"But Mom, I'm not fat."

"No, look here," she said, and grabbed the skin that peeked out between my shirt and my jeans. "This is fat." *Mom thinks I'm disgusting.*

The warning cemented itself in my nightly routine. As my stomach swelled, I prayed: "Please, God, let my chest grow too." In bed, I laid on my back so my tummy would look flat.

I hadn't always been fat. "Fat" didn't become a bad word until a few years after I ran around the house with nothing but shorts on, my tummy hanging over the waistband. My healthy appetite fueled my little body's activities then. Once I was a teen, however, the more my mom criticized my weight, the more weight I gained.

"If you don't lose weight, you'll never find a boyfriend," Mom reminded me.

Okay, I'll eat more, I thought, hoping this would keep boys away. But the catcalls increased. Men couldn't care less that I was fat. They knew that fat stomachs, arms, and thighs were often part of the big-breast package. And they thought I was starved for attention. "You're a big girl," they would say as they tried to wrap themselves around me. Early on, my chest was looked at and fondled without my consent. Guys ignored my face and went straight for my breasts. I thought it was my fault when I was groped. Covering my chest as much as possible, I tried to reduce its come-hither qualities. Hooded sweatshirts were a good solution to the problem of cleavage.

At fourteen, I got my first girlfriend. I was femme to her butch. I don't think I'd ever felt anything as nice as the back of her shaved head. She would lay with her head on my lap, and I would run my finger under the back of her sports bra and up to the nape of her neck. It was calming. She didn't think of me as a fat girl or as a pair of boobs. She thought of me as me, and that was nice.

At sixteen, inspired by my girlfriend and other queer kids around me, I left home for good and shaved my head too. The waist-length hair that I felt was required to be female in my family was gone. Although my teachers were taken aback by my haircut, I started to be listened to. My thoughts and beliefs were what they paid attention to. My shaved head became synonymous with a "don't-fuck-with-me" attitude as well as with being butch. All of a sudden, I was tough shit at my high school, the defender of all things righteous. I spent most of my nights alone, but sometimes curious straight girls and I would pretend we were older than we were, smoke weed, and make out.

At nineteen, I came out as trans. In a community of people who were choosing hormones and surgery to alter their bodies, I also chose these methods to alter mine. My queer, effeminate masculinity was not represented as a diagnostic option by the DSM-IV. One day I walked into my gender therapist's office with a pair of pink tennis shoes on. "Sailor, why are you wearing those? You might want to tone down your flamboyance—at least around me," she said. *Or what, you won't prescribe hormones for me?*

I was encouraged by my therapist and my friends to "tone down" my emotional self as well. "Feminine" parts of me were sacrificed in order that I might pass as male. While it was time-consuming to physically alter myself so I could pass, it was even more emotionally exhausting trying to conform to behaviours that are perceived as masculine.

At age twenty, I weighed 250 pounds. I got a breast reduction. My transition to male had begun a few months earlier and included bi-weekly shots of testosterone. My society and queer community spoke in unison: "Men don't have breasts." I wasn't sold on being a man, but knew for sure I didn't want to be a woman—especially not one with 42 DD breasts. With my insurance, the $10,000 breast-reduction surgery would only cost me $100. A double mastectomy—which insurance didn't cover—was the more desirable choice for FtMs, but I didn't have the money, so it was not an option.

As insurance coverage for breast reduction was contingent upon my being a woman, I became preoccupied with trying to conceal my trans-ness during the pre-surgery hospital visits. I was afraid the doctor might notice my budding facial hair or deepening voice, but the invisibility of trans people apparently made these changes less visible than I thought.

"I would really like As, or the smallest size possible," I begged the doctor while trying to keep my cool.

"I'm sorry, but your breasts have to be proportionate to the rest of your body. You're too overweight to have A cups and look normal," she shrugged. *What's normal?* my whole body wanted to ask her. I settled for B cups.

A few lost hours later, I came out of the operating room seven pounds lighter. I felt free. The next morning, the nurse unwrapped my soiled bandages before she drained the tubes that came out of the sides of my body. My new chest was revealed.

"They're perky!" the nurse squeaked. So much for being a boy.

For the next three years, I was often perceived as male. I spent a lot of time trying to get my "pecs" to blend into my other fat. Binders were uncomfortable, so I tried to get away with the fat-men-have-breasts look. When perceived as a man, I was treated like an average-sized person. I felt invisible in a way that was comforting, like I was on a vacation from sexism, or at least from catcalls. In bed, I made sure my lovers didn't touch my chest. My sides remained numb from the surgery and I still had unpleasant memories about my breasts.

As a white man, I began to experience white privilege in a way I had never felt before. People looked me in the eye. Whenever I went out with a female friend or date, I was always the one addressed. In classrooms, I was often called on first. My thinking was validated as intelligent. These are all good things, but they were at the expense of the people around me who were perceived as female.

During this time, I dated people along and between the butch-femme spectrum. I tried to date people who only objectified me when I asked them to. When my identity ebbed and flowed, my lovers often questioned my motives for dating them. Once I said a girl was cute, and my FtM partner said threateningly, "You're just pretending to be a fag, aren't you?" One night when I dressed up in girl drag to go out, my femme girlfriend said, "I never signed up to date someone prettier than me." It became apparent that I was living under a heterosexist paradigm that insists there is a limited amount of gender expression in society and little affection allotted for it within intimate relationships.

After three years of hormone therapy, my body began rejecting the testosterone. Boils erupted at the injection sites on my thighs. I was tired of the lack of fashion options. I stopped the injections and the buzz cuts. I stopped talking in a lower tone and wearing shoes that were just a little too big for me. One day, I decided to stop trying to pass as male. I went from undershirts to sports bras to cotton tank tops with built-in bras to push-up bras. I grew my hair out. I went out to clubs in girl drag. I went from beefy boy to androgynous-invisible to mistaken-as-femme to mistaken-as-straight.

Now I think I'm perceived as a chubby girl with small boobs. If I'm going to be treated as a girl anyway, *was getting a breast reduction a mistake?* Much to my mother's continuous chagrin, my fat stomach protrudes past my pushed-up chest. A bed of chest hair the hormones left behind complicates my lack of cleavage. My chest hair used to be something I shared only with my most intimate partners before I started shaving it. I feel safer participating in chest-baring activities this way, especially with men. *What if he feels my stubble?* Growing up, I was told it was okay to be fat as long as I had big boobs and an hourglass figure. I'm not an hourglass anymore. I'm more of a bong. *If I had bigger boobs, would I get asked out on dates more often?*

Despite these questions, I have grown into my smaller breasts. I'm not objectified as often. I have more clothing options. I have conversations with people who retain eye contact. My experience with gender has taught me how limiting language can be, especially when I use other people's words to make sense of my experience. When I stopped modelling myself after other people's genders and began settling into my own, I found a gender that transcended the options I thought were possible. As a young person I was told to hate my body for being female, fat, and queer. Now, at the age of thirty, I am having the adolescence I

didn't have. Sometimes I let my lovers touch my chest. My surgery scars are anchors, reminding me that my chest is beautiful,
and it's once again my own.

SAILOR HOLLADAY is a writer, artist, and community organizer living in
Portland, Oregon. Sailor's writing and art have appeared or are upcoming in: *Gay Genius Comics Anthology, When Language Runs Dry #3,
The Encyclopedia Project Vol. F–K,* Chronotopia at the 2010 National
Queer Arts Festival, Colony Collapse Disorder Radio, *Enough.org, Without a Net: The Female Experience of Growing Up Working Class,* and
elsewhere.

baby butch

a love letter from the future

Melissa Sky

this is a love letter
from the future
baby butch

a lingering kiss
blown from a space that exists
where butch
is not an insult
for a girl

consider this
an enlivening embrace
from a time you will find
where the word—butch—is mouthed
with reverence
and longing

right now
i know
you don't know
can't know
your own power
your different beauty
the resplendent, dazzling joy that awaits you
once you find us
the women who will look at you
with awe
with envy
with desire

right now
in these first terrifying forays into
exploring how masculine you might want to be
when your uncle asks
"why would you do that to yourself?"
when the saleslady says
"sir or ma'am or whatever you are"
know that we are here
waiting
wet
wanting you
wanting precisely what confounds and unnerves them
in the future
women will thrill to
such exceptional and exquisite contradictions

trust me
when you meet us
see for yourself the way
our eyes widen, our breath catches
at the mere way you walk into a room
the way you hold yourself in the world
it will no longer matter so much
not when you know us
feel the way
our tongues taste, our thighs open
for the way you transgress the lines daily

trust yourself
your secret subterranean visions
dye your hair purple, pierce your eyebrow, put on the tie
one day
i tell you
one day

baby butch
a rocking hot woman
will use that tie deftly on you
creating knots that would put the boys scouts to shame
and you'll see what power looks like
in black stockings and four-inch heels
she will give you things
you don't know
yet
that you want
and that woman
she will
whisper, whimper, sigh
shriek, croon, sob, guffaw, chant, and cry out
thank you
thank you
thank you, baby butch
for having the courage
to withstand their acrid stares
to contravene their assumptions for you
to become the complex, competent, confident woman
you are already well on your way to becoming

for all the ardent femmes of your future
our latent lover
thank you
thank you for allowing us to be
for me to be
over you, under you, beside you, twisted around you, inside
    you, upside down on the playground monkey bars at mid-
    night with you
but mostly
under you
oh goddess

under you
with your biceps straining and your eyes flashing
that look that screams
woman
you don't even know the things I'm about to do to you

and you'll ask her to take it
and she will
she will open and open and open
to levels of openness she didn't even know existed within her
and together you will smash through limits, transcend bound-
    aries, freefall from the edge and arrive panting and spent in
    evocative territories unsuspected and staggering

then do it all again tomorrow morning
disregarding the six o'clock alarm
so she has no time to straighten her hair
and all day at work, she flashes back to why
the sweet, sweet why

you will learn how to fuck her
with finesse
hard and precise
careful not to mess up the hairdo she spent twenty minutes
    perfecting
you will learn to unhook a lacy push-up bra with one hand
to manage tiny clasps as she holds up her hair for you to place
    jewellery about the exposed curve of her neck
to place your hand at the small dip of her back as she sways in
    kick-ass come-fuck-me boots down the street
to relish the sound of unzipping her dress, letting it fall to floor
    and following its delicious descent yourselves

just wait

when you see yourself reflected in their eyes with distortion,
·   with contempt
remember there will be women who see you
fully embracing everything they scorned as
wrong, ugly, unworthy, disgusting

don't believe them

know that one day you will walk by those same boys
with a woman on your arm so luscious
so succulent in her sexiness that it will drip from
your arm
casually slung across her shoulder
her ass
making music in her jeans
they will stare after you like ravenous dogs
sniffing forlornly at the bitch that got away
they'll scuffle and stare in disbelief
that you, somehow, you got the girl

there's a little somethin somethin to contribute to your swagger
baby dyke
yearning for things only vaguely conceptualized

in the words of a stranger
who is your long lost foremother
you will learn in time to
"follow the scent of a woman
melon heavy ripe with joy
inspiring [you] to rip great holes in the sky"[1]

---

1   From Rita Mae Brown, "Dancing the Shout to the True Gospel or,
The Song Movement Sisters Don't Want Me to Sing" in Robin Morgan,
ed., *Sisterhood is Powerful* (New York: Random House, 1971).

the future
wants to fuck the shit out of you
baby butch
so hold on
the ride is just beginning
and it will rock you

we're waiting

MELISSA SKY a proud femme lesbian, feminist, writer, and filmmaker whose work focuses on bringing fresh images of queer sexuality to the page and the big screen. She has a PhD in English Literature from McMaster University and is currently enrolled in the Filmmaking Boot Camp at the Factory Media Arts Centre in Hamilton, Ontario. You can read her provocative thoughts on lesbian pulp fiction and film in *Twilight Tales* and *Judging a Book by Its Cover.* Her film production company, Femme Fatale Creations, has produced several award-winning LGBT short films and documentaries. Find out more at *femmefilms.ca.*

Female Masculinity, Male Femininity, Feminine Masculinity, Masculine Femininity ...?

Prince Jei and Misster Raju Rage

> *This mutual interview is part of a series of dialogues between two transgender friends of colour, whose years of joint performance, writing, and activism in London now continue from other places. Our conversations have appeared in* Masculine Femininities *zine,* Chroma: A Queer Literary Journal, *and* Race Revolt *zine. They deal with themes such as identity, arts, oppression, and the difficulty of finding home, community, and tools for survival in queer scenes that often force us to choose between the "trans" and the "of colour," the masculine and the feminine.*

Raju: Are your masculine and feminine identities separate or do they correlate with each other?

Jei: I identify as a switch or a pendulum, and my masculinity and femininity are very related. When I present masculine for a while, my femininity comes back with a vengeance. I get depressed when I feel stuck in one mode. Presenting masculine for too long makes me feel grey, lifeless, like all the colour is drained from my life. You know how boys grunt and move their bodies, their shoulders and hips very sparsely? This is the longest I have stayed in predominantly masculine mode. There are times I have to remind myself that I am entitled to express myself, express femininity, to switch and change.

R: Why do you have to remind yourself?

J: Pressure from outside. Even within the trans community. You know how you and I often talk about standards of authenticity that we internalize and pass on to each other, that you are successfully trans if your masculinity is read as "real" in the street.

And then, in the street, wanting to pass, even if it's just from point A to B, that becomes easier if I tone it down on the makeup and the nail polish! Also, I get worried if people now read me as a genderqueer "male." I know how to negotiate being treated as a "gross lesbian," but no one's taught me how to survive as a "faggot." I worry [others] will be even more vicious, as male-assigned people aren't treated as if they deserve chivalry.

Then there are the pressures I put on myself. I look back on longer patches of presenting feminine in my life than most of the FtMs or masculine-presenting genderqueers I know. (Or, to reframe this positively, I have a broader gender repertoire.) I often feel I have to hide that past. Part of me sees it as inauthentic, as selling out my transness in order to fit in, find partners, be liked and loved. But that same femininity is now an integral part of me; if you do something for a long time, it becomes you, and it's something you also need to reclaim and stay truthful to.

I've realized it makes a big difference whether I present as feminine or masculine as a female or as a male. So while either mode is authentic to my body and my personality, my choices are mapped against different constraints—the same presentation could get me either violence or social approval. I miss things I used to be able to do as a "girl," such as exchanging smiles or being feisty. People are friendlier again now that I pass more as male, but for a long time, when I was perceived as a masculine female, that kind of social grease that oils your everyday survival or passage through space—the friendly small talk on the bus—just wasn't there. I felt like I had to keep my head down, avoid talking to people, become hard, invisible, cut off from the world.

How about you? Do you see yourself as masculine and feminine at the same time? At all times?

R: Sometimes I feel it's complicated, and I can't put my finger on whether they exist separately or whether they always exist together. I feel like, at different times different identities are drawn out of me by different people, depending on what they want out of me. But viewing myself, I see them really mingled together. When I was growing up, I never had any sexist ideas. I played with boys and was interested in doing "boys' things," but I still had a feminine identity. I wanted to do what I wanted to do, whether it was considered "female" or "male." I've kind of grown up with that same mentality; I want to allow myself to be both and find it hard to be accepted as that. They're not always equal, masculinity and femininity, but they come with each other. I felt like partners have sometimes wanted me to be more male, or sometimes more female—same with society in general. I obviously understand that's about confusion. I think it's the hardest for me to understand in people who are close to me, but I think there's a lot of sexism that's engrained in people.

J: Like in your partners?

R: I think people who are closest to me have found it more difficult to deal with. When I say I'm femme, I find that partners have felt threatened by that or felt that they shouldn't be attracted when they're femmes themselves. For me, that seemed odd, because I hadn't changed the way I behaved or who I am. It's almost the concept that's difficult for them to accept. As I've struggled to be accepted as male, the male side of me has been harder for people to accept. I've tended to focus more on my male side in my transition, and it's only now that I feel comfortable with that side of myself that I can allow myself to share femininity with others and, more importantly, myself. It's felt like a coming out in itself

J: The femme coming out.

R: And I'm not so afraid to show it.

J: What kinds of reactions have you got from femme partners to your femme identity?

R: More recently, I've attracted partners who are more open and embracing of it. I think it has been difficult for some partners because of how they've been conditioned to behave toward trans men/boys. There are a lot of assumptions, in terms of how you don't want to be touched (and, to a lesser extent, how you do want to be touched), and it's almost like a reconditioning is necessary.

J: Like you recondition them. I used to identify as a femme, as a result of being in a long-term relationship with a butch. I now feel very ambivalent about that phase of my life. On one hand, I loved her, fancied her, wanted to be with her, wanted to be *like* her—and since she only "did" femmes, that was where I could fit myself into her life. I also got a lot out of it; I was treated really well. I still associate this with butches, this gentlemanly, very caring, very female way of being with someone. But I have always been a switch, always wanted to also express masculinity ... I'm struggling with my ex over this, who is still in my life, because she sees my masculinity as inauthentic, she insists I'm a totally different person now, like I invaded and took over that beautiful feminine body. [laughs] This is painful, because I realize how co-dependent I have been in my gender identifications. That I feel much more comfortable in other people's bodies, genders, and sexualities than my own. I would happily do femme for this butch, straight girl for that FtM, and butch dom/me for that bi-curious boy.

What's so beautiful, special, and different about my life now is that I'm giving myself permission to explore in all directions. After trying to fit myself first into a female frame, and then into a transsexual male frame, I now try not to be too fussed about whether this is male with a feminine foreground or masculine with a female background. I want to reclaim all that instability and incoherence as authentic parts of my personality, or as possibilities that I can choose to explore or not, depending on the constraints I currently face, like holding down a particular job, moving safely through a particular territory, or pulling a particular person.

R: I can relate to this; I've also felt like a chameleon; that was my way of surviving as I was growing up in quite a traumatic, abusive situation. It was always about surviving and being the right person in the right moment to the right person. I think I've carried that through with my gender identity. I've noticed, looking back on my past relationships, it was very easy for me to be a chameleon, to change and shift in different situations with different people. I've always honoured others' wants and needs and didn't really think too much about my own. At the same time, I did manage to be myself in my expression, and I've always found people who've been attracted to that. I always accepted it was positive attention and so never questioned the affirmation of who I was and what they found attractive in me. I never really questioned why partners wanted what they wanted from me; I just willingly gave it. I now think that was self-destructive. I wasn't recognizing myself or honouring who I was.

J. By fitting yourself into a butch-femme paradigm and losing out on your femininity ...

R: Yeah. I always felt shameful about it; it was something I hid, and not very well. Sometimes it was acceptable, sometimes it was not, and that was confusing. And because I always felt more male, I felt that I should veer toward that, and that was my goal. But the femininity was always there. That's why I found it difficult to relate to other trans men/boys, who were always more masculine-focused. It's only recently that I've met people like me, who feel a combination of masculine and feminine but who still present in a male way.

J: How would you describe your femininity?

R: It's a good question. It's always been something that I've bonded with my femme partners over and not something I can put my finger on: "This is what makes me feminine." But I've always liked femme company (of all genders). I've often felt like I couldn't show certain parts of myself, even at a young age, and I felt those parts were my feminine self. These were things like dressing up in women's clothes, wearing makeup and nail polish, cooking, and being sexually interested in femme boys/men (as well as girls/women).

J: It was more like a gay man's childhood, wasn't it?

R: So those things became secretive and appealing. My first introduction to my femininity as an adult was to wear my partners' clothes and feel like a transvestite, something I identify as positive now, but not something I would share with them at first. Or it was something I would do privately with them once I had "confessed." I've presented as mainly male in my communities, though sometimes, when I've been brave enough, I explored my femininity separately, and more recently it's been something that's been fused together. I have found that I tend to get more affirmation when I present as more male or as genderqueer. Femininity is something that I now enjoy expressing the most, probably because it's something I've repressed for so long, even though being male feels more real to me.

J: Are you still worried that your maleness will not be seen when you present as feminine?

R: Yes. I feel like I currently pass as genderqueer, so I feel like there are more options. But I also feel that if I express my femininity, people won't recognize my maleness. People still assume that you can't be both. I have had a lot of people tell me that I look very male in my femininity. I'm presuming that's because of the hormones I take. I never felt like putting on makeup when I was younger because my mother pushed me to, but now I really enjoy drag and dressing up. I had allergies to makeup and didn't wear it much, so people read me as butch, as more female-masculine identified, when I didn't necessarily feel that way myself. I've always enjoyed the freedom to explore and not be constrained by boundaries. I can see the difference between wearing makeup to attract a man versus wearing makeup to please yourself.

J: I have become much more extreme in expressing femininity since masculinizing my body. I recently had these drag-queening photos taken and was surprised how much more comfortable I was showing off flesh, my legs especially, which is definitely a result of the T, 'coz its shrinks away those hips. [laughs]

I had a lot of body issues when I was younger. Coming to terms with those issues and coming out as trans were linked for me. Later, I stopped messing around with food and trying to lose weight, which was also about trying to become more petite and attractive and shrinking away those muscles. (This was also racialized, as the white-girl standard of long legs and dainty, bosomy figure was clearly out for me, and the petite-exotic-Eurasian niche I was left with was a huge mind fuck.) When I allowed my body to extend itself naturally, without manipulation, I realized that it was, in fact, more masculine, and that was fine. I really liked it, and I started going to the gym and taking homeopathic T and then synthetic T to express that love and exaggerate those features that I had learned to love. Which is ironic—since "gender dysphoria" is defined as hatred of one's body.

When I think about how I came to identify as trans, I have to be careful not to slip into a "What caused it?" pathologizing frame ... but I do find it interesting. For example, exploring hyper-femininity seemed like an organic precursor to becoming male. It was only in my late twenties and early thirties that I started experimenting with extreme femininity, and I think that this actually freed up space to swing back, or swing into, extreme masculinity. It's all about giving yourself permission to gender your body on your own terms.

I also think that sleeping with non-trans men was very important to my trans coming out. On the BDSM scene, I met a lot of male subs who wanted to do gay things with me, had gay rape fantasies, wanted to be fucked ... And obviously, heterosexual BDSM can be problematic with regard to queer and trans stuff, as it often reduces it to a fantasy or a fetish. But for me, it was a really important space, where for the first time I met people who desired my maleness. I never found this on the queer scene; there, people didn't fancy me that way because I wasn't traditionally genderqueer, wasn't butch. So the BDSM scene was a really important practice ground for me.

You've written about how racism influences your gender explorations. Could you say something about that?

R: I think there are some views about my culture in terms of divided gender roles, strict gender codes, sexism ... that have meant I have chosen a very genderqueer, non-polar expression. I have always wanted to prove that those negative opinions of my culture were not necessarily true. I used to believe, from my experience growing up, there was some truth in those views but it is more complex than that and I resent those fixed assumptions by people who are ignorant about the history and the heritage of my culture. It's something that is idealized. Even though masculinity is something that seems more overtly dominant, I feel that femininity holds more power.

J: Do you feel there are role models of feminine males in South-Asian cultures that you can aspire to?

R: Yes, I've always looked toward androgynous role models, whether within a perceived male or female body. It's something I've seen within my culture, and I feel that's maybe why I have a different way of expressing my trans identity and how I choose to transition. I've never identified with being the hyper-masculine butch, even when I was briefly lesbian-identified. I've sometimes felt that my ideas of what it means to be male are very different from everybody else's, and thought I was just being strange. [both laugh] It was only when I started having more relationships with male-identified people that I realized that I was right—there are many different ways of being male.

J: I often meet white FtMs who are into hyper-masculinity, who really aspire to that huge, studly, broad-shouldered, even macho build. I could never look like that. My dad doesn't look like that. He is shorter than my five-foot-one-inch—and not much hairier. I find it problematic.

R: I've always seen being male as problematic. When I was growing up, it was always the males around me who had trouble being man enough. In terms of femininity and being female, I always saw that people around me were more comfortable with that, even though they still struggled with standards. So, coming into a trans community, I haven't wanted to seek out the ideal gender norms or be preoccupied with "passing." I think it should be a space where people can be themselves, to come away from that. To me, transition has meant acknowledging who I am and being myself. I'm made up of very different elements, which are always changing, and I never want to be stuck or struggling.

J: Definitely. It's funny how changeability is considered problematic, this whole kind of "incoherent, unstable, mad, bad ..." This is something I have also learned from mad activists—that stability and coherence are problematic ideals of identity, and that they serve to stifle diversity, individuality, and non-conformity.

R: A big part of my life is worrying about abuse and violence. I have been a survivor of it, so I'm not so scared of it in some ways, but I know it's a reality. I worry that I spend too much time surviving that or escaping from this than actually exploring. Most abuse I get on the street is about my being a conflict of genders, and it would be easier sometimes to be either masculine *or* feminine. I think everyone struggles with their gender—even those people who are abusive. It's their own gender identity that they are battling with, really.

J: I love how being a survivor makes you feel more free to explore gender, and gives you tools for your gender expression. Because the stereotype is that you're trans because you were abused, that it's a negative thing, and that being a survivor is a negative thing.

R: Yes. If you are a survivor, you have to focus on what makes you more positive and healthy, and I've never felt more positive than when I'm being myself. So I can't see that [being trans] is a negative result of my abuse.

J: In my family, it was considered more dangerous to be feminine. My mum would tell me not to wear makeup because people would think I was a prostitute. (This obviously had a racial aspect to it as well—my mother is white and Thai females are stereotyped as prostitutes.) Heterosexuality was something that was dangerous, that could get you pregnant or HIV positive or raped or people would talk badly about you, and the neighbours already were because we were this strange interracial family. Being masculine or androgynous was definitely the lesser evil. Also, in Thai diasporic spaces, it's okay to be a tomboy; it's even considered cute sometimes.

R: Growing up, it seemed to me that being feminine and attractive was done for someone else, mostly for men in a heterosexual context. So you had to be as femininely desirable as possible but not on your own terms, which is why I rejected femininity for a long time, even though I felt an affinity with it. I became a "tomboy," as masculinity was more comfortable for me. It's only now that I am exploring both femininity and also with masculinity, the way I want to, and it took me a while to get to this place. I also find.it interesting to observe what I express when I'm with different people, but not in the same way as in the past, where I gave up my identity. Now, I embrace it. I would like to be braver in exploring my hyper-femininity more and seeing how far it goes; it's something that really excites me. But there is always something holding me back. I would like to let go of those inhibitions. What about you? Do you ever feel held back in your desires?

J: My desires are very broad and eclectic, so in a way I don't mind not having a ready-made niche to fit into. I am excited about finding more surprising possibilities that fall off the map, the social scripts we have inherited. I feel more comfortable that way. The major reason I transitioned is that I felt claustrophobic and stifled by the existing scripts, including butch-femme, heterosexuality, and even queerness. I just couldn't do it anymore; it killed my spirit. So I have to remind myself of this when I'm overcome by the sense that there is no place for me and nobody will ever want to fuck me again. This is the freed-up space that I have been looking for, that I have fought for. And I intend to savour every inch of it!

Misster Raju Rage is a trans-gender, queer-fem-inist person of colour. Born in Kenya, raised in London, UK, with South Asian heritage, he is a traveller at heart. He is also the editor of a zine about gender, *Masculine Femininities*, a performer in D'Artagnan and the Three Musclequeers with Prince Jei, and co-organizer of the London Transgender Film Festival 2008, and more. An artist and activist in multiple forms, at the time of the interview he was experimenting and performing with femininity and now has an alter ego, Lola Love, who helps him survive this harsh heteronormative world.

Prince Jei identifies as a multi gender trans person of colour. Born and raised in Germany, and in the midst of further migrations, Jei was a Londoner of thirteen years at the time of the interview, above. They have published many political and academic writings and also been involved in queer-of-colour organizing for almost a decade, most recently around homonationalism and the prison industrial complex. Since the interview, they have experimented further with different gender presentations and wants to continue shifting, according to where his or her desires, survival needs, and dreams for community, resistance, and radical transformation take him.

Backstage with Lady Gaga

Ben McCoy

"Sorry, were you saying something or did your asshole just burp?" Miss Taffy deadpanned in the cramped backstage dressing room.

"Maybe you'd know the difference if you cleaned the jizz outta yo' ears," huffed Diana Wrong, applying her fourteenth coat of Wet 'n' Wild Sparkle Vanilla Baby-Cake lip-gloss.

Miss Taffy sat in the corner on a heap of unopened beer boxes. Her arm rested on the makeshift counter that propped up a mirror the girls used backstage. Diana Wrong fluttered about like a butterfly at a rave trying not to get smacked by flailing hands, though it was her own fidgeting fingers darting about, reapplying this, powdering that, readjusting her clip-on fall, false eyelashes, and control-top pantyhose. When it came to being in various stages of undress backstage, Diana Wrong was the least modest of all the other queens. She was singing a Keyshia Cole song in front of the mirror, her tits out, and beige pantyhose just barely covering the outline of what would be her dick, had it not been properly tucked under. In contrast to Diana's constant call for attention, Miss Taffy sat quiet, stoic, fully dressed. Her sequined and feathered shrug glimmered over her ankle-length evening gown while tendrils of smoke rose from her cigarette and circled her zaftig form.

"Girl, you got a light?" Miss Wrong asked, pulling out a Newport. Miss Taffy looked away, ignoring her completely. Diana found Taffy's lighter sitting on her pack of Camel Lights and lit her own cigarette. "Alright, bitch," she snarled, slipping on a dress over her hose.

Jake was coming down the narrow staircase. The backstage dressing room had two floors. The bottom floor was behind the stage, had two mirrors, and was well-lit but cramped, the space a jumble of makeup, wigs, dresses, and coolers, booze, boxes, and standard bar paraphernalia. Jake was the newest performer at the drag bar and always went upstairs, where it was less crowded, to get ready. Jake was the only one who ever got ready up there, except when Miss Wrong made an occasional appearance, fluttering about, singing to herself, and claiming she left a wig up there somewhere. There was a desk, a chair, a full-sized mirror, and room to peel your pantyhose off comfortably or stretch your leg out enough to slip it into a pair of thigh-high black vinyl boots without kicking a queen in her padded butt.

Jake would be going on stage soon and wanted to come downstairs and have a cigarette before performing. Camel in hand, she realized she'd left her lighter upstairs after making the trek down. "Somebody got a light?" Jake asked, trying to fix her wig while Diana hogged up most of the mirror room.

"Miss Thing over there has one, but don't ask *her* for it; she's a cunt tonight!" Diana said, laughing, and pointed Jake to Taffy's lighter.

Miss Taffy rolled her eyes and sighed. "I'd be in a better mood if you'd just shut the fuck up for five seconds, you crazy bitch."

Jake smiled. It was true. Another great reason to get ready upstairs was to escape the non-consensual monologue/R'n'B concert that was Diana Wrong backstage. If, at certain intervals, one wanted a dialogue, a conversation, the opportunity to throw one's own two cents in, even to agree with Diana, it was difficult, strenuous, and almost impossible. Her topics varied wildly, as did her attention. Giving Jake the side-eye, she frowned. "Girl, you can't tuck no better than that?"

Jake was getting ready to lip-sync a Lady Gaga song and was dressed accordingly: a black Fredericks of Hollywood chemise revealing the cheeks of her ass poking out of her hiked-up, size-too-small panties. Her dick was folded down and not quite between her butt cheeks, as some queens do, but held in place by the teeny black panties. Not an obvious bulge, for sure, but, as

Miss Wrong pointed out, it wasn't the best tucking situation either.

"I don't get paid enough for this shit," Jake said. Besides the very specific sensation of having your balls crushed and your dick forced into hibernation, Jake was also dealing with itching and sweating from her wig. Her natural hair, long and black, hung down well past her shoulders to her belly button. But for the Lady Gaga number, she had it all pulled back tightly in a small pony-tail then pinned up in a bun on the back of her head. It would be a struggle to fit the blonde bob wig over it. "Can you see my real hair in the back? I can't tell," Jake asked Miss Taffy.

Miss Taffy stood up and grunted, "Here," pulling the wig down tighter in the back and then fluffing it up on top. "Adds some volume in the back."

"Speaking of volume in the back," the show's hostess, Miss Sally Knows, cooed, coming in from the stage, microphone in hand. "You're on!" she whispered to Jake and gave Jake's exposed cheeks a smack.

Following Sally Knows, Jake waited behind the curtain while the hostess stepped out speaking theatrically into the microphone. "Oh! A few more people trickling in! We have room *right up here*, ladies and gentlemen! Welcome, *welcome ... to the Den!* Life's a *jungle* and in *this* particularly shady spot, we have *lots* to look at, indeed! She-male snow leopards, tranny tigers, and cross-dressing cougars! But don't worry, boys and girls, none of our lovely ladies will bite ... unless you *pay them to!*" A few people laughed. Jake had heard the whole bit countless times and could lip sync it just as well as she could her favourite song.

"Next up, we're saving you an *awful* lot of money, folks. You see, our *next* performer is currently on tour and charges upward of $250 a ticket! She's *very* expensive ... but tonight, you're catching her for a mere five-dollar cover! Lucky, lucky you! It's ... *Lady Gaga!*"

The audience applauded and screamed, but it was a little bittersweet for Jake. When Jake first began performing at the Den, the other queens scoffed, "So, what's your girl name, honey? What do you perform as?" The looks on the faces of the glamazons backstage when Jake replied "Jake. Just Jake Connelly," were heavily made up, with brows etched in disbelief and lip-liner that bled into a scowl. "Look at that face! That fishy face! She has a face like *that* and wants to go by a boy's name?!" shouted Miss Nomi Better. Jake's face was naturally very androgynous. "Well," Miss Sally Knows sighed softly, seeming somewhat disappointed, "how 'bout we just introduce you as Miss Connelly." Jake noticed it was a statement, not a question.

Jake's face reddened, though none could see it through her foundation. She thought it a bit offensive, if not simply rude, to want to negotiate someone else's name. But money was hard to come by, and this was a paid gig, after all. Besides, at least they'd introduce her as Miss Connelly, right? That wasn't so bad, thought Jake, it's kind of like being a teacher. *Miss Connelly*—she imagined it written in immaculate cursive on a clean classroom chalk-board.

But it seemed the matter of Jake's name was one that still made the other queens noticeably uncomfortable. Only a few would call her Jake, most opting for "Miss C," and the hostesses preferred to blatantly introduce her as their "very own Lady Gaga." Jake adored Gaga, and the dollar bills were very much a necessity, but it would have been nice to enter the stage as a performer with her own name. Sure, all the queens were lip-syncing, appropriating music from other artists—Jake knew this—but at the end of the night when audience members would say to the queens before leaving, "Oh, Miss Taffy, I loved your dress!" or "Diana, you worked it out, girl!" Jake most often heard, "Lady Gaga, we love you!" Lip-syncing at a drag bar doesn't pay that much, so any and all compliments were greatly appreciated but would have been even more so if they had been paid to her own name.

Jake could remember her first night backstage, with Diana Wrong rattling on left and right, while Miss Taffy seemed to silently size up the newcomer. "Sally said you go by Jake, so you a boy during the day then?" Miss Wrong asked casually.

"Uh, no. I look like this all the time. I mean, well, clearly not when I wake up," Jake laughed nervously. "But, yeah, this is all me. I'm not wearing a wig; this is all mine." She ran her fingertips through her long black hair. A blonde bob wig that had been curled and spray-painted yellow at the tips lay curled up in her bag.

"So you a tranny, then," Diana turned and said, lighting her cigarette, while Miss Taffy looked bored out of her mind.

"I'm just me. But if you're asking if I look this way all the time, then yeah. Oh, I like your shawl, that's really gorgeous," Jake said to Miss Taffy, hoping to dodge the How-Trans-Are-You? Q & A with Diana.

"Thanks. I made it." Miss Taffy's voice was flat, monotone, and firm. But before Jake could chat about Taffy's tailoring, Diana whirled around, rubbing foundation over her nipples, as though she was about to model for soft-core porn.

"Well, being tranny is a state of mind. You don't need no tits to be a tranny. Please, I seen some bitches with the biggest implants, they face all pumped up, but they still a man, just a man with tits. A doctor can't make you no lady. That's up to you. Don't matter what you wanna be called, neither." And with that she whirled back to the mirror and shimmied into her sequined bra and panties.

"Well, I just always try to be myself. Seems to me you could go insane trying to please everyone else." Jake leaned against the cooler in the backstage dressing room.

"You'll go insane doing this show, if you stick around long enough," grumbled Miss Taffy. They all laughed, and the show went on.

Back from her routine onstage, with dollar bills in her Fredericks of Hollywood water-bra and filling her hands, Jake was out of breath. She had two more songs to do, and she was already exhausted. Some nights, the crowd was more eager than others, screaming as soon as your stilettos hit the floor; other evenings, people stared blankly, unenthused and unimpressed. In the dressing room, Jake pulled her blonde wig off and took a big breath.

"Tired already?" Miss Taffy raised an eyebrow full of rhinestones. They shone while her eyes seemed reluctant to.

"I got a lot on my mind. I have a deadline—"

"A deadline?! For what?!" Diana interrupted as though the word "deadline" was the most exotic thing she'd heard of in weeks.

"Oh, I'm submitting a story. For a book. I'm a writer. There was a call for writing on gender, femininity, and masculinity ... and I'm writing a ..." Jake's voice trailed off. Diana Wrong immediately lost interest, although at what point, Jake couldn't tell. She was already singing an Erykah Badu song. If Miss Taffy even heard that Jake was a writer, she didn't let on. Nicotine, and being dressed in time for her routines, seemed her only interests.

Sighing, Jake went upstairs with her cigarette and glass of white wine with a straw in it. The fact that she had about fifteen minutes to completely undress then re-dress herself, adjust another wig on her head, and re-apply her makeup before taking a big breath and dashing back out onstage was exhausting. The reluctance of many of the queens to call her Jake, the purposeful omission of her name during her onstage introduction was exhausting. The How-Trans-Are-You? Q & A was exhausting. Even the thought of writing a piece on gender was exhausting. Diana Wrong was exhausting, and Taffy being bored was exhausting!

"Ugh!" Jake pulled one stiletto-heeled boot on. She was sweating now and craned her neck in the direction of a small fan that blew slightly her way. Slipping the other thigh-high on, she wondered what she would write about. A letter to the girl who called her out earlier today, sitting at the bus stop, yelling "Dude, she's a *dude*!" to the amusement and evil teenage laughter of her friends? How passing felt like a self-imposed prison? Something praising the theory of inclusivity behind the whole genderqueer thing, then throwing it some seriously snarky shade for its seemingly elitist-group tendencies, birthplace in academia, and adoption by kids who were deodorant-challenged?

"Miss C! Get yer lil' white ass down here, you're on!" Diana Wrong called from downstairs. *Shit*, thought Jake, as she quickly powdered her face and ran downstairs.

Dashing through the velvet curtain, Jake noticed there were two new large groups, both bridal parties, sitting up near the front. One group had little penis-hats on and seemed to have pre-gamed a bit with the booze. The other table seemed just as excited, though much less inebriated, and both bachelorette parties had already begun waving their dollar bills toward Jake.

Jake's androgynous body danced about, her face smoothed over with paint, adhesive holding her false eyelashes tight and liquid liner blending them in. She was wearing a wig that she had hot-rolled, and long wavy curls bounced past her shoulders, over the curve of her water-bra.

The bridal parties hooted and hollered, throwing their dollars at Jake. It was not lost on her that, at this very moment perhaps, the bride-to-be's fiancé was just a neighbourhood or two away, watching a very different performance—an oiled-up lap dance, girls on poles, topless, bottomless, maybe some time in the champagne room, or a private party set up by his male buddies. Meanwhile, here was his blushing bride to be at the Den, a local drag bar where she and her friends would sip sugary drinks and slip one-dollar bills to lip-syncing drag queens and trannies and the bartenders doomed to work there.

Maybe she could write about that? She could say drag bars are the site of post-modern re-enactments of the female worship of the effeminate god Dionysus and the bachelorettes were modern day maenads engaged in pagan ritual. Here they were, about to be married, and before the actual marriage they were offering up gifts and payment to an androgynous god of wine, intoxication, and sacrifice. These maenads were known to sacrifice men in honour of their effeminate god, Dionysus, who had sacrificed his own maleness, his masculinity, in favour of femininity. The bridal parties weren't making a ritualistic sacrifice of any living creatures, it's true (though some of them, upon having imbibed too much wine, would later, on the sidewalk or in a taxi-cab, sacrifice their last meal and that day's dignity), but in celebrating at the drag bar, they were enjoying their last single night out with their girlfriends while also honouring the effeminate, the trans, the queens, Dionysus. Jake seemed to see in them maenad-like qualities—their eagerness to compliment the god's appearance, her costume, her performance, their gushing enthusiasm bubbling like wine into a goblet. And what could be more pagan than a penis-hat?

Jake went backstage, satisfied with the amount of tips she made during that number, but her smile soon faded. *Shit*, she thought. *Camille Paglia probably already wrote something about that.* The deadline for submissions was imminent, and she had no idea what to contribute. She was already so exhausted by the gender ghetto. Every day held a magnifying glass up to the issues of femininity and masculinity and how they shaped her life; they were tyrants, like the gods of Olympus wreaking havoc frivolously upon the mortals below. (*Great*, thought Jake. *Now I'm going to be talking like Paglia all night*.) But it was true; from her daily ritual of shaving this, shaving that, applying this, applying that, and trying to maintain a decent tuck, to avoiding the always possible hate-crime to the limited acceptance and discrimination found in employment and even the catastrophically clichéd gigs lip-syncing, Jake felt oppressed by gender.

At the moment, Miss Taffy felt oppressed by her corset.

"Honey, I'm going on next, and this is too tight! Can you loosen it for me? I can't breathe and I can't reach the strings in the back!" Flustered, her voice lost its monotone and teetered into anxiousness. Already, Sally Knows was making the last of her bar-room jokes before announcing Miss Taffy onstage.

Jake was awful at this sort of thing: she got stressed out and sweaty just putting her own clothes on in-between numbers, but staring blankly at an unfamiliar garment with foreign straps and hooks made it even worse. Her fingers tried to undo the knot that bound Taffy in pain, but fumbled.

"I don't know if I can do it!" Jake whimpered, hearing Sally Knows just moments away from purring into the mic, "Miss ... Taffyyyyyyyyyyy!"

"Move over, I'll do it!" Diana stepped in and worked at the corset, pulling and loosening its binding on Taffy. "Girl, next time you do your corset up, if you a size twelve, don't be try'na turn into no size four, aiight? There, that better?"

"Ugh! Thanks!" Taffy regained her breath and her posture and headed out onto the stage just as her song was cued up. Diana Wrong went back to humming a song while waving a sheer turquoise floral print dress in front of her half-naked body. She then put a long pink gown before her, which had a deeply plunging neckline and long sleeves with beadwork on the bottom of the gown that reached up mid-calf.

"Which one, you think? This one—or this one?" She asked Jake, swishing the dresses over her body, back and forth.

Jake was still trying to decide what to write about for the submission, but deciding which dress Diana should wear onstage was a welcome distraction.

"The pink one. The beadwork is really beautiful and I think it goes with your jewellery. Yeah, do that one."

Miss Diana Wrong turned her head this way and that, tilting it like a seesaw and scrunching her face up. She puckered her lips and said, "I'll do *turquoise*!"

Jake rolled her eyes; she was ready to go home. Finally, Miss Taffy came backstage, and it was time for Diana to scoot out in front of the crowd in her tight-fitting, sheer turquoise gown.

"Please, let this be one of her five- to six-minute numbers, and not a short one," said Miss Taffy, plopping down on a heap of boxes and lighting a cigarette. "Five minutes. Just five minutes without that constant verbal diarrhea!"

Jake laughed and concurred. Finishing her glass of chardonnay through its straw and puffing on her Camel, she waited in silence to give Taffy some peace of mind. She was still trying to come up with an idea of what to write about.

When Diana returned backstage, Taffy quipped, "That turquoise? Again? When are you gonna make a new dress?"

"As soon as you get a corset that fits, ho."

Jake, Diana, and even Miss Taffy laughed. "Alright, now somebody get me out of this thing!" Taffy turned around and Diana undid the strings.

"If you can't throw a little bit of shade at your friends, honey, what are they good for?" Diana smiled a big toothy smile as Taffy pulled off her wig. "We might be fucking cunts, but one thing's for sure ... Without each other, how in the hell we gonna get all this shit on and off?"

All the girls agreed and continued stowing away their various stage-clothes. Zipping up her luggage and shaking out her long black hair, Jake said goodnight to the girls and the bartender. Waving goodbye, she finally had an idea.

BEN MCCOY is a writer, versatile performance artist, and at times, a short-film vixen. McCoy has toured the United States twice, most recently with Sister Spit. He has slung words, stilettos, and slices of LOL-pie to audiences while raising a well-manicured finger to homo-and-transphobia and misogyny everywhere. Surprisingly not a Leo, McCoy is a quadruple Scorpio. Currently, he is enjoying a mutually bewitching affair with San Francisco.

FEMME SHARK MANIFESTO!

Leah Lakshmi Piepzna-Samarasinha

FEMME SHARKS DON'T EAT OUR OWN.
FEMME SHARKS LIKE TO EAT, THOUGH.
FEMME SHARKS RECOGNIZE THAT FEMMES COME IN ALL
KINDS OF SIZES AND EACH KIND IS LUSCIOUS. WE WORK
TOWARD LOVING OUR CURVY, FAT, SKINNY, SUPERSIZE,
THICK, DISABLED, BLACK AND BROWN FINE-ASS BODIES EVERY
DAY. WE REALIZE THAT LOVING OURSELVES IN A RACIST/
SEXIST/HOMO/TRANSPHOBIC/ABLIST/CLASSIST SYSTEM IS AN
EVERY DAY ACT OF WAR AGAINST THAT SYSTEM.
FEMME SHARKS DON'T THINK ANOREXIA IS CUTE.
WE THINK EATING A BIG-ASS MEAL IS SEXY.
WE SAY SCREW "HEIGHT-WEIGHT PROPORTIONATE PLEASE" IN
CRAIGSLIST WOMEN-SEEKING-WOMEN ADS AND IN LIFE.

WE HAVE BIG MOUTHS AND WE KNOW HOW TO USE
THEM. DON'T FUCK WITH US! ASK US IF WE WANT TO FUCK,
THOUGH!

FEMME SHARKS WILL RECLAIM THE POWER AND DIGNITY OF
FEMALENESS BY ANY MEANS NECESSARY.
WE'RE GIRLS BLOWN UP, TURNED INSIDE OUT, AND REMIXED.

FEMME SHARKS ARE OVER WHITE QUEERS' OBLIVIOUSNESS
TO QUEER OF COLOUR, TWO SPIRIT, AND TRANS OF COLOUR
LIVES.
WE KNOW THAT WE ARE A CENTRE OF THE UNIVERSE.
WE'RE OVER WHITE FEMMES AND BUTCHES WHO THINK THAT
FEMME ONLY COMES IN THE COLOUR OF BARBIE.
WE'RE OVER BUTCHES AND BOYS AND OTHER FEMMES
TELLING US WHAT WE NEED TO DO, WEAR, OR BE IN ORDER
TO BE "REALLY FEMME."

FEMME SHARKS RECOGNIZE THAT FEMMES, BUTCHES,
GENDERQUEER, AND TRANS PEOPLE HAVE BEEN IN
COMMUNITIES OF COLOUR SINCE FOREVER.
THAT BEFORE COLONIZATION WE WERE SEEN AS SACRED
AND WE WERE SOME OF THE FIRST FOLKS MOST VIOLENTLY
ATTACKED WHEN OUR LANDS WERE INVADED AND COLONIZED.
FEMME SHARKS WON'T REST UNTIL WE RECLAIM OUR POSITIONS
AS BELOVED FAMILY WITHIN OUR COMMUNITIES.

FEMME SHARKS AREN'T JUST DIMEPIECES AND TROPHY WIVES.
FUCK THAT!
WE MIGHT BE YOUR GIRL,
BUT WE'RE <u>OUR OWN</u> FEMMES.
WE RECOGNIZE THAT FEMMES ARE LEADERS OF OUR
COMMUNITIES.
WE HOLD IT DOWN, CALM YOUR TEARS, ORGANIZE THE RALLY,
VISIT YOU IN JAIL, GET CHILDCARE HOOKED UP, LOAN YOU
TWENTY DOLLARS.
FEMMES ARE WELDERS, AFTERSCHOOL TEACHERS, ABORTION
CLINIC WORKERS, STRIPPERS, WRITERS, FACTORY WORKERS,
MOMS, REVOLUTIONARIES DEDICATED TO TAKING THE SYSTEM
THE HELL DOWN SO WE CAN BE FREE!

FEMMES ARE LEADERS IN TAKING CARE OF BUSINESS/
DEFENDING OUR QUEER AND TRANS OF COLOUR COMMUNITIES.
WE USED OUR STILETTOS AS WEAPONS AT STONEWALL.
WE WERE THE TRANSWOMEN WHO FOUGHT BACK AT THE
COMPTON CAFETERIA.
WE'RE THE GIRLS WHO STARE DOWN ASSHOLES STARING AT OUR
LOVERS AND FRIENDS ON THE SUBWAY.
WE WALK EACH OTHER HOME,
ACT CRAZY ON THE BUS TO GET ASSHOLES TO MOVE AWAY,
AND KNOW HOW TO BREAK SOMEONE'S LEGS.
WE SHARE WHAT WE KNOW.

FEMME SHARKS STAND UP FOR THE NEW JERSEY FOUR AND
EVERY OTHER QUEER AND TRANS PERSON OF COLOUR IN THE
PRISON INDUSTRIAL COMPLEX FOR DEFENDING OUR LIVES.
WE BELIEVE IN SELF-DEFENSE AND SELF-DETERMINATION.
WE BELIEVE THAT WE HAVE A RIGHT TO DEFEND OURSELVES
AND OUR COMMUNITIES AGAINST ANY KIND OF ATTACK—
FROM ASSHOLES ON THE STREET
TO RACIST WHITE CLUB OWNERS WHO WANT THREE PIECES
OF ID
TO FOLKS WHO INSIST THAT WE'RE STRAIGHT.
TO PEOPLE WHO TAKE OUR LAND.

WE REMEMBER OUR DEAD—SAKIA GUNN, GWEN ARAUJO, AND
MANY OTHER QUEER AND TRANS PEOPLE OF COLOUR WHO
DIED BECAUSE OF RACIST, HOMO/TRANSPHOBIC VIOLENCE.
NOT AS A POLITICAL STATEMENT,
BUT AS WOMEN WE LOVED IN REAL LIFE,
WOMEN WHO COULD'VE BEEN US OR OUR LOVES.

WE ARE NOT GOING TO BE LEFT OUT OF "THE STRUGGLE."
NOT THIS TIME.
WE'RE NOT JUST A PRETTY FACE.

FEMMES GODDAMN WELL KNOW HOW TO STRAP IT ON,
CHANGE THE OIL IN THE CAR, AND PUT UP SHELVES.
WE CAN DO ANY GODDAMN THING WE WANT!
THAT'S WHY WE'RE FEMME SHARKS!
FEMME IS NOT THE SAME THING AS BEING OUR MOMS
FEMMES ARE BEAUTIFUL AND STRONG WHEN WE BOTTOM
AND WE'RE HOT AS HELL WHEN WE TOP.
OUR BOTTOMING AND TOPPING ARE BOTH GIFTS TO BE MET
WITH RESPECT.
WHEN WE TAKE OUR LOVERS' FISTS ALL THE WAY INSIDE,
ASK FOR WHAT WE WANT,

BE THE BEST DIRTY GIRL,
OR MAKE OUR LOVERS FLIP,
WE'RE A FUCKING MIRACLE.
IN THE WORDS OF JILL SCOTT, "YOU GOTTA DO RIGHT BY ME.
IT'S MANDATORY, BABY."

FEMME SHARKS SHOP AT ROSS, FOXY LADY, VALUE VILLAGE,
THE HM $5 RACK, TORRID, AND THE DOLLAR STORE, AND
KNOW HOW TO SHOPLIFT.
WE CONCOCT BRILLIANT STRATEGIES TO LOOK FINE
ON TEN DOLLARS OR LESS.
WE'RE ONLY "INVISIBLE" IF YOU DON'T KNOW HOW TO LOOK
FOR US.

WE TAKE CARE OF EACH OTHER,
RECOGNIZE THAT FEMMES ARE EACH OTHERS' WEALTH.
HOS BEFORE BROS, ALWAYS!
FEMME SOLIDARITY AND LOVE FOR EACH OTHER
IS A REVOLUTIONARY FORCE.
WE BELIEVE IN GIRLS LOVING GIRLS, RESPECTING EACH
OTHERS' BRILLIANCE,
NOT FIGHTING OVER BOIS OR BUTCHES,
NOT TRYING TO BE THE ALPHA FEMME.
WE'RE ANTI-DRAMA,
BELIEVE IN THE POWER OF COMMUNITIES THAT HEAL HURT,
APOLOGIZE, LISTEN TO EACH OTHER, AND MAKE THINGS
RIGHT.
WE BELIEVE IN BUILDING OUR QUEER AND TRANS PEOPLE OF
COLOUR COMMUNITIES STRONG.

FEMME SHARKS WERE THERE WHEN FRIDA KAHLO HOOKED
UP WITH HER GIRLFRIENDS,
WHEN JOAN NESTLE, CHRYSTOS, JEWELLE GOMEZ, ALEXIS DE
VEUX, SYLVIA RIVERA, DOROTHY ALLISON, MINNIE BRUCE

PRATT, AND AMBER HOLLIBAUGH MADE QUEER FEMME
HISTORY,
WHEN ZAPATISTA WOMEN HOOKED UP,
WHEN OUR COUSINS WERE MAKING OUT IN THE WOMEN'S
SECTION OF THE MASJID,
WHEN OUR GRANDMAS AND QUEER AUNTIES SNUCK OUT AT
NIGHT,
DIDN'T GET MARRIED TILL LATE—OR AT ALL—
HAD A BEST GIRLFRIEND
AND STOOD UP FOR HER.
FEMME SHARKS WERE THERE.

FEMME SHARKS ARE IN THE BODIES OF COUNTLESS SEX
WORKERS, NEIGHBOURS, AND LADIES WAITING FOR THE BUS
AND IN THE LINEUP AT CENTURY 21.
AT RIIS BEACH, FUNKASIA, LOVERGIRL NYC, BUTTA, MANGO,
MANHATTAN'S, DESILICIOUS, AND BIBI!
FEMME SHARKS LIVE ON THE REZ, IN CAPETOWN, NEWARK,
OAKLAND!!!!!, THE SOUTH SIDE, NEW ORLEANS, COLOMBO,
JUAREZ, AND BROOKLYN, SUBURBIA, THE FARM, AND LITTLE
SMALL TOWNS.
WE'RE IN FOSTER CARE, THE PSYCH WARD, JUVIE, AND ABOUT
TO BE EVICTED.

WE ARE SURVIVORS WHO ARE MORE THAN WHAT WE
SURVIVED.
WE ARE FIGURING OUT HOW TO HEAL
AND HOW TO MAKE IT SO THAT NO ONE
WILL HAVE TO SURVIVE SEXUAL VIOLENCE EVER AGAIN.
WE BELIEVE IN THE TOTAL DESTRUCTION OF THE SYSTEM AS
WE KNOW IT
TO MAKE SOMETHING MUCH MO BETTA,
AND WE BELIEVE IN MAKING OUR OWN WAYS TO FIGHT AND
RESIST ON THE DAILY.

A FEMME SHARK IS ANY GIRL
WHO IS TOUGH, HUNGRY, FIGHTS FOR HERSELF AND HER FAM
AND IS WORKING ON BECOMING THE KIND OF GIRL
WHO FINDS GOD IN HERSELF
AND LOVES HER FIERCELY.

WE'RE YOUR BEST GIRLFRIEND AND YOUR WORST
NIGHTMARE.

LOVE AND RAGE,
THE FEMME SHARKS

LEAH LAKSHMI PIEPZNA-SAMARASINHA is a queer disabled Sri Lankan
writer, teacher, and cultural worker. The author of *Consensual Genocide*
and co-editor of *The Revolution Starts at Home: Confronting Intimate Violence in Activist Communities*, her work has appeared in the anthologies
*Yes Means Yes, Visible: A Femmethology, Homelands, Colonize This, We
Don't Need Another Wave, Bitchfest, Without a Net, Dangerous Families,
Brazen Femme, Femme,* and *A Girl's Guide to Taking Over The World.*
Her second book of poetry, *Love Cake*, and first memoir, *Dirty River*, are
forthcoming. She co-founded Mangos With Chili, a national queer and
trans people-of-colour performance organization, is a lead artist with Sins
Invalid, and teaches with June Jordan's Poetry for the People. In 2010, she
was named one of the Feminist Press's "40 Feminists Under 40 Who Are
Shaping the Future" and nominated for a Pushcart Prize. She comes from a
long line of border jumpers, scholarship winners, middle-class Sri Lankan
feminists, working-class Ukrainian-Irish ladies with hard hands and three
jobs, radical teachers, queers, crips, hustlers, storytellers, and survivors.

A Failed Man

Michael V. Smith

For many years, I have held my head very high to be *this* gay, which is *so* gay. *So* gay, because I'm femme. I like to say I'm one of the gayest people most people will ever meet, though the older I get the less I can tell how true that might be. Yes, I wore skirts to work at the university for a short season, did many nights of boy-makeup, have made lesbian porn, gay porn, wrote about my unfortunate sex life for two years in the local paper, joined the radical faeries with gusto, wore pink at nearly every opportunity worth celebrating, carried my wrist *just so*, and, through it all, have maintained my status as a thoroughbred lesbro. I hang with the most socially progressive, community-minded, fun-party-but-with-lefty-politics bunch of power lesbians any town has seen—but the standards are always changing. What once was the norm is no longer the stereotype. Or vice versa. And the more blendered my gender—the more femme I am and the more butch—the less I can tell which is which.

What I do know is that my sense of myself as an über queer brings me great joy. And is still, every day, hard-won. I have learned by the most excellent examples of human confabulation that the best work—and by best, let's say bang-for-your-buck best—I can do in my community is to be myself, which is a radical act. That's the faerie talking, and I'm sure he's right.

I will admit there is a certain narcissism in writing about butch and femme—a Western privilege even, and yes, it's easier to be limp-wristed as a white bio-male—so let me acknowledge that. Let me admit to being very lucky to be this gay, and, okay, a little narcissistic. But maybe you are too. Maybe you're trying to take the structures of power down one lipstick at a time, or with one black-hankied fist in the air.

Let's say this: you and I believe in a world that is brighter—

brighter being better—because there are those of us who, quite simply, play. Yes, you get it, or you wouldn't have picked up this anthology in the first place. Or you're about to get it because you're as desperate as the rest of us to give yourself the necessary permission to play.

I would like, then—being a little narcissistic and a little apologetic—to explain to you the kind of butch-femme I am so that we may understand ourselves a little better, understand who you are in relation to who I am. That's productive, I think. A little legacy, a little context, a little leading by example and counter-example.

For starters, the best way to explain just how fey I am is to talk about my father, who nearly drank himself to death last spring. He's been hard on his luck, meaning his girlfriend asked him to leave. He's been without a job or social assistance because he's too proud.

Pretty much destitute, he moved in with his brother. They binged for a week. Apart from the idiocy of drinking alcohol at all, which is never advisable for a man with his condition (Dad says his heart is so weak from the diabetes that he can't walk to the car without getting winded), he also made the poor decision to skip meals. All of them, for a week. My uncle Pat said he tried, but couldn't convince Dad to eat—or shower, which he seemed to think was a worse sign.

Seven days in, Pat wakes up a bit more sober on Monday morning and notices that Dad doesn't know where he is. Then my father collapses. Pat phones his other brother, who phones the police and an ambulance. Ted knows, very smartly, for they went through this very thing with their mother, that the police are probably required to force Dad to go to the hospital, which is the case.

He's in the hospital nearly a week, doped up, drying out. When they release him, he picks up his fourteen-foot camper trailer and drives it out of town to an ex-co-worker's driveway. There's no heat in the camper, and he can't afford the payments on what little money he gets from his retirement pension.

I phone to see how he's doing, hoping I can get him into some sort of treatment, for he's nearly killed himself, so now he can't deny there's a problem with his drinking. Well, he doesn't. But he has it in his head, he says, to not drink anymore, so he won't. No manner of encouragement, sense, or emotional blackmail can make him think otherwise. When I tell him that I've had my own struggles with drinking, as he remembers, and that every person in the world who's quit has likely had some form of help, so maybe he should get some too, just to beat the odds, he says to me, with a dead earnestness laced with resentment, as if it's my fault, "You don't know me very well, do you?"

It's everything I can do to be calm and say, "No, Dad, I don't," without putting any hint in my voice that I am all too familiar with our own history, which is also a history of his relationship to the bottle, and his hopeless relationship to masculinity.

Our relationship, or the lack within it, is also my father's relationship to himself, to his blue-collar small-town sense of what it means to be a man. That, I think, has made him an emotional wreck. It's done so because he's a man not allowed to have emotions. My relationship to him has always been restricted by the fence of that manliness. It's a legacy, of sorts, one I chose to abandon, which has made it also a history—a great mammoth germ of an impulse in my history—to be something other.

I can measure my sense of my uselessness as a man in direction proportion to my father's sense of pride. I don't blame my father—or not just my father—for everyone in our town knew, clearly, that I was a failure. They all subscribed to the same narrow criteria on their macho list.

When I was a small, slim shaggy-haired boy in middle school, my best friend's mom always told me, in her hardened smoky voice—usually while turning blood sausages on the stove—that I was a handsome boy, yes, but I would make a *beautiful* girl. I was the skinniest kid anyone had ever laid eyes on. I had a high-pitched voice. I was fey. I used big adjectives I learned watching Phil Donahue. I was way too poor to have any social clout as a cool kid, so I retreated into books, which, you guessed it, meant I was one of those soft boys with big brown eyes who—gasp—wrote poems. In my small town, my redneck neighbourhood of mechanics and the sons of mechanics, I wrote a lot of poems.

So, for five or six years of my young life, I wanted simple, obvious things: to have different parents, a different home, different clothes, a different body. I clenched my little fingers together at night under *Star Wars* sheets and prayed to a random god to make me someone else.

Those kinds of prayers are answered only by making one small, instinctive decision at a time. I didn't throw myself out of my bedroom window. I didn't run into oncoming traffic in the street. I didn't take any of the pills in the medicine cabinet. I grew up.

I think I mostly survived for as long as I did because, without knowing it, I had that magical skill young people in dire situations need: a simple naïve hope that dreams could be answered if you clung to them long enough. Or maybe that's half the answer. I somehow understood that hope put into practice is hope granted. Hope is work. And I worked long and hard. Not at making myself anew, mind you, but at making myself into who I wanted to be—which is a convoluted way of getting to who I *am*—despite the shit that folks might sling at me. I think Donahue taught me that too.

During those desperate, formative years, TV and books were my best friends. I was dangerously, chronically lonely—from the time I began to grip those Star Wars sheets through to, well, today. I carry a deep fear that I'll kill myself from the consuming black pit I know as loneliness, which is likely a product of having been so isolated for so long, so young. I had to find my own kind.

The key to finding my kind—the best thing I ever did for

myself—was to pick up an eyeliner. In my twenties, I began to realize how I could love myself. I had carried around a shame for my body that was the exact size and shape of that body. Every inch was a reminder that I was less than what I wanted to be, less than what was expected of me. Too thin, too girly, and with not an ounce of man to my name, as far as I could tell. Then, one evening, I put on a curly blonde wig and an orange A-line dress ... and the clouds parted, and the sun shone down, and I was gorgeous. Everyone said so. I felt it, through to my bones.

In an instant, my famous chicken legs were now enviable. My slim waist, long arms and neck, my love of colour, my humour, my ability to mix and match, my love of sewing and hair-styling and bobbles, shoes, and shoulder bags all suddenly fit into one terrific soft-lensed portrait of a man gone girl.

I was committed to drag in that instant because it allowed me a means to celebrate my body. In a dress, all the terms were suddenly reversed, and I fit. Drag gave me a way to celebrate the limp wrist, for it was no longer limp but feminine.

Much later, at a warm Sunday brunch, I realized that all my favourite queer women—how could I not have known?—were femmes. Amazed to see the obvious for the first time, I remarked how curious it was and how much I loved it. "Of course you do," they said, and someone patted my hand, "because you are too."

How magical that we spend our lives discovering ourselves. What is so clear to others escapes us until someone taps us on the shoulder and calls us by our hidden name.

That moment, of course, was a long time brewing. I write about it in hindsight as though it was inevitable, when it was really a mess of coincidence, unknown intentions, and random shit—like a pinball machine in which the ball mostly just bounces around by itself, and my job is to hit the flipper every once in a while when it's important.

That femme-olution, then, included my first boyfriend, who transitioned from fag to lesbian after we broke up. She told me a few years later that she couldn't wait for me to transition too, for I was becoming my own kind of genderqueer. I thought about that a long time, for I did feel trans, but I was still a man. I *was* transitioning. I was MtM. Male to Male, though that second male was new, a man of my own devising.

Then my cosmic femme pinball hit the radical faeries—they found me, because that's what they do—and the gender-euphoria blossomed.

This is my favourite part. The faeries recognized that my boy clothes were drag, which is uncommon for fags, but not for faeries, so that magic—the magic of being recognized, the magic of being understood, the magic of being celebrated in any gender mash one could imagine—led me to butch in, I think, one of the most singular moments in human history.

I came to butch through lesbian porn. By a complicated turn of events, a couple of dear friends and I made a lesbian porn documentary in which, dressed in drag, I lost my virginity to a woman, a close friend who was an ex-sex trade worker and bisexual performance artist and one of my favourite people. The video was called *Girl on Girl*. Billed as a "lesbian porn documentary," it was meant to be anti-porn because we were real people with a genuine affection for each other, with very real fears, exploring sex together. I was losing my lesbo-hetero virginity. Kinda complicated. And kinda straightforward too.

Countless times I made the joke that, when I was sixteen, my father wanted to take me to Montreal so I could lose my cherry with a prostitute, and sixteen years later, I was living his dream—with a twist. I chose to have sex in drag because that was when I felt my hottest, my most desirable, whereas my fey male self seemed to me to be a weakness. I only felt hot as a guy when I was cruising for public sex, performing a kind of minimalized self in a ball cap and jeans, not talking, not gesticulating. I was hot when I was a silent, reduced version of my small-town self—and I was hot as Cookie LaWhore.

Magically, in the middle of that film, still in a wig and makeup, penetrating my dear friend and goofing around a little too, the drag somehow got in the way and seemed ridiculous. It didn't feel genuine any longer. A very literal narrow door to something else inside me opened, and a crack of light spilled in, and there, on the other side of that door, was the man I had been waiting for. In that moment, I found butch. Drag led me to my masculinity.

I had loved myself so thoroughly, so comfortably, as a femme that I managed to walk on through to the other side. From that day forward, I have been easing into butch. I feel entitled to it, capable of it, within it, and not as a stance, not as the popular version of butch amongst fags who would rather not appear as fags. I'm judgmental, but it's a short walk from the straight-acting types to the straight men fucking each other in the park, hell bent on not having to give up cultural power, and married to the perception of being straight, which is everything, really. We are hung up on appearances: Fags think masculinity is all in the pose. Forget values—honesty, integrity, courage—we just want the look.

Often I slap palm to forehead, wishing that gay men would look past my biceps to figure out if I'm attractive. I have wished my gender-courage to be so massive that the size of my dick wouldn't matter. I am trying to be an example to young men— fey or butch or anything in between—to show them how to grow into themselves. In no small way, I guess, I am trying to be an example to my father.

It's no wonder I came to masculinity from the opposite direction. How could I understand what it means to be butch—how could I lay claim to that title, why would I lay claim—when the "butch" I knew was fraught with ruin? The "butch" I knew in my youth was clothed in a deep misogyny, racism, and homophobia, which, let's face it, are the other side of self-loathing. The butch I knew best was a pose designed to mask a too-dark vulnerability. The failure was not in masculinity—not all masculinities, at least. It's no wonder I often thought of myself as a failed man. I couldn't see both sides of the masculine coin being offered. One side was a perversely limited life within a prideful blue-collar masculinity by which I judged myself poorly in comparison, and the other was the complicated self-loathing-as-xenophobia, which I was smart enough to know I never wanted. At a young age, I somehow intuited that, in rejecting my father's version of a man for one of my own devising—rejecting the cultural norm and replacing it with individualism, a key ingredient in outsider-status—I was making a better trade. But I still judged myself as less-than. Then, last year, my father drank himself into the hospital on my thirty-ninth birthday and, by some new magic, some evolution, at the confluence of thinking about butch and femme and talking to my therapist about my father's collapse, it occurred to me that my being a failed man was worth celebrating. Being a failed man was the measure of my success.

MICHAEL V. SMITH's most recent novel, *Progress* (Cormorant Books), was released in spring 2011. Smith's previous novel, *Cumberland* (Cormorant Books, 2002), was nominated for the Amazon *Books in Canada* First Novel Award and won him the inaugural Dayne Ogilvie Award for Emerging Gay Writers. His videos have played around the world, from Bombay to New York, Beirut to Buenos Aires. Smith is an MFA grad from the University of British Columbia's creative writing program. He teaches creative writing in the interdisciplinary program of the Faculty of Creative and Critical Studies at the University of British Columbia's Okanagan campus in BC's Interior.

Spotlight

Debra Anderson

My favourite childhood photo is taped onto the fridge.

I stand on a chair and proudly hold up my dress, underwear exposed. The pink elastic waistband hugs my puffed belly. My face is cracked wide open in a smile. My mother sits beside me, arms raised, about to yank my dress back down where it belongs. Her smile is the kind she brings out for company she doesn't want. I am out of her reach.

Femme.

I am frozen in the frame, my image emblazoned from corner to corner. Who I am is imprinted loudly, unmistakably. I am who I am meant to be, long before I understand what that is or all that it means. This snapshot was taken long before I get to that place where I finally embody what I have been from the start, who I already am. Undeniable and persistent. Femme.

When my parents go out, I open up my mother's dresser drawers, flutter my hands through her filmy things. I try on bras so big it's as though they are made for a giantess when held up against my tiny, flat frame. Still, I hope anxiously for the day when I can finally have one of my own, in all of its elaborately hooked wonder, complete with adjustable straps and stiff underwires, like a beautiful work of art.

I rummage through her jewellery box, careful when lifting necklaces over my head. I tighten sparkling earrings against my small earlobes. Their weight tugs at my ears. I make sure to remember where I found each item so I can return it to its place. I don't want her to find out I've been playing with her things. She says that I'm not old enough, yet.

Later, in my grandmother's apartment, I lurk behind the dresses

in her walk-in closet; run my fingers over the skirts that hang
down and cover me during games of hide-and-seek. Her fancy
clothes are draped in flimsy plastic; they tremble like ghosts. She
lets me walk in her strappy high-heeled sandals with the shiny
gold buckles. When I rub my fingertips against their black patent
leather, they squeak. She claps her hands and laughs at the noise
I make as I smack against the floor with each step.

I note the brownish-orange line that rides across her jaw. Un-
touched by foundation, her neck seems barren. I assume that one
day I will also posses this magic mark and cross the line from
child to adult. I tie her vibrant scarves loosely around my neck.
When the tails catch the breeze from the open window, they
float in the air like butterfly wings trembling around my face.

Sitting at her telephone table, my grandmother looks up numbers in her black book. I hope that my telephone book will be
just as full of as many girlfriends as hers is when I get older.
She dials each number with a pen to protect her painted nails,
swings the plastic disk patiently around with the pen tip slotted
into the correct hole. My grandfather sits in the kitchen in his
slippers and robe and reads the newspaper, occasionally rattling
the stiff pages so we don't forget he's there.

On the phone, she tells her girlfriends what to do next. What
the answers are. Her Ruby Desire lipstick leaves marks on her
coffee cup like little rose petals. At the end of her conversations,
all that's left are sticky toast crumbs and blobs of Damson plum
jam dotted across her plate. Brown coffee rings remain like time
stamps. She sets her silver hairclips in a treasure pile on the telephone table and steps into the washroom to remove her pink
plastic curlers. I fondle the sunny yellow headscarf she wore tied
in a knot at the top of her head and then left draped over the gold
vinyl seat of her chair.

In her washroom she keeps a little dish of pink, scented sea-
shell soaps that are not for hand washing. She has an entire bowl
full of lipsticks on the counter. I look at them and hope, deeply,

instantly, that I will have just as many someday. Mine. I open one and inhale the stale, powdery smell. I'm always surprised that the lipstick doesn't smell sweet, like strawberries or red Jell-O. I smear the colour across my mouth and step on the pink, fuzzy toilet seat so I can see myself in the mirror. Because this is a secret I keep for myself, I wipe the toilet paper across my mouth and drop it into the toilet to get rid of the evidence. It looks like a little bright kiss in the bowl.

When I come out as a lesbian, it is after I have come out as a feminist. I know everything about what is sexist and wrong in our society, and I make sure I tell everyone—from my mother to my grandmother to the cashier who sells me pizza bagels at the local bakery. It doesn't immediately occur to me why I always have these conversations with women, except that talking about women with women seems necessary. I wear overalls and sensible shoes and eschew makeup, which I understand is a tyrannical tool of the patriarchy. I righteously tell my mother, No! when she asks, Don't you want to pluck those thick eyebrows? Her tweezers have no place in the progressive future I think I am building with all of my sisters.

Because I come out as a lesbian, I think that now everything is going to click inside of me. All around me, the androgynous in the women's community dress in plaid shirts, baggy jeans, and baseball hats. No one seems to need purses to carry any of their things. I cut my hair short and use a backpack so that everyone will stop treating me like a straight girl. But no one ever cruises me. I want to be seen. Recognized. Welcomed.

I want that big "coming home" feeling you're supposed to get once you come out where, all of a sudden, your whole life makes sense and you can't be anyone but who you've always been meant to be. Instead, I still feel like some kind of alien, implanted in my own life. Like I don't belong anywhere. I don't even know what it is that I'm waiting for, what the big thing is that is supposed to have happened, but hasn't yet. I don't know how to get from here to there, so I sit on a bar stool and I wait.

And then a door opens. A promise. When I first notice them, the older femmes at the bar flash bravely from corners of the room amidst a sea of sameness. Dark eyes. Bare shoulders. Dresses hug and highlight curves, demanding you pay attention. Sharp heels holster pretty legs. Cleavage plunges, and earrings swing against exposed necks. These women coat themselves in fabrics that glisten with metallic fortitude and shine under the pulsing lights. Their magic strips the humdrum off the everyday.

I watch the femmes that everyone always wants, femmes who make people hang from their every word, as if their sentences are wrapped in gold. Cherished. I discover how to make an entrance like it is your birthright—as though you are in the centre of a stage and people lined up all night just for the chance to get close to you. I watch femmes who walk into every room as if they own it. As if it was created just for them.

"Someone is always watching you," a femme I admire tells me, her curls raining red around her face, eyes pressing into me. I can't believe this is true, that I have anything worth watching. I realize that this conversation is a signal; she has been observing me. Inside, something hot and hard glows like she has reached down, wrapped her fist around something I never knew I had, and squeezed tight. I am recognized for the first time. And I start to recognize myself—draped in my mother's costume jewellery, hopeful that some of the sparkle will rub off on me. The reflection of my small, made-up face peering back at me from my grandmother's mirror, a reminder of who I've always been, waiting to emerge. The sound of me walking in her oversized high heels, a loud, clattering declaration.

I begin to learn how. I learn how to work a room. How lipstick stains the end of a white-tipped cigarette, leaving a breathtaking, bold crimson imprint. The beauty of an ashtray full of finished smokes, their bruised red tips packed together like flowers, powdered with the sparkle of grey ash. The snaking exhalation of smoke pluming upwards and the aching heat a slow drag can fetch. The splendour that is imperfection—a nylon run racing down a tensed thigh, the jagged chips in nail polish daring anyone to comment. Realizing that they will want whatever I am, as long as I make it shine. I learn that it is okay to take my time. Not to rush. To act as if I am worth it, because there are those who believe I am. I learn to take up space, my space. It feels like home.

The older femmes teach me that all public adjustments are arresting. A work-in-progress is something to behold. So go ahead—pull up stockings, tug at boots, fix those underwires. Make yourself even more perfect for them. They will wait. Others may rush out of a bathroom, eyes on the floor. But you can stop to redefine all your best details—smudged eyes and a formidable mouth. Your lips leave a mark, hot and brazen, on paper towels you toss in the trash, lingering there for those waiting for a stall to witness. It's not wrong to want to make a fuss. Over yourself. Over each other.

I watch the older butches. They have perfectly shined shoes and crisply ironed dress shirts; ties that point politely down, slung around necks I want to carefully touch; thick belts and square edges and hair that looks like it's been freshly cut at all times; change in a loose jangle at the bottom of pockets calling out an insistent rattle as they walk by; neatly clipped nails on hands that are forever ready to hold open the door. Their postures are straight and stiff, except for the ones who stoop shoulders to hide their softness.

The butches are always quietly determined to get the drinks. I watch their calm circle to the bar and back, nobly presenting cocktails to femmes who take them like prizes. At the end of the night, I see them hold up coats with outstretched arms for their tired femmes, hail cabs with one authoritative arm reaching for the stars, the other wrapped lightly around their girl's waist. They make everything look charmed and easy—rolling coins across the table with a silver flash; arm-wrestling with their sleeves rolled up as my eyes hungrily lock on their tensed forearms; swinging Zippo lighters open before I've even contemplated having a cigarette. I crave their softness, how gentle they can be in touch and gesture; I love their hardness, all of the sharp lines and angles I want to feel the pinch of and press myself against. They wear their difference out there every day in a mostly hostile world. They take refuge in the approving nods of other butches, in the welcoming smiles of the femmes at the bar. When they are here, they are home. When they are here, there is nowhere else.

I want to be a part of this. I want to walk this road and know every inch of tender, every strip of sore, every piece of same and difference. I'm greedy for all of the troubled and glorious bits of us and them that make us femme and butch. That make us exactly who we are when we are together and who we are when we are apart. I want to be the kind of femme who will always fight for a butch's right to be exactly who she is in this community and outside of it. To be a femme who will always stand up for my boy. And for myself. I want someone to ache for me. I want someone to fight for the chance to win my affection. I want nothing less than history spread out before me to pull me into the promise of my own gleaming future.

I shoot each femme I see a shy smile. I wonder if she knows how thankful I am that she has been there. That she has helped teach me what this is so that I have learned each baby step until I can get to where I was supposed to be all along.

These femmes have helped me to unlearn everything I have ever known. There is no shame in spectacle; how wrong it is to be made to want to disappear. I learn that the best moments happen when you look back—or when you choose to look away. I learn to make the butches that I meet work for it.

I learn, relearn, and learn again the hardest lesson of them all—to make sure that they deserve you.

She knows not to assume. Anything.

On the couch in her living room, she gratefully works on my feet after leisurely unbuckling the tiny straps of my high-heeled sandals. She ignores the ugly red marks banding my ankles. A history of each step is bitten into my skin. The shoes lay on the floor, tangled together in a complicated pile of straps and hardened soles. My shoes seem almost taller now that I am out of them. The heels rise spectacularly. I think, *I wore those?*

I know that earlier tonight I strode forcefully across the bar in those heels, my warrior hips sliding back and forth in a delicate figure eight as I wrapped my body deliberately around every step. That was who I chose to be tonight. I know that I make a choice every time I put something on or take it off. That I construct the intricacies of this thing called femme, framed from the inside out.

She tenderly works her way up from the bottom, running over my feet with steady palms, holding me with a lax enough grip that I don't feel that familiar urge to bolt. I ease back against the rough couch cushions and let myself loosen. We both pretend to watch late-night TV. She stops flipping channels and puts down the remote. Lays both hands back on me. Stevie Nicks sings onscreen. She's draped in flowing scarves and sways with the music. I close my eyes and let her voice fall over me in waves. I allow this butch's hands to wander upward, sink into my tight calves, softening me. I stay here, on this couch, right behind the red velvet of my closed eyelids, my legs partly spread, askew in her lap like they've always been there.

Our first kiss is slow, tentative. My hair cloaks her face. I straddle her. My skirt is raised around my hips. The material pinches at my waist. The denim of her coarse jeans brushes against my bare, straining, summertime thighs. Later, my feet grip the sides of the couch, sink into second-hand sofa cushions on either side of her. I press her deep against the back of the couch and feel her arms lightly touch my back, encircling me. A question—*Is this okay? Am I allowed?* When I don't push her away, she holds me more firmly in place.

What's left is only this darkened room, this couch, the heat of her mouth under mine. Her breath is sweet and ragged, hitting against my neck and into my ear, feather-brushing my insides. Her chest is a forced concave, shoulders rolled inward to hide her curves. She raises her face upwards, gently seeking me when I pull away even the slightest bit. Her tenderness ropes me back in.

The soft brush of her lashes against my cheek, a flutter. The beauty in her closed lids, blissful. She palms the cheeks of my ass, coated silky with the tight pull of panties. Although they are unfamiliar, I already know her hands. We are bucking in a quick rhythm, locking necks and pushing against each other. Straining. The light of the TV flickers across her. I grip the short hairs at the back of her head in my fist and tug. Her mouth is left open, a slack circle, gaping slowly for me when I pull away.

I leave her wanting, even though part of me doesn't really want to go. But I would like this to be more than just a tumble after a night out at the bar, for her to think about this, about me, for longer than just tonight. I can feel the imprint of her palm, hot; five fingers spread and wrapped across the back of me long after it is gone. She watches me slip into my shoes. Bends down onto her knees to help me do up the straps. She looks up at me with full eyes as I smooth my skirt.

I kiss her goodbye and leave marks all over her mouth and down her neck, a red stain that trails like a roadmap. She walks me to the door coated in my girl. I don't offer to wipe off my lipstick, and she leaves it planted across her skin. In everything, there is a beginning and a middle and an ending. We are somewhere in between these places.

At her front door, she watches me as I fix my hair and reapply my lipstick in my compact mirror before I go. She isn't afraid of my femme—a femme who fights hard for her rightful spot in the bar, cleavage bubbling over a short skirt and tall boots. This butch is not afraid of someone who feels the utmost delight when she stumbles across the perfect pair of new earrings that will dangle sparkling thrills or of someone who takes her satisfaction from the stretch of lace gloves pulled tight across ready fingers. This butch craves each purposeful detail, yearns for each determined choice that a femme makes, which allows who they are on the inside to shine on the outside, so that they may be recognized and revered.

I leave her holding the door handle and know she is watching me walk away. She can't help it. Just like I can't help walking, knowing she's watching. I walk from this place that I was meant to come to. Femme. I walk from this place of home, my centre. Each step loaded, weighted with history, consequence, desire. Each step mine, prized, leading exactly where I want to go—somewhere that no one else can alter or predict. The pavement is hard underneath my feet; my bare thighs are tense and push me forward. My heels leave a trail of staccato sound behind me, marking my path. The sky is dark, a navy curtain hanging over my head. I pass by a streetlight that shines down yellow bright light, a circle swooning around me. I'm in my own spotlight.

DEBRA ANDERSON is the winner of the Dayne Ogilvie Grant (2009), awarded by the Writers' Trust of Canada to an emerging gay Canadian writer for a body of work. A graduate of the York University Creative Writing Program, her writing has been anthologized in *Brazen Femme: Queering Femininity* (Arsenal Pulp Press), *Geeks, Misfits and Outlaws* (McGilligan Books), and *Benton Writing: Contemporary Queer Tales* (Women's Press). She has recently read at the queer community TRIGGER Festival (2010), Word on the Street (2009), Pride Toronto (2009), and was the guest author at York University's Canadian Writers in Person Reading Series (2009) and at Pink Ink, a SOY Writing Group for queer/trans youth (2007). In 2007, she facilitated a Creative Writing Workshop at Word on the Street. *Code White* (McGilligan Books, 2005) is her first novel, which

Herizons magazine described as "a book that meets your eye, has a good handshake, and looks killer in a pair of fishnets." For more information, visit *debraanderson.ca* or join her on Facebook.

Hats Off

Ivan E. Coyote

To all the beautiful, kick-ass, fierce, and full-bodied femmes out there, I would like to extend my thanks to you. It is for you that I press my shirts and carefully iron my ties. It is for you that I make sure my underwear and socks match. It is to you that I tip my cowboy hat. It is for you that I polish my big black boots.

I know that sometimes you feel like nobody truly sees you. I want you to know that I see you. I see you on the street, on the bus, in the gym, in the park. I don't know why I can tell that you are not straight, but I can. Maybe it is the way you look at me. All of my life I have been told that I am ugly, I am less than, I am not a man, I am unwanted. Until you came along, I believed them. Please do not ever stop looking at me the way you do.

I would never say that the world is harder on me than it is on you. I would never say that. Sometimes you are invisible. I have no idea what this must feel like, to pass right by your people and not be recognized. To not be seen. I cannot hide, unless I am seen as something I am not. This is not more difficult, it is just different.

I know those shoes are fucking killing your feet. I want you to know how much I appreciate that you are still wearing them. You look hot. I love you in them. They look great with that dress. If it makes you feel any better at all, the boots I have on right now weigh approximately twelve pounds apiece and they make the soles of my feet burn like diaper rash in a heat wave, and it feels like I'm wearing ski boots when I have to walk up stairs. But I wear them for you. Even still, my new boots are velvet slippers compared to your knee-high five-inch heels. I notice, and I salute you.

I promise, I am not just staring at your tits. I am trying to look you directly in the eyes, but you are almost eight inches taller than me; please see above note regarding your five-inch heels. At the same time, I would like to mention that while I was trying to look you in the eyes, I couldn't help but notice your lovely new pendant. I am sure it really brings out the colour of your eyes, if I could see them.

I want to thank you for coming out of the closet. Again and again, over and over, for the rest of your life. At school, at work, at your kid's daycare, at your brother's wedding, at the doctor's office. Thank you for sideswiping their stereotypes. I never get the chance to come out of the closet, because my closet was always made of glass. But you do it for me. You fight homophobia in a way that I never could. Some people think I am queer because I am undesirable. You prove to them that being queer is your desire.

Thank you for loving me because of who I am and what I look like, not in spite of who I am and what I look like.

Thank you for smelling so good.

Thank you for holding my hand on the sidewalk during the hockey playoffs. I know it is probably small-minded of me to smile wickedly at all the drunken dudes in jerseys smoking outside the sports bar in-between periods because you are so fucking hot, and you are with me and not them, but I can't help it. That's right, fellas. You want her but she wants me. How do you like them apples?

Thank you for wearing matching bra and panties. I don't know why this makes my life seem so perfect, but it really does.

Thank you for being the daughter my mother always wanted. You are so smart and successful, and you dress so fine that you almost make up for her having me and my sister for her real children.

Thank you for reaching out in the dark at the movie theatre to grab my hand in the scary parts. It makes me feel like I am strong, that I can take care of you. Even if there is no such thing as vampires, and you do so much yoga that you could probably easily kick my ass.

I want you to know I love your crooked tooth, your stretch marks, the missing part of your finger, your short leg, your third nipple, your lazy eye, your cowlick, your birthmark shaped like Texas. I love it all.

I want you to know that I know it is not always easy to love me. That sometimes my chest is a field full of landmines, and where you went last night you can't go tomorrow. There is no manual, no roadmap, no helpline you can call. My body does not come with instructions, and sometimes even I don't know what to do with it. This cannot be easy, but still, you touch me anyway.

Thank you for escorting me into the women's washroom because the floor of the men's was covered in something unmentionable. Thank you for asking me if I had a tampon in my purse really loudly so the lady in the turquoise sweatshirt did a double take before gathering up her daughter and hitting me with a pool noodle. I can't say for sure whether that is what actually would have happened, but thanks to you, I didn't have to find out.

Thank you for wearing that dress just because you knew it would match my shirt. Together, we are unstoppable. When seen through your eyes, I am beautiful. Turns out I was a swan the whole time.

IVAN E. COYOTE is the author of seven books, including the award-winning novel *Bow Grip*, the Lambda Award-nominated *The Slow Fix*, and, most recently, *Missed Her*. Ivan has also released three albums and four short films. A renowned storyteller, Ivan frequently performs for live audiences internationally.